Measuring Up

Measuring Up

How Advertising Affects Self-Image

VICKIE RUTLEDGE SHIELDS
with DAWN HEINECKEN

PENN

University of Pennsylvania Press
Philadelphia

10 9 8 7 6 5 4 3 2

Published by
University of Pennsylvania Press
Philadelphia, Pennsylvania 19104-4011

Library of Congress Cataloging-in-Publication Data
Shields, Vickie Rutledge.
  Measuring up : how advertising affects self-image / Vickie Rutledge Shields with
Dawn Heinecken.
    p. cm.
  ISBN 0-8122-3631-9 (cloth : alk. paper)—ISBN 0-8122-1791-8 (pbk. : alk. paper)
  Includes bibliographical references and index.
  1. Gender identity in mass media.   2. Advertising.   3. Semiotics.   I. Title.
II. Heinecken, Dawn
P96.G44 S54   2001
305.3—dc21   2001041462

For Peter, Claire, and Ava
My sources of inspiration, love, and joy

Contents

Preface

How do you "measure up" against the perfect bodies in fashion ads, in films, and on TV? Do you spend much time thinking about this question? Does trying to measure up have any real or lasting effects on your life? Are you critical of your body, its shape, size, or even color? Or do you consider yourself immune from mass media's powerful prescriptions? If popular culture is an indicator of the concerns of everyday people, then evidence for the popularity of the subject of "how we measure up" is all around us. The lead story for the June 3, 1996 edition of *People*, for example, reads, "Too Fat? Too Thin? How Media Images of Celebrities Teach Kids to Hate Their Bodies." TV talk shows and entertainment specials focus on eating disorders, celebrity plastic surgery, personal trainers, silicone breast implants, pressures from mates to look like models, and so many more ways to change ourselves. In the popular press, feminist critiques of the cosmetics, diet, and exercise industries, such as Naomi Wolf's *Beauty Myth* and Susan Faludi's *Backlash*, hit a nerve with millions of women readers, becoming bestsellers. In the academy, the influential work of Jean Kilbourne in her films *Still Killing Us Softly (I, II, III)* and *Slim Hopes* and her book *Deadly Persuasion*, Catherine Gilday's film *The Famine Within*, and Susan Bordo's book, *Unbearable Weight*, just to name a few, have entered into this terrain, theorizing the relationships among gender, media, and culture.

This book is about a particular, complex relationship between the idealized images of gender we see in advertising everyday and our own thoughts, feelings, and behaviors in relation to those images. Any woman who has ever avoided a trip to the beach because she could not bear to be seen in a bathing suit has first-hand knowledge of this relationship. Any man who has insisted on spending two weeks lifting weights before sporting a sleeveless summer tank top is in this relationship. Anyone who is frightened to leave the house without first rolling on a particular brand of deodorant is in a complex relationship with media images about gender and gendered behaviors. Anyone who chooses to implant silicone in healthy breasts is a partner in the relationship with culturally constructed beauty ideals. And anyone who starves him- or herself in response to cultural pressures and personal desires to be "thin" is head deep in this complex relationship. Whether we are deep in the relationship with advertising images of perfect bodies or in the average maze of everyday existence with them, on a cultural level advertising affects us all.

This book focuses on advertising as a key institution of socialization in modern/postmodern society (e.g., Ewen 1976; Jhally 1987; Schudson 1984). Fueled by the perennial struggle to market goods and services and by the development of a multimedia environment, advertising images increasingly pervade our everyday lives, bombarding us with snapshots of what we supposedly lack and what we need to fill the void. What we supposedly lack typically has more to do with the lifestyles, looks, and aspirations advertisers seek to associate with the products they are trying to sell, than with the inherent qualities and attributes of the products themselves (e.g., Jhally 1987; Kellner 1990; Leiss, Kline, and Jhally 1986; Williamson 1978). Almost from its inception, mass advertising has played a central role in perpetuating particular definitions—often in the form of stereotypes—of gender roles and gender relationships.

Images of ideal bodies, most often female bodies, are some of the most dominant and consistent messages produced by advertisers. The current fashion season's definition of perfection in body image pervades Western(ized) cultural landscapes and gives shape to expectations of what it means to be a "gendered body" in twenty-first century global capitalism. Throughout the history of advertising, messages detailing the perfect female—her beauty, her societal roles, and her sexuality—have occupied a central role. These images, used to sell everything from cosmetics to cars to cybersex, provide prescriptions for how we should look and be looked at, how we should feel and be made to feel, and how we should act. In short, these messages prescribe particular gender identities to aspire to for all of us, but for women in particular. They also prescribe how men should relate to women and how women should see themselves. More recent trends in advertising forefront the perfect male body as an object to admire, suggesting how women should relate to men.

In other words, advertisements show us and tell us how to "gender" ourselves. This statement makes more sense when the concept of "gender" itself is more closely examined. Feminist scholars, particularly in the fields of communication and mass media studies, define gender as the term that describes the cultural and social basis of roles assumed daily by men and women. Gender is the effect of and is constructed in our everyday involvement in culture, whether that involvement is dressing for class or taking the children to daycare or running a corporate board meeting.

Gender is reproduced and continuously assigned according to our actions and behaviors. Gender is not simply the outcome of our biological sex assignments, but a kind of "cultural accomplishment" that is at play in both women's and men's lives in an everyday ongoing way. As communication scholar Lana Rakow explains, "Gender is both something we do and something we think with, both a set of social practices and a system of cultural meanings" (1986, 21). In other words, what we do and how we think about what we do are filtered through gender. Assigning gender to others and gendering ourselves is work we do as members of a culture. We gender ourselves to convey information to others about our gender identities, how we continuously regard ourselves as men or women. This is not to say that gender identity is confined only to male/female heterosexual configurations. Our constructions of a gendered identity for ourselves can be seen as a process by which identities can fall anywhere on a continuum between society's ideal of "femininity" and society's ideal of "masculinity." To complicate matters further, our gender identities are also filtered through race, class, or socioeconomic positionings and personal histories.

For some, a personal gendered identity may be a steadily evolving process. For example, an adolescent girl may only conceive of herself as attractive if she has her make-up on, has her hairstyle just right and is at her optimal weight. In her mid-twenties she may begin to believe that she could be attractive for other reasons, such as when she is showing her intelligence or telling a good joke or helping out a friend. For others, strict, rigid gender behaviors instilled in childhood may be the codes a person lives by most his or her life and never really breaks from or evolves out of. For example, a boy who was raised to believe that domestic chores are women's work may carry this expectation throughout his life, especially if he seeks out and finds relationships where the woman willingly takes up this role in the household.

Studying gender and the construction of gender identities as a culturally constructed process instead of a biologically based fact is particularly important for gaining a clearer understanding of the complex relationship between gender representations in media and our own constructions of gender identities. If gender representations are seen as culturally produced and reproduced, then they can also be seen as malleable and changeable.

Acknowledging that gender representations are culturally produced and reproduced allows us to deconstruct, or analytically take apart, how seemingly "natural" gender relationships came to be and how they are maintained. It allows us to ask the question, "In whose interest was it that gender be defined this way at this time?" For example, it seems "natural" that we gaze upon the female body as an object of beauty and that particular attributes naturally make one female body more attractive than another, refined nose, full flowing hair, straight teeth, rounded breasts, small and long-flowing waist, slightly rounded buttocks, long shapely legs, perhaps. However, the pioneering work of such scholars as John Berger (1972), Laura Mulvey (1975), and a host of feminist cultural studies scholars who have criticized and built upon their work, deconstructs the "naturalness" of looking at the female body and questions the stability of the attributes of ideal beauty listed above. Berger explains that the rise to prominence of the female nude in European oil painting depicts a turning point when women's bodies became the object of the "gaze." At the time it was considered socially unacceptable to gaze at "nakedness," but quite a different matter to gaze upon the "nude." The nude is a form of high culture occupying a space in the lives of the privileged class; the properties of the "nude" have come to define a quality in high art aesthetics. The popularity of the nude, then, was conceived and enjoyed within a particular material context. According to Berger, "in the art-form of the European nude, the painters and spectator-owners were usually men and the persons treated as objects, usually women" (63). The aesthetic value invested in the tradition of the nude in European oil painting has been instrumental, according to Berger, in molding the acceptable way of viewing women today.

The female nude as the object, or repository, of looking (or staring, as the case may be) and assessment is not so much "natural" as cultural. For one thing, if the objectification of the ideal female form were a timeless, inevitable fact outside cultural politics, trends and tastes, then the plump, alabaster-skinned, inactive European aristocratic female would remain our society's ideal female. Of course, we know that the ideal female form has endured numerous incarnations in the United States alone since the seventeenth and eighteenth centuries (Morse 1987–88).

The past century alone has witnessed the following changes in ideal female body types: the cinched-waist ideal of 1900, the flat chested and straight bodied flapper of the 1920s, the full-chested hourglass figure of the 1950s, the skinny waif of the 1970s, the muscular, tanned breast-implanted aerobicized body of the 1980s that continues today, albeit with smaller hair. Trends in ways of seeing the female body are cultural. They are closely tied to the gender politics, economic conditions, and popular culture of an era. The mass media continue to play a pivotal role in reflecting and promoting gender ideals. Representations of idealized bodies and gender roles always have been available through advertisements, whether it be the Sears Roebuck catalogue or a newspaper ad for Pears soap. For over a century idealized gender relations have been projected by way of the silver screen. For at least fifty years most people have received the majority of their representation of idealized bodies and gender roles through television. Today, in a complex combination of cinema, television, magazine, newspaper, billboard, and internet viewing, mass media define, refine, and reproduce idealized gendered bodies and gender roles for all of us in early twenty-first-century global capitalism.

My personal interest in the relationship between the idealized images of gender we see in advertising every day and our own thoughts, feelings, and behaviors in relation to those images has a long history. I grew up in this media-saturated culture. As a girl growing up and now as a woman, I have endured a particular love-hate relationship with idealized images in advertising and across the mass media. I am a feminist media scholar, but that does not somehow place me outside the culture that has socialized me. I hope my training and experience have given me the insights and tools to deconstruct the "naturalness" of the socialization process and to share that deconstruction.

I have fantasized about looking like actresses in Hollywood films, especially brunettes like Demi Moore and Andie McDowall. I dreamed of having the celebrity status to be able to wear designer gowns to fancy parties. I love to watch the Oscars and the Emmys to see what the stars are wearing. It used to be interesting only to look out for the female bodies in beautiful clothes, but the male celebrities are now dressing outside the usual black and white tux and they are very interesting to look at too. I succumb to the seduction of glossy women's magazines, with their waif-thin models and diet tips, but also their intoxicating perfume smell and their slick, satiny pages. These are not fascinations I have given up, but I certainly see them in a different light now. These images used to dictate how I felt about myself. How I measured up to models and actresses in popular culture defined my confidence level and how I interacted with others, both women and men. Now I can enjoy them and critique them at the same time. I can also begin to imagine what alternative images might look like.

Our highly gendered relationships to culturally prescribed ideal bodies begin very young in life. I have distinct girlhood memories of the incredible importance of appearance placed on my older sister and myself. My mother had been "a real beauty," especially in her teens and twenties. She competed in some local pageants and dabbled in modeling. She has always been very conscious of her weight and appearance, so it is no surprise that we two girls became very conscious of such issues too. Of course this hyper-awareness of how we looked to others was nurtured outside the family as well. At school, teachers always had a kind remark when one was wearing a nice dress and a pretty bow. The same remarks were conspicuously absent when one showed up in a sweat shirt and jeans. Another social discourse continuously reinforcing the importance of focusing on how well the body was measuring up was television. Of course all the famous people on TV were tall and thin. In the 1970s, when we were kids, the actresses and models were downright emaciated!

My sister always considered herself to have a "weight problem" and believed that I was the skinny one. Our weights and appearances have changed and flipflopped throughout the years. At one point in the mid-1980s she was super-skinny and I was putting on the pounds. Sometimes she had the great perm and I had the bad haircut. At one point in her early twenties she got braces on her teeth and, although she was confident that the results would be worth it, her self-confidence took a pounding during that period because of her metal mouth. What is important here is not so much how we saw each other at different stages, but that the way we each thought "others" saw us has been a defining component of our relationship our entire lives. Much female bonding in this culture occurs in the exchanging of discourse over how others see us. Why is this so and why is it different for men? This is one of the questions to be explored in this book.

This question has occupied my intellectual life since I was an undergraduate studying interpersonal communication in the early 1980s. This is when I discovered feminism. I had come of age in the 1970s and early '80s with an all-too-comfortable feeling that girls could now be anything and do anything they wanted. I certainly felt that way. In college, however, I began to realize that many doors had opened for me not because I was the smartest or most capable, but because I fit a particular cultural ideal of femininity. I had the right body shape and the right skin color, for example. I began to realize that many of my friends who were not of the same body type or size or skin color weren't getting the same opportunities and were not nearly as confident in a "post-feminist" era as I had been. I was benefiting from a cultural way of seeing I did not yet understand, but was beginning to feel increasingly uncomfortable with. I knew I was smart and capable, but what if I gained a lot of weight? What if I became disfigured in some way or disabled in some way? What would happen when I got older? Would the same opportunities be open to me? Why weren't my male friends feeling any of these fears?

My intellectual pursuit of answers to these questions continued in graduate school. There I was introduced to feminist film theory, critical theory, and cultural studies. I was also introduced to the analytical tools of psychoanalysis, semiotics, and post-structuralism. These influences have shaped my understanding of how advertisements depicting gender relationships "work." In particular, feminist research that examines the content of advertisements depicting idealized images of women, provides the basis for my work. However, these textual approaches always left nagging questions unanswered. How do real people experience the influence of advertisements in their everyday lives? Do men and women experience ads differently? Do different types of women experience ads differently from one another? What about men? In other words, I was as interested in the audience of advertisements as the advertisements themselves, knowing from experience that the relationship between the two is neither easy nor uncomplicated. More specifically, however, I was interested in what kinds of influence, if any, the ubiquitous image of the ideal female in advertising has on both women and men. Understanding the connections between idealized gender images in advertising and the effects they have in the everyday lives of people means unwrapping many layers of cultural and personal experiences. It also involves a certain tolerance for the fact that the connections we uncover, either through research or in our own lives are at any given moment changeable.

There is little doubt that the messages and images that surround us every day via the mass media have an impact on our attitudes, perceptions, and behaviors. Just how this is accomplished and to what degree it is accomplished has been the preoccupation of mass communication researchers and media critics for the better part of this century. There is profound evidence suggesting that girls and young women in this culture are particularly vulnerable to particular kinds of mass media messages: those pertaining to body image, size, and appearance. They are not more vulnerable than boys or men because they are somehow weaker against the power of these messages. They are more vulnerable because the culture they are born into subscribes to the notion that women should be the objects of vision. Female bodies are held up to inspection to a much greater degree than are men's in this culture. Women's worth is judged generally by appearance first and abilities second. Granted, many of these norms are beginning to change in the everyday world in which we live, but in the world of representation, whether film, TV, or advertisements, the premium placed on the sleek, firm, yet shapely female body is at an all-time high. Supermodels are some of the most highly paid individuals in the world.

This cultural overemphasis on female body perfection is not lost on very young girls. My oldest daughter is nine and I have had my work cut out for me for at least six years, trying to counterbalance all the cosmetic and diet ads on TV and in magazines; trying to explain to her why I think little girl beauty pageants are probably not a very good extracurricular activity as compared to, say, piano lessons or soccer; trying to suggest subtly that "being pretty" is not a bad thing, just not the highest attribute a woman should strive for; and perhaps the biggest challenge of all—not to pass on my own obsessions and insecurities about my female body to her. In this regard, I slip up often. One way I consistently slip up is in the mirror inspection (that torturous ritual that most women partake in daily) when I'm dressing. The dissatisfied scowl on my face is my dead giveaway. When my daughter is there she might ask, "What's the matter, Mommy?" and before I take a moment to reflect, the words are spilling out: "I really wish I could lose some weight." These kinds of slipups serve to undermine other moments when I'm thinking clearly, as a good feminist Mom should. One such moment is when I put on the shorts and tennis shoes and pop the aerobics tape into the VCR. I try to tell my daughter that the prime objective of working out is to be healthy, to increase my energy level, and to boost my immune system. To which she might say something like, "and won't you be happy if you lose some weight!" in her most sincere and supportive voice.

These examples point out what an incredible struggle it is to give girls the emotional armor they need in their most formative years to be able to concentrate on developing all of their attributes and not get incredibly sidetracked and waylaid by how their bodies "measure up." Advertising messages are one of the major instigators keeping not only girls and women but the entire culture "body obsessed." Advertising images, then, are the primary media images to be interrogated here. It will quickly become apparent, however, that the basic elements of gender construction so prevalent in advertising resonate across mass media. This book examines how women in particular are mandated to measure up to the perfect bodies in the media on a daily basis. The book is an in-depth look at how these messages are encoded with cultural "ways of seeing" the perfect female form; most importantly, the book examines the gender "decoding" of these messages by both women and men. Focusing on how both women and men relate to the idealized female body in the media is important. Gaining a keener understanding of how these images work on women is extremely educational for them; understanding how men see these images that socialize them is also important to women.

1. Theory and Method

A particular challenge faces researchers interested in how real people experience media in their everyday lives. There is often an overwhelming gap between our theories about how particular media affect us (from a production and content standpoint, for example), and figuring out how media weave through people's lives (Abercrombie and Longhurst 1998; Lull 1995; Moores 1993; Press 1996, 1991; Seiter 1998). As Colin Sparks points out, "Boundaries in actual social life are inevitably messy and blurred. Actual social formations always display a greater richness and complexity than the theoretical abstractions we use to understand them"; however, "We are forced to use those abstractions because we cannot hope to understand reality simply by observing its surface features" (1998, 29). Most of the time theoretical insights guide us in a particular way toward a better understanding of how the discourses of people *might* be interpreted.

Advertising permeates our everyday lives insisting we be its audience. Marketers have made a fine-tuned science out of targeting particular demographic groups to position products. Furthermore, there is now little dispute that the content of commercial television is primarily a vehicle to deliver audiences to advertisers and that glossy magazines serve the same purpose. However, real people do not experience their lives as target audience members. Sometimes we are audiences of many media at once; at other times we choose to tune out altogether (if this is really possible). Sometimes we are passive: the television is on in the background, but we are having a phone conversation, or we have it on just to pass an hour. At other times we are highly attentive, playing along with every question on *Who Wants to Be a Millionaire?* and talking back to the television set.

A useful way to think about the active or passive positions we take up with media comes from Stuart Hall's concept of encoding/decoding (1980). Cultural studies in the past has approached the reader/media text relationship as a series of positions viewers take up given their ideological predisposition to the media message they are attending to. Viewers may be seen as taking up either preferred/dominant, negotiated/resistant or oppositional subject positions in regard to the text (Johnson 1986; Morley 1980, 1986, 1989). To illustrate, consider examples of possible dominant, negotiated, and oppositional readings of the popular television series *Ally McBeal*. A dominant reading of this show might see Ally as a hip professional woman, trying to make it in the cut-throat world of litigation and law practices. She is quirky and unlucky in love, but she shows a lot of gumption, spirit and hope. She's a real '90s woman, trying to have it all (Heywood 1998).

A negotiatied reading of the show might find many elements believable and others not. For instance, the fact that Ally, a young single woman, has achieved success in a prominent law firm may seem very real and believable. Her yearning for love in the midst of a single life may ring true for many also. Yet, an audience member may think many of the silly choices she makes and things she does wouldn't actually be tolerated in such a competitive field, or they might feel that the female competition on the show is really unnecessary and detracts from the show's potential.

Finally, an oppositional reading of *Ally McBeal* might read a lot like some of the critical reviews the show received in the popular press. In her article for *USA Today*, "Ally, Real Life Has No Commercial Breaks," Colleen D. Ball (1998, 27a) talks back to Ally (the way many of us talk back to our television sets) about what would actually happen to her career if her yearnings for Mr. Right and a baby came true right away. Ball explains that having a baby will involve daycare choices and perhaps even part-time work arrangements. Ally's boss probably wouldn't understand, she would be slow-tracked and probably would never make partner—or she can keep up her current work schedule, never see her family, risk divorce from Mr. Right, and maybe even lose custody of dancing baby because she works too much! In *TV Guide*'s "Insider: Smart Women, Foolish Choices" (1998), Beth Brophy called these foolish choices the "Ally McBeal-*ization*" of TV. "Like the Harvard-trained lawyer—who often wins in court but loses control outside of it—these women share a startling disconnect between professional competence and personal ditziness" (6).

Popular TV shows are certainly not the only media we take up various subject positions with. We even take up active "subject positions" with our favorite commercials. Sometimes we don't get a snack or change the station when they come on. We sit in our chairs to watch and sing along. However, generally we experience advertising not as something we actively seek out, as we do a TV program, magazine, newspaper, or website. Even billboards by the side of the road are encountered because we are driving *by* them, not driving *to* them. Advertising comes to us "bundled" with these media and we think of viewing ads as secondary to the medium we seek out.

Ethnography and Sense-Making

Ethnographic methods provide many of the best tools for studying media and everyday life. A methodology used in anthropology, ethnography in the authentic sense of the word is a research methodology that involves extended periods of participant observation and emphasizes extensive field notes and the final ethnography produced (Seiter 1998). "Ethnography is the work of describing a culture" (Spradley 1979, 3). The aim of ethnography is to grasp a way of life from "the Natives' point of view" (Geertz 1983), and to understand a way of living that is usually different from but sometimes a part of the researcher's own experience. It is a method more concerned with learning from people than with studying them.

Cultural studies scholars have held up ethnography as a methodology best suited for studying popular culture's "elusive audience" (see Ang 1989, 1990; Ang and Hermes 1991; Bacon-Smith 1992; Bird 1992a,b; Erni 1989; Fejes 1984; Press 1996, 1991; Radway 1989). Media reception analysis studies by cultural studies and communication scholars tend to be hybrids of ethnography and qualitative interviewing. Influential examples include David Morley's research on lower-middle-class London families and television use (1986); Janice Radway's study of female readers of romance novels (1984); Ien Ang's analyses of fan's letters about the television show *Dallas* (1985); and Ann Gray's research on video cassette recorder use (1992).

More recent influences in feminist reception analysis have built upon this tradition of using ethnographic and qualitative interviewing approaches to study media use in everyday life. Such studies include Camille Bacon-Smith's study of U.S. Star Trek fans (1992); Jacqueline Bobo's study of black women's readings of *The Color Purple* (1988); Elizabeth Bird's examination of tabloids and their faithful readers (1992); Robin Means Coleman's in-depth research on African American viewers of black situation comedies (2000); Andrea Press's study of female television viewing and social class (1991); and Ellen Seiter's research on children's television and computer use (1998).

In studying men and women's relationship with gender representations in advertising I made methodological choices based on what would most effectively draw out people's experiences in their own words and on their own terms. At the same time the methods needed to be informed by theoretical advances in audience reception research and feminist media studies. An ethnographic approach guided the sampling of participants and the coding and writing up of transcripts which resulted, ultimately, in a "writing of culture" that attempts to present a portrait of how men and women experience advertising in their everyday lives, and how they decode the repetitious, ubiquitous image of the idealized female body in advertising in particular.

The Interview Participants

The pool of participants totaled 73. The men and women who lend their insights and voices to this book do not come from one discrete sample, however. The core sample is a group of 15 women and 15 men who were interviewed during a three-month period in the late fall and early spring of 1993. The remaining 43 men and women are from two other studies. The first was conducted as part of a gender and communication class at a major midwestern research university. The second was an independent study I conducted in the fall of 1995 at my current university. In actuality, more than these 73 voices will be speaking. Over the past six years in the undergraduate and graduate university courses I teach on women, mass media, and culture, I have witnessed numerous recountings of students' relationships to gender images in media as well as their explanations of how they see media images affecting other significant individuals in their lives. These testimonies weave their way into the discourse of this book also.

The 73 men and women represent a fairly culturally diverse group, although not representative of the larger population. Their ages ranged from 18 to 45. The sample included 6 African American women and 2 Hispanic women; it also included 3 gay men and 5 lesbians. Obviously the second sample for the gender and communication class were university students. But, the core sample and the independent study sample were drawn from the university area, not from university students exclusively. Some men and women in the sample were not students at the time of the interviews, but working in such self-reported positions as receptionist, psychologist, house painter, artist, and "between gigs."

The Interviews

All the interviews were conducted using ethnographic methods and interviewing techniques from Sense-Making, a set of theory-driven methods developed by communication theorist Brenda Dervin (see Clark and Dervin 1999; Shields and Dervin 1993). Sense-Making assumptions have been used to generate a series of interviewing approaches useful in a wide variety of research settings, for in-depth as well as brief contacts, in formal research as well as informal episodes where one person wants to understand another, in two-person as well as group settings (see Dervin 1983, 1990, 1991a,b, 1993; Dervin and Clark 1993, Shields 1996). Fundamental to all Sense-Making data collection approaches is the assumption that, no matter how much like another human being one person may be, there are always differences between the two, and there is always potential for these differences to change over time.

In the interview, the interviewer always starts by having the respondent identify a real situation the respondent experienced. The interviewer then asks questions that deliberately and systematically implement the Sense-Making metaphor. What happened in this situation—what happened first, second, and so on? What was important to you about the situation? What was difficult about it? What led you to see it in this way? What questions did you have? What kind of answer(s) were you looking for? What understandings did you get? Did the understandings help? Did they hinder? How? What ideas did you create? Did these ideas help? Did they hinder? How? Did they have an impact on your later behavior? thinking? feeling? How? It is assumed that we can better hear what others have to say about their worlds by systematically addressing their views of how they bridge gaps, of how they invent their worlds even in the most externally constrained of situations.

The interviewing protocol used with the core sample of participants was carefully designed to provide a methodological alternative to traditional unstructured, open-ended interview techniques. The protocol presented the viewing of ads to men and women in three different ways. First, they discussed ads they chose for themselves, simulating a natural viewing situation. The men and women browsed through their choice of the five magazines provided, and chose three ads with females in them that stood out for them in some way (because the ad is attractive, eye-catching, pleasing, disgusting, intriguing, repulsive, persuasive, etc.). The five magazines were *Time*, *Cosmopolitan*, *Rolling Stone*, *Sports Illustrated*, and *People*. These magazines were listed as the five most popular magazines of a freshman-level university class that consisted of approximately 130 students.

The second and third portions of the interview protocol were designed to tap into the relationship between how men and women see society's view of the ideal female body in advertising and how they personally see, or experience, the ideal female body in advertising. By rank ordering their impressions of eight preselected ads, the men and women interviewed were encouraged to begin making fine distinctions for themselves that constituted comparisons between how they saw society's ideals of femininity and their personal constructions of femininity. They were asked to relate their assessments of the ads to their own life situations, past and present, and say how they see the ads as having an inpact on their lives, thoughts, and emotions. The goal of this particular construction of the interview was to tap into those moments where men and women see constructions of gender as rigid and unyielding and also those moments of interpretive freedom in response to those rigid constructions.

The next series of Sense-Making questions asks, "When you look at the female(s) in this ad (these ads), what characteristics would she/they have to have to make them *unattractive* by society's standards?" This question and the Sense-Making questions that followed were designed to encourage the participants to take a critical stance toward the ideal body image, that answering questions about what *is* "appealing" might not evoke. For most, framing responses to what society finds ideal and what they personally find appealing was somewhat intuitive, while being asked to express what specifically is "unattractive" ran counter-intuitive for them, demanding higher reasoning and more abstract responses.

The Sense-Making questioning in Parts II and III, then, focused on those distinctions, or more specifically, what led men and women to make those distinctions. Through a series of questions, men and women were asked to compare and explain the choices they made in ranking both individual ads and piles of ads. Through Sense-Making questions, or Sense-Making cues that allow them to circle their own realities and experiences, they were allowed to relate those choices and distinctions to their own lives, society and others.

The final portion of the interview protocol asked the men and women to describe their life histories and, in addition, to trace back to life situations in the past where they saw advertising as impacting upon their definitions of gender, both socially and personally. The goal of this section was to further encourage them to theorize if, how, and in what ways advertising played a part in their social and personal development as gendered subjects.

The Ads

The ads selected for Parts II and III of the interviewing procedure were chosen from past or present issues of the same five magazines used in Part I, for the sake of consistency. Seven of the eight advertisements were chosen as representative of sex-role stereotypes and gender ritualizations widely identified by scholars of gender and advertising and widely recognized as repetitive themes in representation of the female body in mainstream print media. The eighth ad, for Nike shoes, is representative of an alternative aesthetic to the conventions of the other seven ads.

1. *Sex-object/passive*. Figure 1, for Budweiser beer, is representative of a highly sexual stereotyped ad. The women in the photograph are ornamental, the female body is objectified, positioned clearly for visual gratification of a male gaze, and the pose is one of complete passivity, both because the women are lying down and because their swim suits are a part of the beach towel, suggesting restricted movement.

2. *Sex-object/active*. Figure 2, for Johnnie Walker scotch, offers a slight contrast to the Budweiser beer ad. The female bodies are again the object of the voyeuristic male gaze, however the women in this ad are engaged in a moment of activity. They are unrestricted in movement.

3. *Pleasure/danger*. Figure 3, for Jordache, is representative of the male gaze incorporated in the photograph as well as suggested from the positioning of the female body. The voyeur of this scene is offered an ambiguous scenario: the woman featured is in a moment of either pleasure (enjoying the attention of three males) or danger (attempting to flee the attentions of three males).

4. *Body cropped*. Figure 4, for Montana fashions, is representative of the convention of photographic cropping of the female body in ads. Headless and feetless, the whole woman is represented by the torso and one arm.

5. *Mother role*. Figure 5, for Pier 1 Imports, is representative of ads that present motherhood as a woman's primary role. This image, however is updated for the 1990s and places the young mother in an ambiguous setting of nature, as opposed to the more traditional setting of the home.

6. *Businesswoman role*. Figure 6, for Virginia Slims cigarettes, is representative of the genre of "new woman" ads. The businesswoman is supposedly a symbol of progress and sexual equality. Like many ads in this genre, this one incorporates "progressive signs" (man's suit, briefcase) within very conventional codes of ideal femininity (make-up, slimness, long hair, pink coat).

7. *Face shot*. Figure 7, Isabella Rossellini for Lancôme cosmetics, is representative of ads that focus on the face in lieu of objectifying the body. This particular ad was chosen for the recognizability of the model, lending to the significance of the ad the possibility of intertextual references.

8. *Alternative aesthetic*. Figure 8, for Nike shoes, was chosen for its alternative aesthetic value in comparison to the other seven ads for several reasons. (a) The model is pictured in a moment of self-absorbed activity in a

Figure 1. Budweiser.

Figure 2. Johnnie
Walker.

Figure 3. Jordache.

Figure 4. Montana.

Figure 5. Pier 1.

Figure 6. Virginia Slims.

Figure 7. Lancôme.

Figure 8. Nike.

traditional masculine domain, sport. (b) She is not addressing the camera directly, lending a sense that this is a candid photograph. (c) She is not made-up and her hair is not coifed; she in fact appears to be perspiring. (d) The body is not cropped, she is "embodied." (e) The photograph is shot with a soft-focus lens.

2. Stereotypes and Body Parts: Advertising Content

I view advertisements always as stereotypes. Stereotyping, whether consciously or unconsciously, always has some effect on how I view others. It also creates an environment, also affects the views of other people. It also provides a pressure for me to have society views, because it either directly influences my views, or it influences other views of the people who are close to me. And they can directly influence my views. It kind of influences me to have this group consciousness of stereotypes. . . . First of all [advertising] tells me to stay young, it tells me to stay thin, it tells me to be very social. The majority of advertisements I see are geared toward cliquish type of atmosphere where a lot of people are always involved in a lot of things. All these, ironically, I have found to be untrue. I've been very solitary. I can do something about my weight, but I am going to grow old. (Richard, 24)

To a certain extent I think advertising has an effect on how we lead our lives because it shows the type of symbolism we should appreciate as males or females. It shows how one should act but I don't necessarily see that it is the way I should act. I mean I have always thought, for me, I try to be as independent as possible and not be influenced by others. I mean the only way [advertising] influences me is the type of products I buy. It generally leads me to believe that this product is superior to another product. (George, 22)

We see on TV and the media that life is like this for a particular family or group of people, and advertisers just play along with the image. If it's right or wrong, or true or false. Advertisers tend to do more of creating a situation than trying to represent society. (Jamie, 22)

In the passages above, George, Jamie, and Richard, who are all similar in age, begin to address the question, "How do advertisements show us and tell us how to 'gender' ourselves through the use of stereotypes?" Researchers have been actively addressing this question for about thirty years (see Shields 1996). Serious scholarship on gender and advertising flourished in the 1970s (some influential work such as Betty Friedan's *The Feminine Mystique* precedes this date). In a climate of second-wave feminist politics, increasing support for an Equal Rights Amendment, and the increase of female researchers in higher education, scholars in departments of mass communication, journalism, and marketing raced to produce empirical analyses of sex-role stereotyping found in print and television. This type of research originating in the 1970s and, to a lesser extent, continuing today is commonly referred to as *sex-roles research*. Through the use of the research method *content analysis*, these studies investigated questions pertaining to gender difference and inequality within the *content* of ads. Specifically, sex-roles research has revealed that women in advertising are portrayed by restrictive categories, such as housewife or sex object, and that advertising reflects a false picture of women's real lives (see Courtney and Whipple 1974). This type of research fit in nicely with the research methods already established in communication studies while serving a political imperative, the improvement of the representation of women in the media (Rakow 1986).

Early researchers in the area of sex roles in the mass media examined a large number of ads at a time in order to classify and count particular types of representations. For example, a typical content analysis might have examined 500 ads in popular fashion magazines. These 500 ads would be examined for qualities such as how many times males appeared in business roles, how many times females appeared in bathrooms, how many times females were posed as sex objects, and so on. The aim of this research was to demonstrate how prevalent sex-role stereotypes were in advertising. Thus, it is important to define what is meant by stereotype in order to grasp the aims of this research. A stereotype is

1) The social classification of particular groups and people as often highly simplified and generalized signs, which implicitly or explicitly represent a set of values, judgments and assumptions concerning their behavior, characteristics and/or history; 2) A conventional, formulaic, and usually oversimplified conception, opinion, or belief; a person, group, event, or issue considered to typify or conform to an unvarying pattern or manner, lacking any individuality. A standardized conception or image of a specific group of people or objects. (O'Sullivan et al. 1994, 299–300)

By shining a light on the gender inequities in advertising through empirical analysis, these researchers hoped to show where the most harmful and most frequent stereotyping occurs. The expectations were that the results of this type of research would have two types of effects. First, the research would reveal to the producers of ads where and how they could improve their campaigns to more adequately reflect "real" gender relations in society. Second, the research was intended to reveal to all audiences of advertising how the images viewed each day, and generally taken for granted, were really showing us a warped, sexually inequitable vision of our society.

The rush to research the image of gender portrayal across the mass media in the 1970s could be attributed to at least two major factors. The first was the reemergence of feminist writing in the academy spurred on by Betty Friedan's *The Feminine Mystique* (1963). Friedan was one of the first to raise pointed questions about the portrayal of women in women's magazines and the advertisements contained therein. She saw these images on "women's pages" not only as documentation to support her arguments, but as powerful shaping forces in the social fabric and a "critical moving force in creating for women a view of her ideal self" (Courtney 1983, 4).

Friedan found that the portrayal of women between the 1930s and the 1950s had changed considerably. In the late 1930s "women were more likely to be portrayed in fiction as autonomous heroines seeking to fulfill their own personal goals, but as the forties progressed, the autonomous heroine gave way to the glorified housewife, praised and rewarded for her efforts to run the household and nurture others" (Courtney 1983, 3). For Friedan, advertising, perhaps even more than the magazines themselves, were reflecting (if not fostering and perpetuating) a limited lifestyle for U.S. women by portraying household care and the embodiment of roles of ideal mother and wife as the ultimate goal for women. According to ads, these roles constituted a woman's most creative opportunities.

Friedan's insights highlighted a second factor driving the insurgence of sex-roles research in the early 1970s. Advertising and print journalism received special attention because women were dominating, more than ever, many of the consumer groups targeted by advertisers and common sense dictated that the ways in which women viewed themselves in ads might greatly impact the effectiveness of commercial marketing campaigns (Lundstrom and Sciglimpaglia 1977; Morrison and Sherman 1972; Wise, King, and Merenski 1974; Wortzel and Frisbie 1974). This research was concerned with advertising "effectiveness," examining whether, and under what conditions, more progressive, less stereotyped portrayals may be preferred to traditional ones. Of foremost concern was the measurement of causal relationships between women's heightened attitudes about "Women's Liberation," role portrayal, and product desirability. Several studies, for instance, hypothesized that women would view products more positively if the role portrayal were that of women in jobs or careers (Wortzel and Frisbie 1974).

Taken as a group these studies resulted in findings about particular segments of consumers. They found that traditional roles were not displeasing to everyone, but tended to irritate many consumer segments. One consistent finding that emerged from this research showed that "the sex of the product representative in the advertisement, the role portrayed, and the setting for the advertisement should match the product image" (Courtney 1983, 98). Realism in advertising *was* important, therefore, whether the roles were more traditional or progressive in style.

Alice Courtney and Sarah Lockeretz's (1971) content analysis of the portrayal of men and women in print advertising was one of the first and also one of the most widely cited and replicated research studies on the subject. These authors concluded that four general stereotypes of women existed across advertisements in eight major general-interest magazines in the years 1958, 1968, and 1978: (1) a woman's place is in the home; (2) women do not make important decisions or do important things; (3) women are dependent and need men's protection; and (4) men regard women primarily as sex objects (Courtney and Whipple 1983, 7).

Issues and findings from content analyses of television advertisements showed very similar results. Television studies showed that: (1) prevalent female roles were maternal, housekeeping, and aesthetic; (2) women and girls were seen less frequently than men; (3) women were shown to have different characteristics from males (less authoritative, decisive, powerful, rational); (4) women were housewives or in subservient, low-status occupations; and (5) women were depicted as less intelligent (Ferrante, Haynes, and Kingsley 1988; Kimball 1986; Lazier and Kendrick 1993). It is important to note that the findings in the print advertising research and the television advertising research revealed similar results. Because we as audience members do not generally experience only one mass medium in any given day or week, but are instead positioned within a web of media viewing, the greater the consistency of messages, such as gender stereotypes, across the media the more powerful their potential effect on how audiences transfer that knowledge to their social relationships.

Studies charting progress in these images in the next few years also charted new problems. Louis Wagner and Janis Banos (1973) found that the percentage of women in working roles had increased, but in nonworking roles women were being seen less in family settings and more in decorative capacities. Further, women were seldom depicted interacting with one another or making major purchases without a male also in the picture. These authors concluded that stereotypes predating the women's movement remained and advertising was not keeping up with the times in failing to portray realistically the diversity of women's roles (see also Belkaoui and Belkaoui 1976).

Little attention was paid to male sex-role portrayal in print ads at this time, with the exception of one major study replicating Courtney and Lockeretz's sample from a male standpoint (Wohleter and Lammers 1980) and one minor study (Skelly and Lundstrom 1981). These studies found that men were more likely to be shown working outside the home and to be involved in the major purchases of expensive goods. All these studies concluded that roles of men and women in print advertisements had changed little over twenty years (Busby 1975; Dominick and Rauch 1972; Fejes 1994).

In the 1980s and early 1990s there was a decrease in the number of sex-roles studies conducted compared to the 1970s. Furthermore, recent empirical studies investigate highly specialized areas such as "women's adoption of the business uniform" (Saunders and Stearn 1986), sex-role stereotyping of children on TV (Peirce 1989), women in advertisements in medical journals (Hawkins and Aber 1993), perception studies (Rossi and Rossi 1985), achievement studies (Geis et al. 1984), and self-consciousness variables studies (Gould 1987). Additional recent studies have examined cross-cultural or international perspectives on gender representation in advertising (Furnham 1989; Gilly 1988; Griffin, Viswanath, and Schwartz 1992; Mazzella et al. 1992).

Most recent sex-roles research, however, has used the vast data collected over the last 20 to 25 years to: (1) advance theory on sex-role representation and possible debilitating effects stereotypical images can have for society or (2) revisit this early research, replicating studies to see whether advertising images have progressed in the past twenty years (Whipple and Courtney 1985). According to Lazier and Kendrick, stereotyping of portrayals of women is still important to study because the portrayals are not only debilitating and demeaning, but they continue to be inaccurate. Advertisements today "do not reflect the significant strides (both socially and statistically) made by women in the past two decades into the work force" (1993, 201). Furthermore, women are still not seen as decision makers for major purchases (although women actually make more family financial decisions than do men) and finally, "by using outdated stereotypes, ads are simplistically ignoring the complexities of modern women's lives" (201).

Lynn Lovdal (1989), in a study of 354 TV commercials, found that men's voices were still dominant in voiceovers and that men were portrayed in three times the variety of occupational roles as women. Other recent research has found that men were more likely to be portrayed in independent roles compared to women who were portrayed in a variety of stereotyped roles such as wife, mother, bride, waitress, actress, dancer (Bretl and Cantor 1988; Gilly 1988; Lazier and Kendrick 1993). Even the feminist publication *Ms.*, whose editorial policy states the it will not run advertising harmful to women, did not fare well under the scrutiny of content analysis. A 1990 study by Jill Ferguson, Peggy Kreshel, and Spencer Tinkham found that a substantial proportion

Table 1. Comparison of female portrayals, 1973 and 1986

	Consciousness scale for sexism (%)	
Level	1973 (N = 447)	1986 (N = 530)
1. Put her down	27	37
2. Keep her in her place	48	35
3. Give her two places	4	3
4. Acknowledge equality	19	15
5. Nonstereotypic	2	11

Source: Lazier and Kendrick 1993.

of advertising promoted products considered harmful, such as cigarettes and alcohol. Furthermore, although images of women in subordinate and decorative capacities had decreased overall in the ads in *Ms.*, the number of ads depicting women as alluring sex objects increased. The editors of *Ms.* found that pleasing advertisers and offering serious feminist-oriented articles were often in conflict. In 1990 *Ms.* adopted a no-ads policy. Although the magazine is now more expensive to purchase, the policy has allowed *Ms.* to "present a renewed vision of feminism" (McKinnon 1995).

In 1988 Linda Lazier-Smith conducted research replicating the three major studies of Suzanne Pingree et al. (1976), Erving Goffman (1976), and Jeane Kilbourne (1987). In her research the author replicated the method, categories, and procedures of Pingree and Hawkins's "Consciousness Scale of Sexism" and reapplied it along with Goffman's and Kilbourne's sexism in representation categories to one full year of advertisements run in *Ms.*, *Playboy*, *Time*, and *Newsweek*. Lazier-Smith found no significant change between the 1970s analyses and the 1988 representations. The results appear in Table 1.

In updated research examining the same issue, Linda Lazier and Alice Kendrick reported preliminary results showing a decrease in Level 1 (sex object/decoration/bimbo) portrayals. Furthermore, "Goffman traits from the 1988 study did show some improvement, with three categories (relative size, function ranking, and family scenes) appearing so infrequently that they could be considered to no longer apply" (1993, 205). However, the categories applying to women's subordination to men were still as prevalent.

Sex-roles research, in particular, has played an important part in diffusing the concept of the "sexual stereotype" throughout the language of this culture. A review of Alice Courtney and Thomas Whipple's (1974) four categories of sexual stereotyping in advertising are instructive here: (1) a woman's place is in the home; (2) women do not make important decisions or do important things; (3) women are dependent and need men's protection; and (4) men regard women primarily as sex objects. Although the variety of roles of women represented in ads has increased, current feminist literature on gender and advertising argues that these content categories have changed very little. So we can argue that it is an illusion that women's roles in ads have really changed. These roles are masked by the appearance of variety. Stereotypical representations seem less harmful when served up smorgasbord style.

Decoding Gender Content

In April 1998 I gave a keynote address at an all-day forum at St. Cloud State University in Minnesota. The talk was about gender representation in advertising and whether or not many of the newer images we are seeing are truly progressive, or the same old codes wrapped in new garb (we will return to these issues in later chapters). I presented approximately sixty slides of ads, current and historical, to support my major points. In a follow-up session to my address, two very creative and successful professional advertisers discussed their craft with the audience. One of them alluded to the slides I had shown during my presentation, saying, "these ads are really hardly worth talking about because they are just 'bad.' It is easy to take a half-naked beautiful woman and place her next to a product. Making good ads is difficult. It is hard work."

The point she was making was a good one and one I have made myself in other contexts. I call this point the "least common denominator factor in advertising": when one can't think of anything else, use sex to sell it. It was a good message for an audience of future advertising executives to hear, that sex is a tired old formula and not at all creative or original. However, I've always been interested in how people deal with the images they actually experience every day. The reality is, as decades of sex-roles research has shown us, we experience this bad sexist imagery everyday. Until the landscape of advertising images drastically changes into the ideal these advertisers spoke of in St. Cloud, I want to know how people experience these "bad" ads. The remainder of this chapter explores how women and men discuss their reactions to stereotypes and sexism in ads.

Gender differences in the ways men and women decode images of women's bodies in advertising content today are subtle, yet distinctive. By subtle, I mean that the significant gender differences can no longer be read directly from language and topic choices, as may have been the case in the past. In a cultural environment of imposed "political correctness," men are learning to avoid the words that offend, such as "chick," "girl," "baby," and are also learning to employ the words that gain favor with women when addressing outmoded representations such as "sexist," "exploit," "objectify." This informal cultural reeducation program, due in large part to thirty years of second-wave feminist discourse, has penetrated the everyday awareness and language of both men and women in this culture. In general, males are aware of the politics surrounding the use of women's bodies as ornaments and sites of objectification more now than ever before, and females are better equipped than ever before with the language to name and protest their experiences as the objects of such cultural objectification.

Perhaps the most enduring and profound legacy of second-wave feminism has been its ability to imbue our language with the capacity to name those images, remarks, and actions that are sexist. Of course, the legal definitions of what constitute sexist remarks and actions (in the form of harassment, for example) are being currently hammered out in this country's court systems and contested in public and private forums. However, the *naming* of sexist images, remarks, and actions has circulated in the common parlance and in the popular culture of this society for the last thirty years or so. Although men and women still are probably worlds apart on agreeing to the *boundaries* of sexist remarks and sexually harassing behavior, sexist images are a more agreed upon and more easily identifiable phenomena. Phrases such as "sex object" and "sexually exploited" are common descriptors that both men and women employed during interviews to discuss certain images, especially the images of women in particular advertising genres such as beer commercials and music videos. Jane, 32, said, "I think [ads] definitely exploit women. The sexual content of them is focused on it. Beauty and very little brain is demonstrated and it's just the male attraction to them."

Images of women's roles in advertising have greatly expanded beyond the dichotomy of the sex-object/household drudge, and perhaps the largest expanse in imagery has been in the realms of women in the work force and women in sports and fitness. These changes will be explored later on. Further, through this informal liberal feminist cultural reeducation program, both men and women have gained the vocabulary to cry "foul!" when confronted with overtly sexist images either on television or in print.

I guess the most evident thing is the sexism issue. The fact that they just show pictures of pretty women, or parts of pretty women as opposed to women with a cause, enjoying themselves, doing something social whether it be social or motivational, that would be the biggest difference [between sexist and nonsexist ads]. (Richard, 24)

Not knowing what the ad is for, I couldn't imagine a product where it would be appropriate [for a woman to be licking the floor]. That probably helped me to decide it was rather sexist because as there is no product that requires one to lick the floor, I assume the only reason she would be doing it would be to be blatantly sexual and pleasing to men, I suppose. . . . The woman [in this ad] appeared to be in a somewhat submissive position and I feel particularly sensitive to these things, as men go. (Bill, 26)

I just don't like the idea of women being portrayed as these kind of objects that when they're wearing really skimpy clothes and have guys hanging all over them, they just have that kind of arrogance about them that I don't care for. (Craig, 26)

Do I look at it as being potentially degrading to women or something? There's a certain part of this ad that says that this is the way that we portray women, and that's not appropriate. At least in my opinion, it's not appropriate. (Mario, 28)

If the mission of 1970s liberal feminist politics, epitomized in early sex roles in advertising research, was to increase women's public visibility, challenge traditional stereotypes, and raise the consciousness of the general public to issues of inequality in representation in order to begin changing those representations, then some small victories were won. A 1989 *U.S. News and World Report* article, in fact, professes that "Madison Avenue's stock in trade is sensitivity to popular values. Yet lapses into sexual stereotypes still pop up 30 years after the feminist movement exploded into national consciousness" (12). "Madison Avenue" is a popular nickname for the mecca of the advertising industry on Madison Avenue in Manhattan. The short article goes on to name two recent ad campaigns that had consumers crying "foul!" The first was an ad in *Fortune* magazine featuring the line, "You don't build a company like this with lace on your underwear." The ad drew protests from employees of Time, Inc. who managed to get the ad pulled. The second incident involved an ad insert for college newspapers produced by Miller beer. The ad insert was aimed at college-age consumers heading for spring break and included sketches of bikini-clad women and features such as, "4 sure-fire Ways to Scam Babes." Protests of outrage were leveled against Miller beer by the constituency they were trying to sell to—college students.

For many men and women interviewed, the beer ad seems to present the clearest example of consistent gender stereotyping. The sexually available party girl as a sign for beer is almost an advertising genre in itself and a formula that beer companies are reluctant to give up. When I shop for groceries at either of my local supermarkets, I must look at lifesize cardboard cutouts of Carmen Electra and other lesser-known models, exhibited beside pyramids of 12-pack boxes of beer. The heavily air-brushed images feature models in tight dresses, T-shirts, or sweaters inviting the consumer toward the pyramid of beer stacked on the floor, as if to say, "Step into my brand of beer and you can step into a full sexual fantasy with me. I'm available to you. Use my image to do or be whatever you want." For many men I talked with, the images seemed unnecessary and out-of-date:

It disgusts me. Again, just the association with the traditional notion of beer companies using really degrading ads of women to sell beer. To promote their products to men. I guess using women as tools to sell products. . . . This [Bud ad of three women as part of a towel] was a very popular poster when I was a freshman in the dorms. . . . Obviously a lot of men had this poster on their door and in their rooms and things like that so it conjures up images for me of that macho, masculine attitude that I hate. (Camron, 22)

'Cause you go to the beer store and you buy beer nine times out of ten they hand you a poster and the girls would be wearing bikinis. It is nice to look at but you know. I think it is more of an everyday occurrence to see people wearing work clothes. I don't think you see people wearing bikinis. . . . I don't know. I am just comparing it [the Bud ad] to other ads I have seen. Every Coors ad I have seen tends to exploit women and some- times men but not as often as women. This ad just seems to do it in a trendy, yuppie fashion. Not like high school. (Shawn, 20)

The men and women I spoke with agree that sexual stereotypes serve as guidelines for lived behaviors. As Erving Goffman (1976) suggested, there is a familiarity in gender displays in advertising because these displays are conventionalized portrayals of the correlates between biologically defined sex and culturally defined gender. Advertising offers up, in ritual-like bits, ideal- ized notions of gender relations. However, cut off from context, and taken as a group, advertisements supply us with an exaggerated distortion of a world with which we are intimately familiar. We will return to the ideas of Goffman in Chapter 3. However, statements by men and women suggested they believe that advertisers do more than reflect gender inequality through sex-role stereo- typing; they actually help to create it.

They're all the same. . . . The rustic Madonna with the child was once maybe a more real or less glamorized person, but now they sell that wholesome thing too. . . . I guess if you thought you looked like all the others [ads in study], you'd feel guilty about not looking like the mother in cowboy boots. . . . It doesn't please me that people waste their time on advertisers' dreams. (Mike, 40)

A surface reading of male and female responses on what constitutes a "sexist" image or a "sexual stereotype" presents the illusion that men and women are now of like mind on issues of equality in gender representation. On a definitional level, this may very well be true. However, gender differences about sexism and sexual stereotyping do not appear at the level of identification and naming, but at the level of experiential knowledge. The remainder of this chapter discusses how female responses to the subject of sexism in advertising extend beyond naming to experience.

How Women Read Sexism

Women I spoke with were far less likely than men to brush aside the cliched sexism of beer commercials and other such advertising genres as a benign nuisance. Many women suggested that the danger in such images is the fact that they are not isolated, but merely the extreme of the ubiquitous and repetitious portrait of femininity circulated and recirculated throughout this culture. Sexist representations in beer commercials are only the most profound symptom of sexist representation, they are not the disease. Many women felt that the effects of these images on cultural ways of seeing women in this society are cumulative in nature. Ignoring the most obvious sexist representations, like beer commercials, would defeat the purpose of naming the real problem.

I would say now maybe because I'm so tired of seeing ads like this, like there's a lot in the music industry, of seeing a woman sprawled out on a car to sell blank tapes. The whole scenario of women being made into objects leads you to question, "what's the point?" . . . I'm angry because women are not objects and they're continually shown that way. It makes me angry. And the more it continues the harder it is to drive it home to people that women are equal as human beings and not objects. (Rachel, 20)

I mean, every time you watch a car commercial, which is what every other commercial on TV, or a beer commercial or all of those . . . it has women like that [the Bud girls]. This one commercial for the Eclipse [car] came on, two heavenly bodies coming together, there's the car and there's the women with long legs and a skimpy dress walks by. So many of them are like that. . . . It makes me mad that they always use women to sell things just like they were products themselves or something. (Laura, 33)

It just makes me angry that they use women's body parts to try and sell something. It is not done so much on men as it is done on women. Women have traditionally been in that position where they have been exploited and they let it happen. . . . I want to be taken seriously as a woman and these kinds of ads, men can look at them the wrong way, it could hurt you. . . . The fact that women always seem to be exploited in ads has led me to become more of a feminist than I would have been otherwise. It takes so much more to be respected as a woman and not be an object. That is like the main thing. I don't like it when men look at ads and then just think about sex. It makes me really angry. Like the women in the ads make me angry too because they are hurting other women. (Claire, 22)

She has a good body and nice hair. She has the whole look but she has this helpless look on her face like, "I have a good body and that is it." That is why I think she is selling out. The way they portray her is not the typical woman. . . . It hurts me just being a woman. Her representation hurts women all around the world. This kind of hurts me because once again the way they are portrayed in these bathing suits, lying there, degrades women. (Nicole, 22)

Stereotypes provide prescriptions for how women should look and be looked at, how they should feel and be made to feel, and how they are expected to act. Many women feel that men see them in terms of stereotypes, therefore oversimplifying who they are and what they have to offer as human beings. The mass media has succeeded beautifully in training all of us in this culture to assess the attractiveness of the female body in minute detail. Most women I spoke with carried around in their heads a list of sexual stereotypes continuously perpetuated by advertising, and can easily tick off the list when the subject is broached.

I see these women as the perfect mother, thin, younger, beautiful, with a child on her back, having a good time. I think that men have thought we should be this. Despite that, we're supposed to be happy with our children and ourselves. Men are behind these ads. . . . I grew up with these [images from]—MTV. I used to watch it when I came home from school. I am not these people but I always want to be because you think if you are these people then you're going to be happy—if you're a Bud girl or tight and small in a bikini. (Rachel, 20)

It disturbs me greatly. I'm sick of people wanting me or women to be all sensual and sexy. I'm me. People buy into that type of behavior when they read articles, or look at magazines. We have models who get paid for selling their looks. That's disgusting. Advertising and women are just a business, but the business is negatively affecting society in a way that it stereotypes women. . . . I don't want to see women's personal body parts. . . . For me it's a turn-off. I watch music videos all the time and see women exposing their bodies and I don't care to see it so I turn it off, or turn the channel. Why must women show their bodies all the time to prove their true potential? I don't know why they bother. It's temporary satisfaction. (Jamie, 22)

Unlike Rachel, who blames the male-dominated advertising industry for such stereotypical images of women, Laura believes the women who pose for the ads and the women that buy into the stereotypes are also to blame for their perpetuation.

They [women in beer ads] are always stupid, in addition to being dressed this way. So that's why I think they are bimbos because they are in a beer ad. And her [Jordache ad, fig. 3], she looks so stupid. Somebody wants to be with three men dressed like that. They are missing a screw somewhere. . . . Same old stuff. I wish women weren't like that, and they would think a little about being their own person. And yet at the same time, I think about real human beings making decisions for all kinds of reasons. I hate that I am judgmental about it. . . . I don't see why I should care about how anybody dresses, or what kind of choices they make. I wish women weren't sometimes the way they are, that they didn't act that way. I don't know, I wish they didn't want to, or they knew a little more about, or they think about it and make a decision to dress that way. (Laura, 33)

Another way to interpret these comments is that these women believe stereotypes in ads help to circulate the message that women are the "other" in society. Women's sexuality itself has been held up historically as the dark "other" of culture. For example, the male-dominated medical profession has traditionally employed the euphemisms of "women's problems" and "nerves" to cover a wide range of feminine physical problems ranging from menstrual cramping to postpartum depression to menopause. Further, the supposed female susceptibility to "hysteria" has historically been used by male medical professionals to separate women from men as the psychological "other." As Christi, 35, states, "I still think there is somewhat of a feeling that 'we have uteruses and therefore we are hysterical,' you know [laughs]. God, every 28 days we are just going to blow someplace up. It's ridiculous."

Placing women in the position of "other" in society is consistent with what feminist scholars of gender and advertising have identified as the ideological gender divisions of "male-work-social" and "female-leisure-natural" found consistently throughout advertising. In Judith Williamson's classic essay, "Woman Is an Island," she explains that:

In our society women stand for the side of life that seems to be outside history—for personal relationships, love and sex—so that these aspects of life actually seem to become "women's areas." But they are also, broadly speaking, the arena of "mass culture." Much of mass culture takes place, or is consumed, in the "feminine" spheres of leisure, family or personal life, and the home; and it also focuses on these as the subject matter of its representations. (1986, 101)

A trend particularly evident in advertising of the 1970s and early '80s placed females in the role of the exotic. The exotic female "other" is outside of culture in nature, and outside of the conventions of the social. The ideological construction of placing female sexuality in nature or the home (the private sphere) and male sexuality in culture (the public sphere), allows the naturalized coexistence of very different ways of seeing gender in this culture.

I was just looking at these three ads [Budweiser, fig. 1; Jordache, fig. 3; Montana, fig. 4] versus this ad [Isabella, fig. 7] and the thing that sums this one up as an ideal was "Puritanism." This woman is the put-on-the-pedestal woman. She is supposed to be admired. She has a quiet strength about her. Puritan, putting a woman up on a pedestal. Don't let her get dirty. . . . The women when they are shown in ads such as this are rarely shown in business suits. They are often shown either naked or in typical quote "homemaker outfits," taking care of kids while the man is walking around with the briefcase. Which I don't think there is anything wrong with the role if that is the role the woman has chosen, but women are always shown in that role rather than roles that are typically portrayed by men. (Ginger, 28)

Well, she's with her kids, kind of representing the mother image, I guess. Women are always associated with babies and children and housework, things like that. That is supposed to be our role in life. I don't think so! I want children and all, yet that's not my goal in life. This ad makes it seem as she's happy with it, and you should be happy too, instead of pursuing a personal goal that you might have. . . . I wish people would stop associating all women with children. Everyone always assumes that all women want to have children. I mean, I do, but I know some people who don't. Classify me as a human being before a mother, or sex symbol or businesswoman, please. (Jamie, 22)

The naturalness, or "common sense," of these differentiations of woman-in-nature (private sphere) and man-in-culture (public sphere) began to disintegrate with the reality of women entering the work force, and therefore the public sphere. The legacy of this ideological division, however, remains. A woman's sexuality still plays an integral part in how she is seen and treated as a "worker." For example, a woman's ability to bear children has been, both formally and informally, held up as grounds for inequality in pay and advancement in industry. Women I talked with cited the concrete examples of inadequate in-house daycare facilities and maternity leave policies as the types of prejudices against the needs of female workers:

Or there is still this feeling that you will just get married or pregnant and you will leave us. Or you will need 6 weeks off to have your baby and we just can't have that and that's part of it. Also, this is a bit far afield, but women in our culture have been the primary caretakers since the industrial revolution and males have formed society. Women are still idealized as the mother and the housewife and for example how many companies have daycare, or novel services for taking care of an elderly parent? Because traditionally that burden falls on females. If healthcare companies were run by females you could bet that you would get more than 6 weeks off for maternity. So that adds into it for me. (Christi, 35)

The Power of Advertising

When my oldest daughter was 7 she still believed most advertising claims to be true. One day I was complaining that at age 35 I still had adolescent skin. I had several unsightly pimples on my face and as I washed, I was muttering, primarily to myself, that it wasn't fair that I was dealing with pimples at the same time I was getting wrinkles. Shouldn't there be some kind of lifecycle trade-off there? My daughter, being the helpful person she is, said, "You should get that cream. They showed it on TV. You just put a little bit on your pimples at night and in the morning they just *vanish*!" I could see in her face that she was wondering why I would spend a moment worrying about pimples when there was this wonder drug just sitting at the store waiting to be purchased. In the process of explaining that I did indeed own a tube of Clearasil, and that by the way, it doesn't make pimples, mine at least, vanish overnight, I got a chance to impart some wisdom absolutely essential to parenting today: "Honey, you shouldn't believe everything you see in advertisements."

After an episode that happened one Christmas, my parenting message needed more teeth. I found myself telling my disappointed four-year-old, "Honey, ads lie." Luckily for me, up to this point my girls hadn't been too interested in Barbie dolls. Although it became clear a few years ago that I couldn't ban them from the house—they arrive in the insidious disguise of birthday and Christmas presents—I have made it very clear why I don't think Barbie "is a woman's best friend." However, this holiday merchandising season my littlest was intoxicated by a commercial for a Barbie who was shown making her own cookies and decorating them. It was the only thing she specifically wanted. I knew how disappointed she would be when she found out Barbie only stands by the mixing bowl while the child makes sickening strawberry icing—cookies and oven not included. She cried a little as we made the pitiful miniature bowl of icing and spread it on graham crackers. Later that day she proceeded to tell anyone who would listen that the commercial lied! Barbie doesn't do anything! The doll herself held no fascination and hasn't been played with since. Although the experience was a little hard on her, the knowledge she now has will serve her well throughout life.

As we get older, as early as nine or ten, we begin to develop a keener sense of the distinction between fact and fantasy in the media. Furthermore, most of us begin to develop a strong sense of the role the media plays in our lives—a source of entertainment or information, a pacifier for boredom, a connection to our world and universe. Men and women interviewed recognized that advertising images increasingly pervade our everyday lives, bombarding us with snapshots of what we "lack" and what we need to fill the void. Both men and women recognized that each new day brings with it a barrage of images attempting to market goods and services directly at them as consumers. Each day these men and women employed strategies in attempts to filter out desired from undesired messages, and/or to resist or to ignore those messages. Men, in particular, reported feelings of being barraged by advertising images.

You're just bombarded with different images every day. Anyone that watches television 20–25 hours a week, reads the books and magazines and journals. You're just bombed with images and so you just kind of . . . I guess I use my values, and my personal life experiences, and things that I feel are right and wrong. . . . I use them as filters. (Mario, 28)

I mentioned a beer commercial earlier where you have the beautiful women and the good-looking guys who are with the women and having a lot of fun and whatever else is going on. And I think they take advantage of that. I think it kind of makes it seem like, with them flooding the media or whatever, when you see these kinds of commercials, they make you think that's the normal, that it's normal to have these kinds of feelings. And it's normal to expect to have a beer commercial with beautiful women in it. Basically, what's normal—kind of like a mass consent thing. (Art, 30)

While both men and women recognized the pervasiveness of advertising images in their daily viewing experiences, sharp gender differences arose in response to whether advertising is seen as a powerful organizing social structure of values and behaviors in this society. Most men saw themselves, their values, emotions, behaviors, and so on, as relatively unaffected by the dominant messages in advertising. In sharp contrast, most women considered the dominant messages in advertising, especially pertaining to gender identity and gender relations, to have immense influence on how they view themselves, how they behave, how they perceive others as viewing them, and how others behave.

Therefore, most men and women interviewed saw the influence of advertising differently. At a fundamental level, the difference can be explained in terms of two competing theories of media effects. The men interviewed tended to speak of the power of advertising in terms of one ad's ability to directly influence one's behavior or values. These conclusions, drawn by many of the males in the study, correspond to the findings of most limited effects research. This research has found that the direct causal effects of messages on individual behavior is extremely limited. Men were confident that the content of advertising messages did not directly affect their purchasing behaviors, much less their actions regarding others.

Illustrative of this confidence were overt statements by men interviewed that advertising is *not* "powerful." Males often described advertising as a nuisance, but rather innocuous and benign. Although both men and women described strategies for resisting advertising, only the males saw resistance as easily achievable. When men stated that advertisements are not powerful, or have no effect upon them personally, almost all references were made in the context of the one-to-one correspondence between seeing an ad and buying a product or buying into an idea.

A basic assumption here is that media effects occur at the conscious, rational level and that the viewer (consumer) must employ rational decision-making capabilities in order to thwart potential influences. Feeling confident that they possessed such skills, many of the men interviewed felt they also possessed the ability to easily distance themselves from the messages and images in ads. A word used repeatedly to describe this ability to distance oneself from the influence of advertising was "immunity." Men possessed a sense that the overexposure to all these images had inoculated them against the ads' effects:

I've been impressed by advertising but I don't think it's ever changed my life or made me go out and say, "I just got to have that to be fulfilled." I don't think it's ever really been part of my past experience. I look at a lot of ads and I think sometimes, wouldn't that be nice to have, but I don't see an ad or buying a product as something that's going to change me. . . . I'm just not really affected by ads, to tell you the truth. (Kevin, 33)

I think I'm pretty much immune to this kind of advertising by now. I'm not overly disturbed or shocked or impeded. (Bill, 26)

It [advertising] doesn't do anything for me. I'll turn the page before the advertisement bothers me. (Shawn, 20)

I don't think I'll be suckered into anything that I don't need or want. So, for me, I see it as a positive. Advertising for me is a kind of nuisance. (Greg, 19)

The commercials, there's nothing really wrong with them. I just don't believe that if I splash on some Old Spice that all of the sudden a great-looking women is going to walk up to me ask me what I'm doing tonight. (Craig, 26)

I think I know what the ad is for as soon as I look at it and I am not deceived when I look at it in greater depth. (Jake, 21)

As stated above, most men were adamant that the content of an ad has very little to do with what they purchase. Some men made some minor concessions to the idea that advertising may help them choose between name brands, but beyond that, advertising had little influence on purchasing decisions:

The only thing that an advertisement does to me is that it shows me it is a name brand. . . . When I go to the store I look at two things, can I afford it? and, do I want it? If I want and can afford it, I'll buy it. Not because Jane Blow is in the ad. (Shawn, 20)

This perceived distance from the seductiveness of the content of ads plays a very important part in defining a male "way of looking," which will be explored in depth in chapter four. Male distancing suggests a certain comfort in looking at ads, and the females portrayed in ads, without the anxiety of being seduced by the image. Some of the men interviewed stated that it is possible to enjoy ads, especially of attractive women, with the enjoyment having little or no effect upon whether or not they buy that particular product. In this schema, therefore, the male, not the image, is always in control of the seduction:

I look at ads and think whether they have sexual content or not. Usually that's about it—more of a curiosity thing. If they do [have sexual content], it pleases me in that regard but for the product itself, if I use it, I use it, if I don't, I don't, and the ad doesn't really do a lot to change it. (Art, 30)

Advertisements don't make me run out and buy something, no matter what's in the ad. If they put a sexy woman, half-naked in an ad for a six-pack, I don't run out and buy it. . . . No matter what they put in the ad, I'm not going to go out and buy the stuff. When I shop for something I'm very careful. . . . Putting a half-naked woman in a car is not going to make me go out and buy a Toyota over a Honda. (Jim, 37)

Women were far less likely than men to describe the power of advertising in terms of one-to-one causal relationships between viewing a particular image and buying a product or adopting a particular behavior. Instead, women described the influence of advertising in terms of pervasive images and repetitive messages that reverberate throughout culture, not just in certain media, such as advertising. This more complex reporting of the many levels of media influence suggest the adoption of a cultural/ritual theory of media effects—in contrast to the limited effects model influencing the male responses. Women described their experiences with advertising in terms of subconscious as well as conscious viewing, suggesting the possibility that resisting the messages of advertising on a conscious, rational level may not be enough to protect them from the influence of advertising messages:

There are so many things. They expect people to make this connection and then there's no reason to make the connection. . . . All you have to do is think something through, you know, two steps and you realize that the claims are totally bogus. "Can't you come up with anything better?" [Advertisers] have been deceptive or whatever. . . . I hope [advertising] doesn't get any cleverer. It's already too powerful. It has too much control over people's opinions and values. I hope it doesn't get any more powerful. (Laura, 33)

Indeed, the inner conflicts women often described when viewing advertising images, especially of other women, were generally couched in terms of a conflict between what their logical mind was telling them they should ignore and what another part of them could not ignore. For these reasons, among others, none of the women I spoke with stated that advertising was *not* powerful. Each woman stated advertising was powerful. In one form or another they all suggested that advertising images of women have influenced their lives either now or in the past.

I feel basically advertising has tried to shape my way of thinking. And has made me, I think everyone, view life from the advertisers' eyes or stereotypes. (Jamie, 22)

Usually when I see commercials like that [for Nike, fig. 8], I want to go out and do some aerobics or something or buy some shoes. Either way I think they're getting their point across. It's good to once and awhile see these and go do something. Half the time that's why I go out and do something, it's because I saw it on TV or in a magazine and I'm thinking, "Yeah, I bought these shoes for that reason." (Collette, 21)

I think it [advertising] helps to contribute to people . . . and how they think about women. I think it is harmful, what we are seeing is the one-dimensional things and we are not—men are not trained to deal with us like regular human beings. Not a lot of them. . . . Everybody including women and including myself, who thinks I'm sort of aware of this, still is influenced by what you see in advertisements, so we are all going to be influenced to see women as one-dimensional things. (Laura, 33)

The women I spoke with did not view the effects of advertising only in terms of direct causal relationships with buying products or ideas, and therefore they made far fewer references to their purchasing decisions than did men. In further contrast to male responses, when speaking of purchasing decisions, women were more likely to allude to times when advertising *did* affect their buying habits than when it *did not*:

I have some pretty strong feelings about what products I endorse, or what advertisements I endorse. When I see an ad I don't care for I tend to remember not to buy that product. . . . If I like a product and especially if I like the ad that goes along with it, I try to buy that so I try to balance it out—its not all negative. . . . It [advertising] helps me remember because if you go to Drug Emporium or Phar-More or one of those places and there are a million things lined up, a lot of them there isn't much difference who makes them or the price or that type of thing. An ad might make a difference to me whether I might choose to buy a product or not. (Christi, 35)

[There's a] difference in day and night ads. The difference is who it is that they were trying to sell to, who was watching TV at that time. . . . it's just that the ones at night you ignore. When you are watching football games you get up and leave when the commercials come on because you know that what you are going to see is the Swedish Bikini Team and that kind of stuff. Really how many times do you want to see it? You get up or you don't watch. What you learn is to not pay attention. (Heather, 29)

How Women Read Sexism in Gender Relations

Women I talked with were far more likely than men to connect the sexism they see in the content of ads with sexism they experience, or see others experience, in everyday life situations. Women expressed their experiential knowledge of sexism in gender relations in two forms. The first is in the realm of sexual harassment and the second is in the realm of double standards.

In 1993–94, when the majority of these interviews were conducted, a cultural event fresh on the minds of many people was the confirmation hearings of Supreme Court Justice Clarence Thomas—tainted with controversy after the testimony that Thomas had sexually harassed law professor Anita Hill. Dr. Hill was subpoenaed to testify against Thomas on charges of sexual harassment in the workplace. This event was seen by many women as the turning point in this society for heightened awareness of sexual harassment as a serious lived experience instead of an abstract concept. The hearings themselves are often held up as a mockery of equality in gender relations. Over a two-day period, an all-white, male Senate panel relentlessly questioned Professor Hill about her professional and personal involvement with Clarence Thomas. Professor Hill's character seemed to be on trial rather than Judge Thomas's actions.

In spite of these negative assessments, however, women interviewed suggested that many positive things came out of the hearings in the form of raising the male consciousness about what constitutes sexually harassing behavior. However, there exists a lag between this awareness and naming of sexually harassing behavior and the legislation to deal with such behaviors. Women felt that this lag is a result of the fact that men still hold the most powerful positions in society. The hearings are said to have shaken up the legal system and led to pursuing legislation that more clearly defines sexual harassment and victims' rights. Christi, who is a psychologist by profession, explained her thoughts this way:

The Clarence Thomas/Anita Hill hearings were hopefully a great realization to the people who run this country how badly women are treated and how upset women are about that. . . . It was very interesting to hear—to even just listen. There was "Judge Thomas" and here's Professor Hill and those who supported her were calling her Dr. Hill and Professor Hill and those not of allegiance it was "Miss Hill" this and that. So, it was a one-up, one-down position. Here is Judge Thomas and here is Miss Hill. Let's forget she has a Ph.D. Let's forget she is an attorney. Let's forget she is a professor. It really showed a lot of people, males and females, the inequity of the whole system because not only was it a question of whether she had been harassed by him, the whole hearing became a harassment of her. And that really shows why we have not come very far. . . . And I think the other thing is if we look at the Fortune 500, or you look at top managers, or you look at organizations such as APA [American Psychological Association], that I am in, I would say that APA is 54% or more female in body, but in upper levels it is almost all male. That is true in rehabilitation, it is true in law, it is true in universities. It smacks you in the face all of the time. Even if you choose a profession that is dominantly female, it is very interesting that the people in power are males. (Christi, 35)

A second realm where women discussed sexism in gender relations was the double standard they perceived between a male fantasy of ideal femininity as projected in advertising images and the ideal female who is fit to marry in real life. Women perceived that although the females in beer commercials and music videos are seen by men as the perfect sexual playmates, males define a life mate as someone beyond reproach, and certainly not sexually promiscuous. In feminist literature this double standard is referred to as the "Madonna/whore" phenomenon. Feminist historians trace this double standard back to Victorian era morals, where women occupied two different stations in society for the needs of men. The wife was supposed to be frail and pure, ashamed of her sexuality, guarding it at all costs. For the wife, sex was endured for the purpose of procreation only, and a good woman did not enjoy the experience. The whore fulfilled men's other needs for sex and warmth. However valued the whore's company, however, she was never fit to be a wife. Some women suggested that this double standard is alive and well in this culture today:

I mean I'm sure that a lot of people don't look down on [women in beer ads] because they are, they must sell something, so somebody has got to think that they are hot, right? But in terms of that sort of women, I wouldn't think of that sort of woman as society's ideal. Maybe the men buying beer . . . even for them, that wouldn't be their ideal woman, I mean to marry or something to live with. You know what I'm saying? That same old thing, not the kind they would marry. (Laura, 33)

But as far as women go and females go, if you would really ask the males if this is really the way they want their wife to be it really wouldn't be. So I think in some views they would say yes, this is society's ideal and everyone should look like this and act like this. But in reality, I don't really think they do. It's nice to have it out there, but at home you don't really want this kind of thing. (Jane, 32)

Second-wave feminism has imbued our language with the ability to name those images, remarks, and actions that are "sexist." Both men and women readily employ such descriptors as "sexual stereotypes," "sex object," and "sexually exploited" to discuss certain images, especially the images of women in advertising genres such as beer commercials and music videos. A surface reading of male and female responses about what constitutes a "sexist" image or a "sexual stereotype" presents the illusion that men and women are now of like mind on issues of equality in gender representation. However, female responses to sexism reached beyond naming to female experiencing. Most women suggested that the danger in sexist images is in the fact that they are merely the extreme of the ubiquitous and repetitious portrait of femininity circulated and recirculated throughout this culture, and therefore the effects of advertising must be viewed cumulatively and not as isolated images.

Although in agreement about the sheer quantities of advertisements consumed or actively avoided each day and strategies for coping with this barrage of messages/images, men and women see the power of advertising very differently. Many men judged advertising's power by the ability of an ad to directly influence purchasing decisions, behaviors and values. These men, therefore, felt that the direct influence of advertising on their lives was extremely limited. Women, on the other hand, saw advertising in terms of pervasive images and repetitive messages that reverberate throughout culture, operating not only at conscious but also at subconscious levels. Women, therefore, felt that advertising is powerful, affecting their everyday lives in very profound ways, through their own actions and emotions and through the actions of others.

3. What Do Ads Teach Us About Gender?

When we explore how people discuss the content of ads, we are really asking how advertising images that we see over and over again affect our thoughts, emotions and behaviors. In Chapter 1 we discussed a body of literature about gender in advertising commonly referred to as "sex roles research." Cultural studies scholar and Media Education Foundation video entrepeneur Sut Jhally levels an important critique at sex-roles research in *Codes of Advertisements* (1987). According to Jhally, content analysis research of gender stereotyping in advertising places its emphasis on the truth or falsity of representation, when in fact "advertisement images are neither false nor true reflections of social reality because they are in fact *part* of social reality" (135). As such, advertising needs to be studied as a constituent part of our social reality, not as a distorted reflection of it. Therefore, emphasis must shift from questions of truth or falsehood to processes of "signification," or the ability of advertisements to "communicate" to social actors. This change marks a theoretical and methodological shift in advertising research focused on gender from analyses of manifest content to analyses of the symbolic potential of that content.

Gender Advertising as Ritualized Display

In the midst of the flurry of content analysis research, Erving Goffman published his own empirical manifesto on the nature of advertising portrayals in *Gender Advertisements* (1979). Goffman, however, asked very different questions of his data than sex-roles researchers and also employed a very different method for analyzing his results. Guided by the tenets of symbolic interactionism, Goffman suggested that the most relevant questions we can ask of advertising are: of what aspects of real life do advertisements provide us a fair picture, and what social effects do the advertisements have upon the lives purportedly pictured in them?

Goffman's research was unique at the time for employing a method now being labeled "semiotic content analysis." His analysis focused on message structures across the entire discourse of print advertisements containing gender components. Goffman revealed patterns in messages about gender that when repeated constantly and consistently provide a picture of reality that seems natural and real. Goffman's work provides the base for textual analyses that will be reviewed later such as poststructuralist and psychoanalytic approaches. Prominent feminist scholars on gender and advertising, like Jean Kilbourne (1999, 1987), for example, build their highly persuasive and widely circulated findings on the nature of gender in advertising on Goffman's original categories: relative size, the feminine touch, function ranking, the family, the ritualization of subordination, licensed withdrawal. Therefore, sex roles research and Goffman's original study on gender advertisements are presented here as the cornerstones of research on the nature of advertising portrayals of gender.

Goffman's *Gender Advertisements* was one of the first and is to this day one of the most influential textual analyses of the symbolic potential of advertising images. Goffman was intrigued by the signification (although Goffman would call it symbolism) of advertising images in their ability to look familiar and natural, when on close inspection they portray a world which is really quite peculiar. This approach is most interested in how advertisements offer up ritualized bits of real gendered behaviors in order to offer a familiar picture of gender to consumers. Taken as a whole, however, or as a system of meaning, advertising, in fact, offers up a very distorted and hyper-ritualized picture of real gender relationships.

Goffman's discussion of gender and advertising is based on a symbolic interactionist perspective on communication in which the way individuals view themselves and how they choose to behave evolve out of their interactions with others. These interactions are shaped by roles, the communicator's social self (Fisher 1978, 174), and rules, prescriptions that indicate what behavior is obligated, preferred, or prohibited in certain contexts (Shimanoff 1980). An important concept in symbolic interactionism is the "generalized other." The "generalized other" is representative of typical members of a culture or society with which the individual identifies him/herself. The role-taking function allows the individual to align his/her behaviors with those of others within a social setting, and as such, a social collectivity is organized that can perform identifiable actions. In cultural studies this process is referred to as "cultural mapping." In order for communication to take place at all, we must have some common cultural maps in our heads. Although your cultural mapping of the exact meanings produced by, say, an episode of *Melrose Place* will never be exactly the same as mine, we share cultural maps of American urban life in the 1990s, male/female relationships, fashion, "Southern California," and the codes we expect in nighttime TV drama on a network like Fox.

Mass media are one way that the prescribed roles and rules of a society get disseminated, and advertising plays a very large part in our experience of the mass media. For Goffman, advertisements offer highly stylized versions of social mores, definitions, attitudes, values and behavioral tendencies whose meanings must be clear enough to be interpreted in an instant. "The task of the advertiser is to favorably dispose viewers to his [sic] product, his means, by and large, to show a sparkling version of that product in the context of glamorous events. The implication is that if you buy the one, you are on the way to realizing the other—and you should want to" (Goffman 1979, 26).

In *Gender Advertisements* Goffman compares the "job" of the advertiser—to dramatize and make salient the worth of his/her product—to that of the "work" of society. Both function by infusing "social situations with ceremonial and ritual signs facilitating the orientation of participants to one another" (27). Both must use limited resources to tell a story, both must transform the opaque into the easily readable. When studying gender in advertising, according to Goffman, the uncovering of sexual stereotypes is important, but not nearly as important as attending to how those who produce advertisements, and for that matter those who pose for them, can "choreograph the materials available in social situations in order to achieve their end" (27).

Central to Goffman's view of how gender operates in advertising is his notion of "gender display": "if gender be defined as the culturally established correlates of sex (whether in consequence of biology or learning), then gender display refers to conventionalized portrayals of these correlates" (1). The key, then, to understanding how gender is communicated through advertisements is to understand the notion that advertisements present to us familiar ritual-like displays. However, displays in real life or in the world of advertising can be, and usually are, *polysemic* (containing myriad possible meanings). More than one piece of cultural information may be encoded into them. Further, once a display becomes well established and sequentialized—say, for example, the steps and gestures involved when a man opens a door for a woman—parts of the sequence can be taken out, or bracketed. A still photograph of a woman standing on the curb looking toward a parked taxicab with a man reaching toward the door of the cab invokes in our minds the entire sequence of a man opening a cab door for a woman. The stylization itself becomes the object of attention, and we the social actors then have the ability to comment upon it. According to Goffman, this is the process of "hyper-ritualization," wherein "the human use of displays is complicated by the human capacity for re-framing behavior" (3).

Partly because of this web of hyper-ritualization, individuals feel that gender is one of the most deeply seated traits of human beings; femininity and masculinity are the prototypes of essential expression. Gender display, therefore, is at once something that can be expressed fleetingly and at the same time has the ability to characterize a person at the most basic level (7).

Advertisements, then, are actually "ritual-like bits of behavior which portray an ideal conception of the two sexes and their structural relationship to each other" (Goffman 1979, 84). Actual gender expressions are artful poses, too. However, advertisements exist in a constant state of "hyper-ritualization." Standardization, exaggeration, and simplification are found to an extended degree in advertising. The gender displays in advertising are familiar because they show us rituals in which we engage in real life. However, advertisements further serve to conventionalize our conventions. Cut off from context and taken as a group, advertisements supply us with an exaggerated distortion of a world with which we are intimately familiar.

Goffman adds empirical support to his arguments by suggesting six general categories of hyper-ritualizations that showed up consistently throughout the over 500 advertisements he analyzed. In one categorization, titled "The Feminine Touch," Goffman concluded that in advertising, women, more often than men, were pictured using their fingers and their hands, whether to caress an object, cradle it, or outline its surface. Self-touching was also viewed as a feminine domain, indicating that the body was a precious and delicate object (29–31).

Further, Goffman concluded that advertisements rank the importance of the individual by the function they perform, much as in real life. In his category called, appropriately, "Function Ranking," Goffman explained that most often it was the male who is pictured in the executive role, when only one executive role was shown. The hierarchy of functions was pictured both within, and outside of, occupational frames. In these depictions the male was the one executing or overseeing the action or giving instruction. When instructions were given in advertising, generally deference for the instructor by the instructed is also shown.

Interestingly, when males were pictured in the traditional domains of female authority, namely the home, three trends emerged. The first was to picture the male engaged in no contributing role at all, "in this way avoiding either subordination or contamination with the 'female' task" (36). The second was to make the male ludicrous or childlike, therefore distancing the image from real life and preserving the male image of competency. Third, a more subtle technique, was to picture the male undertaking the task under the watchful eye of the female (36–37).

Another of Goffman's categories of hyper-ritualizations that is important for understanding current gender representations in advertising is what Goffman calls "The Ritualization of Subordination." A classic stereotype of deference is to lower oneself, in one way or another, either to bow one's head, slump in one's posture or to sit or lie below another. Holding the body erect and the head high "is stereotypically a mark of unashamedness, superiority and disdain" (40). Advertising embraces these conventions as if they were universal in value. Women and children seem to be pictured on floors and on beds more than are men. Men also seem to be located higher than women in much advertising—drawing on our society's convention of elevating, quite literally, those of superior status, as in a courtroom setting, for example. Further, women, much more frequently than men, are pictured with one knee slightly bent—a convention of unpreparedness, and also in "canting" (bending) positions which can be read as an acceptance of subordination. Another subordinating image continuously found in advertising is that women smile more than men do. The smile can be read as a type of acceptance and as a mollifier of the male's activity or emotions.

Goffman's analysis forces the reader to reconsider the relationship between advertising and reality. "He also uncovers the assumptions underlying the interpretive codes buried in advertisements and the way advertising acts as an accomplice in perpetuating regressive forms of social relations" (Leiss, Kline, and Jhally 1986, 169). In all its familiarity, advertising does not merely reflect reality. Although it draws its materials from everyday life, from real gender displays for instance, the bits of everyday life used are selected carefully and much is habitually omitted. By selecting some things to integrate continuously into the message system of advertising (a good example is the ideal female body image), and continuously omitting others (say, the "fleshy" female body), ads create new meanings that are not necessarily found elsewhere.

Cultural critics of communication have attempted to build upon, as well as push beyond, Goffman's ideas of gender display. Taken in historical context, these new directions in theory are beginning to address more adequately how gender relations can be reproduced when viewed across time and symbolic conventions. Since *Gender Advertisements*, many scholars have expanded upon the concept of gender display in advertising and what these rituals communicate to us when viewed over and over again (Coward 1982; Hay 1989; Kilbourne 1999, 1987; Masse and Rosenblum 1988; Millium 1975; Myers 1982, 1986; Williamson 1986; Winship 1981, 1985). Prominent themes have emerged in this body of work which are of particular relevance to this chapter. The first of these themes involves the "photographic cropping" (Millium 1975) of female body parts to substitute for the entire body in advertising representations, a recurrent ritualization of considerable concern to these authors. Women in advertising are very often signified in a fragmented way, by their lips, legs, hair, eyes, or hands. The "bit" (lips, legs, breasts, etc.) represents the whole: the sexualized woman (Winship 1981, 25). Men, on the other hand, are less likely to be "dismembered" in this way in advertisements. Jeane Kilbourne (1999, 1987), in particular, describes the cropping of photographs of women in advertising as one of the major elements that presents the female as dehumanized and as an object, which is the first step toward the legitimation of committing violence toward that person. This, she argues, contributes to a general climate of violence against women.

In her analysis of the relationship between the positioning of hands and sexuality in advertising, Janice Winship (1981) brings together the theme of photographic cropping with a second theme, "the public male and the domestic female." Male and female hands are a part of an entire message system of social representation signifying appropriate gender behavior. In her analysis, Winship juxtaposes an ad of a man's hand holding an open pack of Rothman's cigarettes, the "world leader," and a woman's hand pouring a pitcher of Bird's custard over a dessert, the caption reading, "home-made goodness." A switching of the hands would disrupt the meanings with which each gender imbues the ad:

A woman's hand does not signify "world leader"; a man's hand does not signify "homemade." But as it is, the appropriately gendered hand allows us to key into familiar ideologies of masculinity and femininity. Those ideologies see "naturally" masculine or feminine, and the represented hand is "naturally" a man's or a woman's. (30)

Decoding Gender Displays

In the language of semiotics (which will be explored more fully in Chapter 4), gender displays are cultural codes. Cultural codes are the store of experience upon which both the advertiser and audience draw in their participation in the construction of "commodity meaning." Images of gender are highly structured cultural codes in this society. The transfer of codes from sexuality to commodities are probably more widely accessible to more people than other cultural codes. Therefore they are continually recycled in the symbolic world of image production. However, Goffman tells us that advertisements further serve to conventionalize our conventions, to codify our codes. Cut off from context and taken as a group, advertisements supply us with exaggerated distortions of the world. When we decode advertising, therefore, the process involves an intricate process of viewing, always through the lens of gender, the encoded displays that are intimately familiar, yet stereotypical, exaggerated bits of lived experience.

The women and men I spoke with discussed many particular gender displays in advertising. At times their responses intersected with categories of gender display discovered by Goffman, such as "function ranking," a hierarchy of functions that places men above women and children in terms of executing action. Further, some responses expounded upon categories of gender display discovered by Jean Kilbourne and other feminist cultural critics such as the process of "body cropping," and the gender divisions of "action vs. appearance." Two other gender displays were discussed at length by both men and women, the displays of "the new working woman" and "motherhood." Finally, this study uncovered the possibility of an "alternative aesthetic" in gender display, as described by those interviewed. These five forms of gender display are discussed below in the context of gender similarities and differences.

Body Cropping

Using female body parts to represent the entire woman in advertising is an often used and hyper-ritualized convention, familiar to anyone who has consumed print advertising, in particular. The practice of photographic cropping only became politicized, however, in the 1970s when scholars such as Jean Kilbourne in her lectures and films, *Killing Us Softly*, *Still Killing Us Softly*, and *Slim Hopes* proposed that the repetition of this practice across time helps reproduce a cultural climate where it seems "natural" to view women in terms of their parts. In this climate, Kilbourne (1999) argues, a woman, seen as an assemblage of parts, is more object than human.

Kilbourne carries this argument one step further to suggest that the act of objectifying a human is the first step toward committing violence against that person. When stripped of humanness, the woman is undifferentiated from other objects that one might not think twice about committing violence against. Individual ads don't cause violence against women, but the dehumanized gender displays across the discourse of advertising contribute to a callousness towards violence against women in this culture (see also Kuhn 1985; Root 1984). Kilbourne's arguments resonate in Ginger's words.

But I think a lot of people are not taught to question the images they see. You see an image like this up on a fraternity wall, and you think of gang-rape. You hear about all these things—the degradation of women. There is a book out about fraternity gang-rape and the brotherhood and how the degradation of women is a big part of that. That is part of the culture.

This is all part of the culture, so you get desensitized to these images we no longer think there is anything wrong with them. Just like the images of war that we see on television and movies like Rambo. We become so desensitized to the killing, that when we actually become engaged in war with Iraq, for instance, the people seen as deviant were the people who protested the war instead of the people who kill. I think it is because of images like this, or other images in general desensitize us to violence, to degradation, to humiliation. So I think it is all related. (Ginger, 28)

Both men and women expressed strong reactions against body cropping. However, it must be cautioned that these responses were all directed toward an ad used for this study where the head and feet are cropped (fig. 4). If another ad with subtler cropping techniques were used, different responses might or might not have been generated. In reaction to the ad used, however, two prominent themes defined men's and women's responses. First, body cropping was seen as a form of depersonalization of the woman, and a form of detachment. They explained that the ultimate objectification of the female is to picture her headless and feetless—unable to think and unable to move. This leads into the second theme: a headless woman suggests no brain, no mind. Therefore, objectification is much easier. There is no need to decode what is happening behind the eyes, because there are no eyes, no soul:

This one it's fairly obvious that she isn't a person, she is just a body. Maybe that's part of what bothers me about this one. She is just a body. There isn't a mind or a head attached to these women. Even though this woman physically has one, I question whether she does have one . . . she has no head, she has no voice, she isn't really a person. I don't like that. . . . Well, I don't like it when I'm headless. That's not comfortable, that's offensive. (Patricia, 35)

This one, no head. I know no one like this in my personal life. This is so detached. There is nothing that makes me feel connected to this person. With the Lancome woman there is more of a chance of some kind of connection. I can see her eyes. This woman here, there is nothing at all. . . . This is the ultimate detachment. I think this is very harmful as far as the feelings. It makes me angry. Purple is my favorite color. So, I'm drawn to that. It is also ironic that purple is considered a powerful color for women, a feminist color . . . I'm looking at this image and thinking, how ironic. *The Color Purple* showed the degradation of women and how awful men can be to women, although the ultimate triumph. In this particular image, there is nothing triumphant about this woman. She is beheaded, she has no mobility, she is simply ass and tits. So I find that very degrading. I can see nothing positive in this image whatsoever. (Ginger, 28)

What strikes me here is her whole body is cut up. You don't even see a head! There's from the shoulders to mid-thigh. I mean, that's chopping up, and what is that saying? I mean, it's saying that she's to be put back for, as a sex object, for her body. That's her main purpose, and its products . . . Yeah, it's just kind of body parts. I mean it's showing a blatant disregard for the person. It's almost as if they're dehumanizing this person. You know, they have statues and things along that line with the heads cut off. Here, they don't even have the dignity to keep—to put the woman's face—up in the advertisement. So, nothing is shown about her, her as a human. It's just her as a sex object. That's all. (Greg, 19)

I just realized that all that is in this picture is the woman's chest and her behind. It disturbs me. No head, no brain, nothing. That's part of the annoyance. (Lynn, 38)

She's a form to me because I don't see a face. Your eyes have to do with your soul, hence your face has a lot to do with who you are. Her head. Where's her head? It's really strange. You don't have dolls with no heads on them. Well, normal kids don't. This ain't the Addams family here. . . . Even if I wasn't in this interview situation I would be wondering why they didn't show her head. Not that I'm better than anyone else, but I know a lot of people who it wouldn't even cross their mind why there is no head there. (Collette, 21)

This is like the ultimate depersonalization. This woman has no head. She has breasts and a hip and an arm. Maybe that is the perfect female [laughs]. "Can't talk back and can't run away!" That kind of really grabbed me, although these [Budweiser ad, fig. 1] are objectifications of females as sex-objects, this one—you have no head, you have no feet. (Christi, 35)

Like Christi, several men and women speculated that, sadly, the headless, feetless woman might very well represent society's ideal female. These men and women suggested that in very stark symbolism, this image accurately represents women's place in society. In this schema, women are seen as body parts that can be objectively assessed without the complications of a thinking human being inside the parts. Further, the woman in this particular ad cannot move, having no feet. Therefore she is completely immobile and available, in both a visual and physical sense:

Starting with the Claude Montana ad [fig. 4], I guess I look at that and I look at the silhouette or what you get to see of the woman, in the ad, and . . . at least from the male society's perspective, of the way they view the ideal woman, I mean, you see the light— just the lighting in the ad—what it highlights. It highlights the woman's breasts, highlights her behind. It's obvious she is very well constructed [laughs], might be a somewhat non-sexist, but probably still a sexist way of putting it . . . I find it somewhat disturbing, but I guess it's how I view society's view of woman, and what I guess they think of women. If you don't get to see her head, and so, you get the impression it's kind of like her head doesn't count. All we're concerned about is how she looks and she does look very beautiful . . . Someone would look at this and say, "This is the ideal woman," and I mean, because she's got the looks, she just looks really, really great, and that's all that really matters. (Mario, 28)

I saw this as society's ideal because of the appealing curves, her breast is stuck out. No [real] women would stand like this. . . . So, we are drawn toward her breasts and she has no head. I think that was very telling that we are not even introduced to this person as a person. She is merely a body. A torso and some legs. I think in many ways that is society's ideal of woman—to be enjoyed, to be looked at, not to be admired for intellect. Children are to be seen and not heard and women are to be enjoyed but not appreciated for other attributes. I see nothing wrong with a nice body, but that is the only way women are portrayed in these pictures, as a body. We are not getting any other idea about what these women are about other than their bodies. (Ginger, 28)

A significant difference existed between female and male responses to photographic cropping in advertisements. The difference involves moving beyond recognizing and reacting to the use of body parts in images, to the internalization by women that attractiveness in this society is ultimately defined in terms of body parts. As females in this society we carry in our heads a ready checklist of body attributes that we feel are society's ideal of beauty. Many women couched their discussions of body cropping in terms of "men's definitions" of what is attractive. These responses suggest that advertisers supply the public with a male vision of beauty, centered on the perfection of individual body parts and virtually nothing else. These women saw the fragmentation of body parts in ads as a reflection of men's fetishes about female body parts:

. . . so many of them are images, society's ideals that have been conjured up by men and what they want to see. They are unattainable, these thin bodies, perfect hair, fine clothes, faces. . . . I just remember commercials telling me I had to be 6′ tall, incredibly thin, long hair, and blue eyes. That was my physical image. I also had to be extremely sexy and provocative to men, feeding who I was for men, not for myself. (Rachel, 20)

Well, this is the kind of figure you want—most women want. We'd all like to have long legs and flat stomachs and just overall perfection—no spotty skin . . . I would just like to be that way. Probably eating anything you want as well. (Jeannette, 22)

The main thing I looked at was their bodies and their facial attractiveness. . . . She is blonde, she's got big boobs, skinny arms, skinny stomach. I mean she is built perfectly as far as what men like in women. Everyone knows who she [model Paulina Porizkova] is. She is very beautiful. She is society's ideal. She sells top products so she must be society's ideal. (Claire, 22)

She's symmetrical. She's got big eyes and big lips. [It's] classic beauty . . . I mean its all cultural, this look here is very cultural. She's got curves, right? Long and curvy. I guess that's why it is classical. She's not stumpy, all bones, or something. I guess she's [Nike runner, fig. 8] classically beautiful too, I think because she's not all sweaty but her face looks a lot like Isabella's [fig. 7] and she's long and sleek too and curvy. (Laura, 33)

If these women were more realistic looking [they would be unattractive to society]. Say, they have 36″ busts, but also 26″ waists and 36″ hips. Because most of us are not 5′10″ and 130 pounds or even 110 pounds. (Christi, 35)

Action Versus Appearance

A second gender display that occupied the discourse of men and women inter-viewed was the "active male" versus the "passive female" in advertising rep-resentations. Jeane Kilbourne (1999, 1987) and Judith Williamson (1986) make very similar points about the ideology of the active and "public" male and the passive, dependent, "domestic" female. Williamson names these divisions in representation the "male-work-social" and the "female-leisure-natural." Men are often positioned in very culturally specific and purposive poses and attire, such as in moments of working, conversing on the telephone, or conveying a commanding stare. In this manner, man is positioned as the consumer of the object being advertised. Women, on the other hand, are rarely positioned in a way to give a commanding stare, but instead are positioned in such a way that they are the object of the stare, the product to be consumed. As Williamson (1986) explains, "he needs the product with a drive that comes from his own masculinity, his activity at work, while she needs the product to bring alive her universal femininity, which is represented as passive and completely separate from the social world" (105). He is society/culture and she is "nature." Janice Winship (1981) describes this odd mix of female subjectivity as both passive, yet actively sexual:

This ideology of sexuality in the ad context admits both to a passive, virginal and inno-cent sexuality—waiting for men, typified by the image of a young woman in long white robes and flowing blonde hair—and to an active experience of sexuality. However, the active experience of sexuality only takes place in a fetishistic mode. Women are in-vited by the ads to respond to themselves through the imagined fetishes of men—the tights/legs, the lipstick/lips which fragments or distortions of them stand for all their womanness. (219)

Men and women who collaborated in this research recognized a promi-nent dichotomy that is often established in representations of gender in adver-tising as well as other popular iconography: females appear and males act. The defining feature of female representation, therefore, is appearance (a quality Laura Mulvey (1975) referred to as to-be-looked-at-ness) most often in a passive or submissive pose, and deferent to the male. Conversely, the defining feature of male representation is activity. While in agreement that the dichotomy of action vs. appearance is a definitive gender display in advertising, men and women invoked this dichotomy to describe very different phenomena. Males, for example, used the action vs. appearance dichotomy to discuss their personal preferences of images of females. When explaining the differences between an active vs. inactive female in ads, males confined their discussions to the spectrum of ads presented to them in the study. Mainly, men stated that the use of female bodies for mere objectification is unappealing. An attractive woman caught in a moment of purposive action was seen as far more desirable than the passive woman. In other words, the defining factor between whether an ad was personally appealing, for example, was whether the ad simply showed an attractive woman "appearing," or whether the ad gave the male respondent hints of what the substance of the woman was, what her motivations are or what her personality might be like:

Well, put it this way, it pleases me that these ads do appear to have some aspect of substance. I guess the fact that I consider being athletic something of substance. I consider spending time with your family and relaxing and being active having substance. But I guess it's also been my personal experience with life and dealing with people and my thoughts about society that society doesn't value some of these substantive things as much as they value how good something looks.

. . . I look at both these images [Montana, fig. 4; Johnnie Walker, fig. 2] and I see that they are both aesthetically pleasing. They are nice to look at. But then my brain kicks in and tells me there are other things to life than looks. . . . Let's put it this way, if the person in the Montana ad had not only this aesthetically pleasing-to-look-at body, but had a wonderful intellect, and a great personality and all that kind of stuff, you would put it over in most personally appealing, but by just looking at this ad there is no way you can determine that. (Mario, 28)

Well, both pictures [Isabella, fig. 7; Montana, fig. 4] don't show any action in women at all. They're more or less inactive. The fact that there's nothing actually being done. It might be a consideration, the fact that women are just being and not being something. Also, there's more of a flavor of sexism involved in these advertisements. The women are more or less exploited for who they are or what they look like instead of what they intend to do or what they really stand for. . . .

In all these ads, the women seem to be very attractive again, but I don't see them doing anything else other than being attractive. I think society expects a little more out of women than just to stand around and look good, which is what they all seem to be doing. . . . The image I would get would be of a person who doesn't think or do anything but worry about being attractive and that would not be attractive to me. (Bill, 26)

The image of presenting a female as a human is what I see these as doing more, is more of an image that is pleasing to me personally. Whereas these other [ads] are almost nonhuman. They're there to be gawked at, to be looked at, and that's the only purpose they serve. And so, I guess, the actions help to make them more human. (Greg, 19)

Instead of confining their responses to particular ads, women saw the action vs. appearance dichotomy as a microcosm of the way women are assessed in larger society. Many women suggested that for women, a judgment based on appearance always precedes judgments based on other attributes, such as motivations, intelligence, ability, and personality. Women at times seemed resigned to this ordering. It was commonly expressed that no matter what the accomplishments are of a woman in society, she will always be judged foremost on appearance, with all other attributes ranked after:

I mean the standard by which they judge women isn't, you know, it's how they look, not really what they accomplish, right? Like this businesswoman, or doing something. What I'm saying is all these achievement things, that's not what we [women] are judged by. It's how we look and everything . . .they [Virginia Slims, fig. 6; Nike, fig. 8] are sort of out of that realm. . . . I wish it wasn't the criteria that we were judged on. It seems like that's the only one, the physical beauty and in that sense, it bothers me. (Laura, 33)

All the women are showing off their bodies and shapes. I think society wants us to show off our bodies, otherwise they are not showing off their true potential. They are less than they could be. Basically, we are judged on our looks, the outsides and not the inside. (Jamie, 22)

When I was looking at it as what I thought society's ideal woman should be, there are some very pleasing ideals. There is nothing wrong with being a woman who fits that, that makes choices around being married and having children and all those things. I think that too many times in advertising you only get the sexual appeal and not the combination. When I'm looking at women I'm looking for the combination of these things. (Megan, 25)

Advertising just in general teaches all women to be beautiful only in the physical sense. To be thin, beautiful, passive, sexually available, non-threatening, not intellectual, not to be powerful in any way that would threaten men. It is OK to be powerful in a pose like this [Jordache ad, fig. 3], but that is only in the sexuality domain. Once in bed, for instance, she is not supposed to dominate the man. The man is supposed to control the mood, the pace, the orgasm, etc. Advertising in general sends women all kinds of negative images. (Ginger, 28)

When I first saw it [a Jordache ad in Cosmo] the first thing that came to mind was that the woman looked inferior to the man. He looks like he is scolding her the way he is pointing at her, the way he is looking down at her. Also, the way she is holding on to him. She needs to hold on to him like he is a father. Also, what caught my attention was the wording, Jordache jeans, and neither of them are wearing jeans. It is not selling the product it is just selling the woman. There is a sexy look on her face while the man is yelling at her. It is really degrading. (Nicole, 22)

The New Working Woman

In the past 20–25 years, a highly recognizable gender display was added to the advertising repertoire, the image of the "new working woman." A snapshot of gender equality in the workplace, without any of the stresses of real life, this image is now a sign for every kind of product from New Freedom bras, to L'Eggs pantyhose, to Virginia Slims cigarettes. In most cases, the encoding of images of the new working woman in advertising involves what feminist cultural critics call the process of "incorporation." Incorporation means that what appear on the surface to be progressive images are not progressive or alternative at all. An incorporated image still adheres to traditional patriarchal conventions of advertising. For example, although a woman in an advertisement may be dressed in business clothes and have a businesslike hairstyle, she conforms to traditional conventions of femininity in advertising in almost every other way, such as model thinness, flawless skin, hair, and make-up, a nurturing concern for domestic and personal matters, and youth.

The advertisement for Virginia Slims cigarettes used in this research features an image of a youngish woman, dressed in a tailored business suit and a bright pink coat (fig. 6). She is carrying a briefcase and, according to the accompanying text, is supposedly employed in middle management. Responses to this advertisement uncovered stark gender differences in how men and women see women's place in the work force and how they decode the gender display of the "new working woman."

Men gave what Stuart Hall (1980, 1981) has coined in his model of encoding/decoding, the "dominant reading" of this advertisement. Men mapped the codes of the Virginia Slims ad in similar ways to that preferred by the text. For men interviewed, the Virginia Slims ad represents an image of equality for women in the work force and a sign that women have truly "come a long way" from previous subordinated positions in society. For these men, the Virginia Slims image mirrors women's progress in achieving equal status in the public sphere of work. Moreover, this type of ad signals that women have arrived, and much of the struggle to achieve those ends is in the past.

Further support for the assessment that men gave a dominant reading of the Virginia Slims ad is found in the evidence that men not only approved of this image because of its message of equality, but because this message is presented within the traditional conventions of advertising and gender. Men suggested that this is an image of the "complete woman." For them it was the combination of a progressive image with conventional codes of femininity, such as youth, thinness, and flawlessness, that defined this complete woman. Men saw the Virginia Slims woman as someone to be envied in the

1990s. Not only is she successful at work, but she is intelligent, independent, happy and, perhaps most important, has managed to remain feminine and attractive:

I think motivation comes under society's ideal due to the women's liberation movement. I think society has relinquished some of its hold of women in the past. I feel society is more accepting of women pursuing office-type careers, management careers, professional careers. . . . It pleases me to think that society has changed enough to be more open about the roles of women and allowing them to pursue what they think they might want to do, but in the past were shunned from. . . . It's motivational the image of the briefcase, I feel that society might associate that with success, the office-type image, the manager image. . . . It pleases me to see that [women] have the chance to be office-oriented if they want to. (Richard, 24)

She seems to have it all. Work, family, this, that, and the other . . . [It's] what I think nowadays, is what is perceived to be "the complete woman." You know, she obviously looks like she's got a job. . . . Successful with that, and she's attractive, and you know, happy . . . content with what is happening with her life up to this point. . . . She's got, I guess, the best of all worlds, in this picture. . . . Who wouldn't want to be in that situation? . . . I don't know too many people who wouldn't want to have a successful job. (Greg, 19)

She looks very intelligent. She looks like a woman of the '90s. She can do as well as me financially. Plus she is very pretty "to-boot.' " (Shawn, 20)

In this case we have this apparent business woman on her way to the top, but she's also appearing attractive and feminine and all that good stuff. So she's managing to combine a professional life with also being the stereotypical attractive women. (Bill, 26)

The Virginia Slims ad is like society's ideal because she is in corporate drag, she is in what looks like a man's suit and tie so she looks like a very successful, professional business woman. She has a real fluffy pink coat on and what looks like a pink suitcase and pink socks. . . . She is proving that she can make it in a man's world without being threatening to them and then the little phrase that says, "You've come a long way, baby." (Camron, 22)

Many men interviewed did depart from their dominant readings of the Virginia Slims ad in one respect. Men, much more than women, commented on the conflict they perceived between the very positive image of equality and contentedness they saw in the Virginia Slims ads and the fact that the image was promoting a harmful product. More specifically, men saw a distinct conflict between the image of female professionalism and the habit of smoking. Men saw no integrative features between these two components. Instead, imposing a negative behavior—smoking—on a positive image was seen as an act of deceit in the process of encoding. It can be assumed, therefore, that men would have decoded the image of the young business woman in the Virginia

Slims ad as unequivocally positive if it had not been attached to the product of cigarettes:

I like the idea of a woman being professional and having career-type jobs and that kind of stuff. On the one hand, . . . but the fact that she's holding a cigarette in her hand . . . to me, just puts it automatically way down on the end of the spectrum and I know that this is probably a little bit my own feelings rather than what I feel society's feelings are. . . . Most of the people I know don't look at smoking very highly, especially smoking for people that are supposed to be business professionals, or health professionals. Smoking is one of those things that you "just don't do." If you do, you don't tell anyone about it [laughs]. (Mario, 28)

I don't understand why cigarettes or alcohol contribute to these kinds of images of people. . . . Again, you've got a lady running along. She is a business-type lady. And at first I thought that would be quite novel, but then I realized it was for cigarettes and I just completely don't understand the ad altogether. It possibly says that if you are a business-type person then you need cigarettes to relax you or to make you look at the world in a different way. (Jake, 21)

For one, this one shows I'd say a woman in middle management by how the ad is and she smokes, giving the impression that all woman in middle management smoke, which is not true—maybe it is, I don't know. Saying that if you want to be successful, you should smoke. I'm against smoking. I've seen what it's done to people. (Paul, 23)

In stark contrast to the men's dominant readings of the Virginia Slims ad, women rarely identified this image as a positive one. Like the males, those women who did find the image positive deemed the ad an image of female achievement and advancement. However, unlike the men, the women who approved of this image did so on a personal level, seeing it as a role model, but never deeming this an image of social equality. Instead, several women stated that they could identify personally with this woman. They either saw her as someone they would like to be or as a strong figure in her own right:

She's got on a pants suit and a tie and she's got a briefcase. She just looks like a business woman. I am a business woman. I can relate to her because that is what I'll be doing. . . . I was a business woman with my intern[ship] and I will be one in the future when I graduate. . . . It pleases me because that is what I am going to be. (Claire, 22)

This one is emotionally strong. She's made up her mind that she can smoke if she wants to. She doesn't care what the Surgeon General has said. She's tough enough to take it plus she has a man's suit on and she is saying I can do anything a man can do plus she is carrying a silver briefcase and a purse. . . . Sure, this is me. I'm tough and do I care what society thinks? Not really. (Patricia, 35)

In terms of Hall's categories of decoding (dominant, negotiated, oppositional) the majority of women decoded this image in highly negotiated or even oppositional ways. Many were able to read against the grain of the text by using the lens of their own gendered experience with the dynamics of the work force. Female negotiations with this image were defined primarily by the incongruities they saw between the image of the young business woman in the ad and the reality of work life, as they perceived it.

The first incongruity is rooted in the belief that liberal feminist ideals of increased visibility in representation are not only highly inadequate, but when held up as an end-point of achievement for women, these images actually can be counter productive. More than one woman rewrote the famous Virginia Slims jingle to read: We have *not* "come a long way, baby." These women were highly critical of the on-going theme of the Virginia Slims ad campaign that suggests women have "arrived." This theme suggests that the struggles of their grandmothers and mothers were certainly worthwhile, but are now a thing of the past. In the Virginia Slims campaign, women have achieved equality with men in the board room *and* in the bedroom. Women, however, suggested that this image is actually a thinly veiled facade that masks the continual inequalities between men and women in this society:

Because I think that although we try to pretend that women have come a long way . . . baby, we have not. And the Clarence Thomas/Anita Hill hearings were hopefully a great realization to the people who run this country how badly women are treated and how upset women are about that. The connotation here is that this is a female executive running off to a business meeting and woman are not really accepted in executive-type positions. I think that is true emotionally and also statistically. What are they calling it now? The glass ceiling? It is the same stuff over and over and over again. Although there are slightly more women in the US than men, society is still run by males. And they more than dictate what ideals are seen, and this is not an ideal. (Christi, 35)

Anytime I see Virginia Slims I think of this phrase [you've come a long way, baby] and I don't like it. . . . I was mostly offended at this ad because you are always drawn back to an earlier time in Virginia Slims ads and you are always supposed to appreciate the progress that has been made. I see nothing wrong with appreciating the progress that has been made, but these images are always supposed to lead us to believe that we have progressed, period. We've gone all the further we need to go. We've come a long way. Be satisfied. Be happy. Don't complain. I think that this is still a long way to go yet. (Ginger, 28)

A second incongruity women identified between the Virginia Slims ad and their own experiences involved the one-dimensionality of the image. Women discussed the fact that the woman in the Virginia Slims ad looks as if she could not possibly juggle the many roles that real women in the work force do, such as worker, cleaner, cook, mother, chauffeur, accountant, and so on. Because she seems so perfect in her role as a business woman, she must have made conscious choices not to be married or to have a family. Women were often openly skeptical of the feasibility of this image, describing the woman in the picture as most likely single, self-centered, and aggressive:

I'd say that it is great that women can have a career and be well-educated, but the reality is that it is not OK in extremes. Like, it is really easy for women if they make a choice not to have a family, not to be married. Then they're sacrificing and being grouped into an extreme and not caring or some way being less of a woman. . . . This woman seems like she wouldn't be the perfect family woman. I was thinking this woman looks like she, not because she doesn't look educated or like a good mother or any of those kinds of things, she seems more career-oriented, therefore maybe more independent [than one] who opts to have a family and marriage. (Megan, 25)

The modern woman . . . she's dressed in this business suit so she's really not just a woman who has a job and a family, right? The woman who can juggle everything. She's one who apparently is also headed to try and take over some territory. (Laura, 33)

We are supposed to look at her and say, "look what progress we have made." Definitely progress has been made, but there is still—she's got to have all the pink, and she's got to be beautiful. Putting her in a man's suit. You know I don't think too many women would be able to go to a Wall Street office would be allowed to dress in a man-type suit like this. Women are still expected to be in skirts and jackets or dresses. So there is a teasing thing going on here. To me there hasn't been that much progress made. The woman has to act like a man in order to get power in society. In order to make it on Wall Street. So this to me is still a negative image. (Ginger, 28)

Motherhood

In general, the gender display of young motherhood was deemed positive by both men and women. Most discussions about motherhood were made in reference to a particular ad for Pier 1 Imports (fig. 5). This ad pictures a youngish woman with long flowing hair, dressed in jeans, a sweater, and cowboy boots. The setting for the ad is somewhere in the country. The young woman has a young girl riding on her back, piggy-back style.

In contrast to the gender display of the new working woman, both men and women gave dominant readings of the image of young motherhood. For most who collaborated in this research there seemed to be a close ideological connection between femaleness and domestic happiness. As was explored in relation the "action versus appearance" gender display, feminist critics of advertising have uncovered a dominant theme in media representation of gender that presents a dichotomy between the "female as nature" private sphere, and the "male in society" public sphere. Images of women caring for young children epitomize the female private sphere. One can argue that this ideological fit is so seamless partly because traditionally males have placed the persona of mother and child on a pedestal: (a) because it is a relationship they are unable to reproduce, both biologically and culturally and (b) because it is a sphere where they are supposed to have no interest or ability. Further, the elevation of domesticity to a privileged position ensures a clear division of labor. In this schema, males labor in society for economic gain, and females reproduce their man's labor in the home through non-economic means and in the market place as consumers.

The ad of a young mother can be read as a literal representation of female-in-nature. This ad for Pier 1 Imports places the image of the young woman carrying the child on her back in an ambiguous country setting, removed from society. The image is pure, free of stress or problems, a frozen moment of pleasure in simplicity and regenerative youth:

She's playing with kids, kind of a motherly figure. She seems happy. She's having fun and smiling like she's enjoying herself. It seems to me that she's glad to be with them. (Jamie, 22)

Just going out and having fun with your kids, and out in the field or something like that you know, it reminds me kind of where I came from. I'm from Wisconsin and we've got lots of corn fields and dairy cows and all that kind of stuff, and that's a lot of the time what we did. Put on a pair of "clod-hoppers" and a pair of jeans on and went out in a field, and played around . . . I'm attracted to the family aspect of it. I'm attracted to, "let's go outside and play and have a good time." (Mario, 28)

It's just ideal when a mother and a child. . . . It's just society's ideal vs. not having this kind of relationship. It just looks like they're having fun. It looks like they are enjoying each other. (Gene, 22)

Most men and women found this image of the young woman with the child riding on her back enjoyable and wholesome. For many, seeing this image encouraged them to launch directly into stories about their own families and what family bonds mean to them. For others this image gave them a hopeful feeling about adult-child relationships in a troubled world where children are not always loved and cared for:

For me, families are top priority. Look out for family members. Respect family members. Do whatever you can for family members. . . . And so this image with the family is an appealing one. It's kind of the "all-American" image, a lady with a young daughter, or out for a day with them. The two seem to be enjoying the company of what they're doing. . . . So I guess I have a lot of respect for females that are raising a family. Well, even a lot more respect for those that are . . . you know, there are a lot of single females now trying to hold the family together, nowadays. And you know how much work has to be put in to it. (Greg, 19)

This one [Pier 1 ad] reminded me of my sister and her daughter. Really, two sisters and their daughters. Just together as a family, being very important. Trying to be together as much as possible, taking advantage of it. Don't take it for granted. . . . I'm a volunteer firemen, EMT. I get an emergency call to an address that sounds really familiar. Person in labor. My sister's in labor. I delivered her baby. . . . Two years ago I had a call, my Dad was in cardiac arrest. I had to drive, they would not let me in the back. I almost got into an accident. Something about the family, something clicks. My family comes first, my friends come next, then my work. . . . Just being so close that you're almost there—you're a part of keeping a relative alive draws that bond closer. Delivering two nieces, one nephew doesn't hurt either. (Paul, 23)

I think that in our society, even though it is starting to change, the mother image has been around for some time and with her holding the child and playing with the kid . . . I've always been from a real close family and that has always been a real strong family value. So I guess that's why I still hold that as a family value although I can see that shifting in society's values. (Jane, 32)

Society's ideal is the bonding between adults and children. I guess with all the problems in the world today with respect to abuse and child neglect it's ideal to see a mother and her daughter or a child and an adult being happy and loving toward each other. (Gene, 22)

Motherly, comfortable, relaxing, fun, energy/career . . . I am a mother, I think mother, that's me. I do things with children, I used to live in the country, playing doing things with kids. . . . Yes, a pleasing concept to have a good relationship with children. (Lynn, 38)

Gender differences appeared in responses to the display of young motherhood when this image was discussed in terms of being a societal ideal. Both men and women commented that this image of the young mother in the Pier 1 ad may be closest to society's ideal of the woman who has it all, or society's "everything woman." This assessment was most often made by weighing the stereotypical gender roles that women have been assigned in this society against the personal appeal of the particular lifestyle depicted in the ad. Men saw this ideological construction as a fantasy based in reality. In other words, the type of woman in this ad does exist, although, in the troubled and tarnished world we live in she is hard to find. This woman, unlike the playmates depicted in beer ads, is the type one marries and has a family with.

Well, I picked this woman as most appealing because I think she has it all. She is independent, and strong willed. She is attractive and also believes in family. Well, the fact of the picture with the kid there. It is also the way she is dressed. She isn't dressed to be a sex symbol person. She is dressed to work, basically. I think she gives off a certain image of the intelligent type. Hard worker, strong, independent woman. . . . It is hard to find a woman like this. (George, 22)

As ideal as the image appeared to women, they expressed a deepseated anxiety and even anger at the impossibility of achieving this type of lifestyle today. Women were not content to read pleasure straight off the surface of this image. Instead, they pondered the economic conditions of such a life. If this woman does not work and is free of stress, who supports her? How does she maintain her lifestyle, looks, and happiness? Are all these things dependent on a man who is not pictured, but who is financially holding this picture in place? For women this image presents a lifestyle that is desired, but, they find it all but impossible to *be* this woman.

This one harkens to the maternal ideal that women have children and men take care of them and you can be well-dressed and fashionable at the same time. . . . Because this is a print as in an American magazine. This isn't "Outback R Us." This isn't what most women can be. You can't be relaxed all the time and running around with your kids. The reality is that most women have to work and most mothers have to work. And many mothers are the heads of single-parent families, so I don't think they would be running around the woods. I think they would be working two jobs somewhere. . . . I guess the only way I see this as relating is that for years woman have been this natural resource that has not been tapped for the work force and there for about 10 or 15 years there was choice, you work or you stay home with the kids. But now there isn't much of a choice. I feel badly for women who want to stay home with their children, who want to stay home with a parent. Who do not have a mother or father with them as has been in the past. (Christi, 35)

There was also something about the woman that looked kind of natural and I think that's another expectation of society, she is in her blue jeans and a sweater and her hair is blowing around and she is laughing. Women are supposed to laugh, they are supposed to smile or they are supposed to really look sexy like this one with the guys in the Jordache ad [fig. 3]. . . . They are images for me. Women with children, women with men, women looking attentive and women without heads. It's almost, there are so many roles for women and I think society puts women into these roles and I think these are the roles that society finds acceptable to men, highly acceptable to men. Companion, men's companions or as listeners or headless people or nonpeople. (Patricia, 35)

I guess, well, for the first picture it was more the mother aspect of society for females, the wholesomeness. The woman is supposed to be the catch-all and the nurturing type. . . . I think women can serve as role models, a good mother and have a career also. (Jane, 32)

The Pier 1 Imports [ad]—I think this is another one of society's ideals because she is a really attractive woman, down-to-earth, mom, good wife, fun loving, adventurous, always up for something, ready to do anything. I think that is what society definitely wants. Someone that is attractive, a loving wife, someone who can cook, clean, and do everything. (Nicole, 22)

Consistent with their very material concerns for the structural impossibilities of the image in the Pier 1 ad, women pointed out another very material possibility of this image that they deemed positive. They pointed to the fact that the woman pictured could be a single parent and therefore a positive image for alternative families. Offering a much broader frame of ideological construction of "family" than their male counterparts, these women saw this image as a positive and contemporary representation of an alternative family unit to the nuclear family.

It's a single woman and a child. More modern than a family-type thing. The woman is smiling. They just aren't very serious. . . . You always tend to get this image of the family—the mother, the father and the child all together. This is just the mother and the child, which is quite a common thing now. . . . It pleases me that they are not unhappy images. (Jeannette, 22)

I guess it is pretty much because here is a Mom and her daughter and another kid, I assume it is her son. There is no father and no other kids. The assumption I make is that it is a mother and a child. What the ad seems to be telling me is that you can be a Mom and still look OK. . . . It's kind of a neat set-up. It looks like they are in an out-back jungle situation—wilderness as opposed to the hectic, nine-to-five, New York City kind of ad. So it is very relaxing to look at. (Christi, 35)

I plan on having a child. My partner and I both do and one of us would have to be artificially inseminated and so to see a woman interacting with a child on her own I think is a positive image, because the traditional nuclear family is not any longer a man and a woman and 2 kids, or 2.8 kids, whatever it is. There are alternative families now. So this allows for a little bit of flexibility. Although many might assume that her husband is waiting for her at home or at work. But there was something in this that I thought was good, showing a woman alone interacting with children. I wouldn't be alone raising my child as a single mother, but this allows for some alternative notion of what family is. (Ginger, 28)

This looks like a very stable Mom. Strength is very appealing to me, it's positive . . . I see this ad of a single Mom. My Mom is a single Mom and she's very strong. . . . The thought of being a strong, independent woman is very pleasing to me. I think it is to any female. It helps me realize it's OK to be happy and independent as who I am. (Rachel, 20)

An Alternative Gender Display

The gender display of the "new working woman" in the Virginia Slims ad (fig. 6) and the gender display of young "motherhood" in the Pier 1 ad (fig. 5) fall into the category of ads examined by Goffman. These advertisements offer highly stylized versions of social mores, definitions, attitudes, values, and behavioral tendencies whose meanings must be clear enough to be interpreted in an instant. However, if gender displays in advertising consist of overcodified and exaggerated ritual-like displays of the very familiar, what would an alternative image look like? If most progressive images of gender representation are mere incorporations of old conventions in new garb, what characterizes an alternative gender display for viewers? Further, within the conventions of advertising, is it possible to offer alternative images of gender from the familiar and still promote a product?

For many of the women, the answer to these questions, in the abstract, involved an expansion of the dimensionality of representations of women in advertising. By presenting images of females that are three-dimensional as opposed to the traditional one-dimensional images, women envisioned an alternative aesthetic in advertising that was not antithetical to more traditional conventions. These three-dimensional women, as described by women interviewed, would be attractive and feminine, but also active, responsible, strong-minded, independent, confident, and intelligent (to name only a few of the attributes mentioned). Further, the three-dimensional woman would be appreciated for her humanness above her attractiveness:

We need to see more women who are just being themselves in every facet of their lives, not just women who always are at home, or partying with several types of men. There's more to a woman than that. We need to get away from those ads that just focus on exposing the woman's body and those ads that always have a woman depending on a man. We need more positivity, like this ad [Nike ad, fig. 8]. . . . We need to show women doing more realistic things than just sitting around a swimming pool drinking beer with 20 men. More than just playing with the kids. More than just packing school lunches. Women are much more than that. (Jamie, 22)

A combination of different things as far as pieces from different ads kind of complete a multidimensional woman for me. There is one of each in each ad. One is very nice and sensible. The other one, the Nike ad, there is a woman being very physical and athletic and the one ad, the woman has a lot of attitude and seems very sure of herself and the last one the image is pure sexuality. I put all the ads together because I think they make a complete woman, all of those things are part of what I think is appealing about women. (Megan, 25)

I think anytime that ads encourage people or females to live their own lives it's encouraging. . . . It's the kind of person I like being, and the kind of person I want my children to be like. . . . Some ads do lead you to do it your way . . . I like doing things my way, so whenever I am encouraged it's appealing. (Lynn, 38)

In more concrete responses to particular advertising images, the ad for Nike shoes used was frequently described by men and woman as an alternative image, or an alternative aesthetic. Both men and women saw this ad as positive in the form of its message, the promotion of health and fitness. Men and women also agreed that the woman in the Nike ad showed commitment and determination, two attributes not often seen in traditional conventions of female representation. Although deemed positive, these attributes seemed somewhat unfamiliar:

I put the jogger in as society's ideal because of the importance and stress on fitness these days and keeping up good health and kind of being like the all-American woman. (Jane, 32)

I like the ads that show an independent and hard-working person. It shows her running. She looks like the person that would get up everyday and do exercises. She looks like a very hard working, diligent person. I mean that's appealing to a certain extent. But, she also looks kind of fanatical about it. She is almost a jock type, but I don't see her as a jock, per se, but getting there. She is appealing. She is independent, good looking, and hard working. (George, 22)

Similarities in gender decoding stopped, however, with this agreement that the message of the ad is a positive one. Men found the woman in the Nike ad to be unattractive, specifically because she did not meet the conventions of attractiveness of femininity in advertising with which they were familiar. Ironically, the woman in the Nike ad *does* adhere to several of the dominant conventions of female beauty in advertising. She is tall, thin, and young. In complete contrast the image of the new working woman, men saw the image of the woman in the Nike ad as falling outside the boundaries of attractiveness both by society's standards and by personal standards. Only men cast judgments about the individual attractiveness of the woman in the Nike ad based solely on appearance. For them she was an "incomplete" woman:

She's drab, ugly, nasty, and does not look like she is having a good time. . . . I am not very attracted to her. She is running. I really don't want to be with her. (Shawn, 20)

The runner's a little blurry, not quite as attractive perhaps. . . . I'd be afraid she'd make me go out and run with her. (Jim, 37)

Compared to how I categorized the other pictures, these just weren't as appealing to me. The black and white of [Nike] caught my eye, but just the fact of what the picture is just didn't appeal to me that much. I thought of it as a woman out running. Women are out jogging past our house all the time. I just don't give it a second thought. (Art, 30)

I guess my theme here so far is that one thing society wants is for women to be attractive. I didn't think this one was particularly attractive. I think society does not yet accept athletic women and this woman looks very, very athletic. She looks a little muscular and I don't think society is ready to accept that. (Bill, 26)

Women saw the Nike ad as a positive alternative aesthetic, both in composition and in content. Some of the reasons women saw this ad as an alternative aesthetic include the facts that the woman in the Nike ad was not posed for the direct consumption of the male spectator and the soft focus lens added a sense of amateur photography, more like a candid photograph than a professionally posed and shot image. Furthermore, the viewer was forced to look up at her. She was, therefore, in the more powerful position, above the viewer and in motion, in a moment of flight. The photograph caught her in a moment where she was driven by internal motivations and was unconcerned, even oblivious, to how she might look to others. She was not made-up or coifed and although tightly fitted, her apparel was not sexy, but practical.

This one [Nike] has a very sweaty, athletic woman and it's not what you normally see. Also, there is this distorted photography and this strange camera angle. It's quite unlike what you normally see. . . . She is so different, so muscular and active and sweaty. Her face is strange, too. She is not beautiful, but she is attractive, but it is forceful. . . . I find it interesting because it is different. (Heather, 29)

She is in a powerful position because of the way this is taken, we are in some ways looking up at her. In some ways a direct gaze, but with this angle and the bridge being such, it looks like perhaps we are looking up at her, which is the very opposite of the way most women are photographed looking directly at her or down on her like the Budweiser ads. So, she definitely looks like she is in power. The way this is photographed the trees are in the background. Her height even exceeds the trees' height. She has just come over a bridge that looks uphill and now she in on the decline. She has conquered the hill. . . . She looks strong. She looks fit, although she looks exceedingly thin to me. . . . She's got her arms pumped in a position, so she's not . . . she is not trying to look appealing, feminine, no head tilted back. She doesn't have what is generally considered a seductive pose. She's running. Her eyes are pointed away from the camera. She's looking ahead where she is running. She has a sweatshirt on. . . . She's in motion. She is still moving. (Ginger, 28)

Women went on to identify the entire Nike "Just do it" ad campaign as alternative advertising primarily because of a shift of emphasis from pictures of posed athleticism to pictures of real athleticism. In other words, they viewed traditional representations of women in fitness and wellness campaigns as posed scenarios in which the goal is to picture the *product*, or result, of working out: a toned body to be objectified as a spectacle. In contrast, the Nike ads were seen as showing the *process* of working out—how real people look while in the process of toning the body. Therefore, authenticity in representation was cited as an alternative to "staging."

She is very active. She's got tennis shoes, and it's a Nike ad so of course she has tennis shoes on, but I like the imaging that Nike does, "just do it." I like that phrase. "Just" implies, don't worry about, you know, "Oh God, am I going to be good enough at this?" or "Am I going to look good while I'm doing it? What are my friends going to say?" and, "I'm not very good at this sport, I shouldn't try it." They are saying just go out and do it. "Do," an active verb—do it. Do whatever you want. Just be active. Do something. I like that phrase. (Ginger, 28)

I think that they're [Nike] good ads. They're pretty real. They don't have girls dolled up because girls don't always have make-up. Likewise, when they have guys, it's just pure and raw. It's real. These are some real ads. Even the TV ads are real. It's basic in its message, "just do it." Don't wait for anyone, just do it. It would be kind of neat if it was the same slogan and she wasn't doing something athletic, but something else that's important I think it's a really neat ad. Once again, the "just do it" part, I really like that. The fitness aspect, how she's doing something for herself. I like Nike stuff a lot. Maybe that has something to do with it. I like it. It's real. I like that a lot. . . . "Just do it." That's what she is doing. She's not waiting for anyone else . . . and that is just a nice little motto for anybody. And you can relate that over to yourself, that doesn't have to stay on the page. (Collette, 21)

Women anticipated that the image of the woman in the Nike ad would be seen as unattractive by men because of all the positive attributes mentioned above. By identifying male tastes in attractiveness as synonymous with society's definitions of female attractiveness, women saw this image as out of synch with male fantasies of submissive femininity. Certainly, the men's negative assessments of the Nike model's relative attractiveness suggest their discomfort with such nonsubmissive images. We see in Shawn's assessment, for instance, of the Nike model as "drab, ugly, nasty," how women who stray outside culturally determined boxes of appearance and behavior are punished, labeled as unattractive. The discomfort of these men is also indicative of how their male privilege, both socially and in ways of looking, is threatened by nonsubmissive images of women. For example, Jim is worried that the Nike model would make him go running (a statement evocative of fears of female domination and of demands of effort on the part of the male in order to enter a relationship with the model). Shawn deems the model as unattractive since he wouldn't want to be with her, share her company either sexually or as a companion.

Given this, it is not surprising that women went so far as to speculate that if they were to present themselves this way in public the effects could be detrimental personally. In the opinion of these women, society is not ready for women to present themselves this naturally and confidently.

All of these women are kind of, they look kind of self-sufficient and they are involved in things [that] are not necessarily female, but they are not the stereotype or the ideal woman like the beautiful woman who's dressed always that way. . . . This one is active in sports, right. Okay I don't know if society wants to know about that. She has a good figure of course, but who cares if she's out doing sports. "Something not feminine about that." (Laura, 33)

She is jogging in one picture. She doesn't care how she looks. Her hair is all pulled back. She is not in this ad to be attractive. . . . I think I'm somewhat of a tomboy. I don't like to wear tons of make-up or fix my hair. Sometimes that can hurt. If you are around women who look more feminine than you are, they are not going to look at you as well as other people. (Claire, 22)

I was very content putting it [Nike ad] under [pile] five because athletes are such individual figures. This ad would be very ideal for some, and not at all for others. A strong woman athlete is still very questioned—whether it is ideal for women or not. (Rachel, 20)

This chapter has explored a perspective on how advertisements are encoded and decoded building on the work of Erving Goffman. For Goffman, advertisements offer highly stylized versions of social mores, definitions, attitudes, values and behavioral tendencies whose meanings must be clear enough to be interpreted in an instant. The task of the advertiser is to favorably dispose viewers to the product, to show a sparkling version of that product in the context of glamorous events. Advertisers must use limited resources to tell a story and to transform the opaque into the easily readable. Advertisers do this by choreographing the materials available in social situations in order to achieve their ends.

Central to Goffman's view of how gender is communicated through advertisements is that advertisements present to us familiar ritual-like displays. Standardization, exaggeration, and simplification are found to an extended degree in advertising. The gender displays in advertising are familiar because they show us rituals in which we engage in real life. Images of gender are highly structured cultural codes in this society.

The codes of sexuality transferred to commodities are probably more widely accessible than other cultural codes and are therefore continually recycled in the symbolic world of image production. Goffman's additional insights are highly instructive here. Advertisements serve to further conventionalize our conventions, to codify our codes. Decoding of gender in advertising, therefore, is not only a process of recognizing ritual bits of the very familiar in gender relations, but at the same time processing highly structured and "hyperritualized" images of gender. When men and women brought their own lives and experiences to the viewing, they were not simply reacting to the gender displays they encounter, they were also responding to the over-codifying of gender relations in advertising. Decoding gender displays in advertising, therefore, involve an intricate process of viewing, always through the lens of gender, the encoded displays that are intimately familiar, yet stereotypical, exaggerated bits of lived experience.

4. Signs of the Times:
A Semiotics of Gender Ads

My two young daughters are both very tall for their age and most people, both kids and adults, think they are older than they are. I let people know the girls' ages so they don't expect more than they should from them. I have encountered some interesting observations from friends and strangers alike about my tall, pretty girls that say volumes about how our culture views idealized notions of the female body — its attributes and its uses. Some people comment, "Oh, they're going to be basketball players!" This always makes me smile and think about how sports is a very active and healthy activity, one that girls were virtually barred from for centuries. It makes me think of how my girls can be anything they want and no matter what their career choices I hope sports and physical activity are always a part of their lifestyle. Smile, smile.

However, the majority of women who comment on my girls' heights say, "Oh, maybe they'll become models!" It is not only what this comment says but the way the well-wishers say it that always puts me back on my heels. It is like when a stranger finds out you have won the lottery. It is a strange mixture of excitement and intense envy. It is as if they are saying that if my girls are so lucky as to beat all odds of female flaws, such as being under 5′8″ tall, or over 120 pounds, or having an imperfect nose or ill-defined muscles or thin hair or myriad female body blunders, if they emerge out of the other side of puberty with all the right body attributes in all the right places — well, then it is better than winning the lottery, much better. In these women's eyes I see the cultural knowledge that in a society where women have always been judged by appearance first, if one possesses the attributes of the supermodel, life will be good on all fronts.

The prize — in these women's observation — on the surface alludes to the fact that models in our culture are held at such a premium that, like movie stars, musicians, and male professional athletes, their market worth is the highest in all our society—much more than the president of the United States, much more than the average CEO, and certainly more than any of the women I've talked to who commented in awe, "Oh, they could be models!" When they say this there is more behind their words than saying my girls could have lucrative careers, reserved for only the smallest percentage of women in the world. What is behind their comments, their glow as they look into my eyes as if the fortune is mine as much as the girls', is that they know, at least they think, that life is easier for pretty girls. Although some recent studies have shown that the handsome man usually gets promoted in the work place more readily than the homely man, a woman's "success" in the work place, in relationships, both with others and with herself are so closely tied to societal ideals of attractiveness, that a multi-billion-dollar industry can convince us every year that if we buy the right products, join the right health clubs, adopt the right weight loss method, we too can achieve the ideal set by the supermodels and strived for in vein by the rest of us.

So, what if one is so blessed to grow up and look like a supermodel already? Well, in the eyes of many women, that is winning the lottery. The odds are almost as high, but the rewards are enormous and life-long. At least that is a myth that average women labor under. Of course, whether it is true is another matter. Regardless, the myth has great power.

When women say about my rascal girls, "Oh, they could be models!" I don't smile inside the way I do when they say, "Oh they could be basketball players!" (which is usually half a joke anyway, as most people still do not envision women being professional basketball players). When I envision my smart, athletic, funny, aggressive, sensitive, lovable, pretty girls as models, I see them trapped in plastic see-through cages, on display for all to look at, but not to know, to use their images for their own voyeuristic pleasures, but not to communicate with them. I envision the multifaceted nature of their selves being stripped away as the two dimensional image of their appearance takes precedent. The caretaking of the body as perfect specimen becomes their primary concern, after all, that is what they are getting paid so much money for— that is what they are being valued for. The other aspects of their selves may get in the way. What if they bruised their legs while rock climbing? What if their aggressive posture made it impossible for men to fantasize using their pictures? What if their love of science made them come across too snotty in publicity interviews? What if their joyful personalities caused them to develop too many laugh lines? What if their love of chocolate ice cream made them gain weight? And then, what if they age?

The Semiotics of Gender in Advertising

Many of the most illuminating studies of advertising images have employed some variation of semiology (see Barthes 1977, 1988; Leiss, Kline, and Jhally 1986; Nichols 1981; Williamson 1978, 1986). By treating the advertising image as a text, semiotic analyses concentrate on the relationships between the ads' internal meaning structures as they relate to the larger cultural codes shared by viewers. Semiology's relationship to advertising is explained succinctly by Sut Jhally (1987):

Semiology is the study of signs, or more specifically the *system of signs*. A sign is something that has significance within a system of meaning and is constituted of two key elements: the signifier (the material vehicle) and the signified (the mental construct, the idea). The two elements are equally necessary and can be separated only analytically. . . . This is the difference between the signifier and the sign. A diamond as signifier is *empty* of meaning. The diamond as sign is *full* of meaning . . . production produces commodities as signifiers while advertising produces them as signs. (130)

A sign is the smallest unit of analysis for discovering how meaning is generated and conveyed. It is widely recognized that there are primarily three types of signs: icons, indexes, and symbols. An icon is a sign that closely resembles, and therefore signifies, its material object. For example, our driver's license picture is supposed to closely resemble us, in order to "stand in" for us as identification. An index is a sign that *points* to something else. For example, smoke is an indexical sign of fire and physical symptoms are indexical signs of illness or disease. To return to our photograph example, a driver's license picture is an icon; however, certain types of portraiture, such as "Glamor Shots," where the person goes through a makeover and then is photographed through a soft-focus lens, are more of an index. In other words, the finished photograph *points* to the person who posed for it, but the image is enhanced, it is "better" than the person it points to. Finally, the symbol is a sign that has been arbitrarily imbued with meaning, either through culture, and habit, or through the intentional strategy of marketing. For example, the signifier of a rose is literally the plant (its petals, stem, leaves, thorns, pigment). However, in this culture the most prevalent signifieds of rose are "love," "affection," and "beauty." These meanings are arbitrary in that there is nothing in the plant itself that either resembles or points to these things. However, culture has "naturalized" these connotations for us. The rose is a symbol of "love," "affection," and "beauty." Advertising operates in the realm of symbols, drawing from those already familiar, and inventing new signs where none existed before. In one final example of the photograph as a sign, when a clever marketing campaign for Guess? jeans repeatedly used the photographic image of super model Claudia Schiffer in their ads, the image of Claudia Schiffer became a symbol of Guess? jeans, or, more accurately, a symbol of the Guess? style and "look." This pairing of Schiffer and Guess? jeans was arbitrary.

The meaning of any given sign is culturally defined and culturally specific. In Jhally's example of the difference between the diamond as empty signifier and full sign, he is speaking of the difference between the material substance of the "rock" called a diamond (signifier) and the connotations that rock has for us in culture. For example, a diamond is a sign of "engagement" (index), "romantic attachment" (symbol), "affluence" (symbol), "taste" (symbol). The diamond is a full sign that has the potential to "stand for" or signify any one or any combination of these things. When advertising and marketing campaigns attempt to sell commodities (signifiers) to the public, they either work with the cultural connotations with which the commodity is already imbued, or, in the case of a new product, or a generic commodity, the significance of the commodity is invented entirely in the process of advertising. For example, the long-running "Diamonds Are Forever" ad campaign draws on cultural meanings of a diamond familiar to consumers, but then imbues particular types of diamond rings (signifiers) with very particular signifieds. The eternity diamond ring, for example, through the magic of this advertising campaign now signifies to us "marriage anniversary" or "milestones within marriage" such as the birth of a child. The ad campaign draws heavily on the persuasive appeal of guilt to convey, especially to the male consumer, that if he lets these milestones go by without rewarding "her" with an eternity diamond ring, he is some kind of clod. So, in this regard, the "Diamonds Are Forever" campaign signifies as much about what it means if one has reached these marital milestones and does *not* own an eternity ring, as it signifies about what it means *to* own and wear a diamond eternity ring. The campaign presents us with the diamond eternity ring as a full sign, both in its presence and in its absence.

For Roland Barthes (1974, 1977) advertising is a mythical structure where any given advertisement has the ability to produce meaning at many different levels of signification. Barthes's essay, "The Rhetoric of the Image," is considered germinal for understanding the semiology of advertising. Scholars such as Sut Jhally, Bill Nichols, and Judith Williamson have refined and also expanded Barthes's ideas in order to analyze the intertextuality of advertising as a "discourse." In other words, these authors are concerned with how individual advertisements are interdependent on one another for meaning—as a *code*. "Signs do not occur singly; they occur in groups . . . placing signs into appropriate groupings stresses that meaning arises not solely, not even primarily, from the relationship of signifier to signified but relations between signs" (Leeds-Hurwitz 1993, 51). A code is not a mere grouping of signs, however. A code is a system of associations governed by rules agreed upon (explicitly or implicitly) between members of a culture. The code unifies the different elements of the process of meaning construction. In advertising, a code is the store of experience upon which both the advertiser and audience draw in their participation in the construction of "commodity meaning" (Jhally 1987, 140).

Dominant ideologies in a culture can change and be reconfigured, while other competing ideologies remain as "master narratives." For example, master narratives of American culture are "rugged individualism," "democracy," "freedom," "equality." Of course, these narratives were not always valid for everyone. In times of slavery the slaves were not free. Before the suffrage movement women could not participate in democracy. However, the ideologies of the times accounted for their own contradictions—those who were outside of the master narratives, blacks and women in the examples above, were inferior and therefore unfit to participate in them. Freedom and liberty for all meant for those worthy by virtue of not being inferior, namely white males.

As cultural codes shift within dominant ideologies, some signs acquire different signifieds, sometimes in direct opposition to the previous signifieds—such is the case with the sign of the cigarette. At an antique store I picked up a 1951 ad for Chesterfield cigarettes featuring Donna Reed and John Derek! Donna Reed was a 1950s icon of "femininity and domesticity," exemplified in her leading role as dutiful wife and mother in *The Donna Reed Show*, and perhaps her most enduring film role, as Jimmy Stewart's wife in *It's a Wonderful Life*. Donna Reed, a smoker?!

Similarly, in *Seven Year Itch* Marilyn Monroe portrays an innocent young starlet who is ignorant of worldly ways. She is concerned with getting enough sleep and making sure her mouth is "kissing fresh" by using the right toothpaste—and she smokes. Smoking in the 1950s was not signified as "toughness" or "worldliness" as in recent decades. In the 1951 ad there is no contradiction between Donna Reed's squeaky clean image and smoking Chesterfield cigarettes. The ad positions Donna Reed and John Derek as stars. But when it comes to smoking, they "are just like you and everybody today. They want the cigarette that gives them the most for the money." In the 1950s, cigarette advertisers had the luxury of investing their product with the images of TV and film stars. Because at that time the product itself was a somewhat empty signifier, the challenge for advertisers was differentiating between brands of a fairly generic product. They could choose the type of signified that would give their product a particular appeal. Chesterfield wanted its cigarettes to be associated with beautiful celebrities. However, a very particular kind of celebrity was chosen. These celebrities are "just like you and everybody else" when it comes to cigarettes. By smoking Chesterfields one is participating in the wholesome image of Donna Reed and John Derek. (Of course, John Derek's taste in much younger women would prevent his image from remaining wholesome for long.)

In the 1970s the Marlboro man was an incredibly good-looking model with real "star quality." A bit later in the decade this handsome model broke into acting, and TV and film enthusiasts soon came to know him as Tom Selleck. Would we ever see Tom Selleck in a Marlboro ad today? What about Tom Hanks? Or what about a modern-day Donna Reed figure, Kathie Lee Gifford? Martha Stewart? In fact, when was the last time we saw any celebrity advertising cigarettes?

Today the cigarette itself is a "full sign" of negative connotations *before* advertisers try to invest it with a particular image. The challenge for advertisers today is to deal with the fullness of the sign in the first place, and then attach some kind of positiveness to it. Camel has done it with a cartoon character, Marlboro is still using the image of the rugged outdoorsman, and Virginia Slims has attempted to incorporate advances from the women's movement into its campaigns. However, these campaigns use models, not celebrity endorsers. The cigar may be enjoying a new life as celebrity-endorsed sign, but no Hollywood agent or publicist in this current cultural climate is going to allow clients to endorse cigarettes.

Judith Williamson's (1978) analysis of how advertisements can be "decoded" employs the conceptual tools of semiotics and structuralism to explore the meaning structures of individual advertising images in relation to the larger structure of advertising as a "currency." For Williamson, advertising can be thought of as a "currency of signs." Advertising helps invest commodities with value: not merely a utility value, but a value attached to an "image" or a "look." Williamson points out that the way advertisers invest their products with value is by differentiating the image of their product from the images of other products in the same marketing category. The value of the image, therefore, is dependent upon the viewers' abilities to make references to the other products in the category.

The systems of meaning from which we draw the tools to complete the transfer from meaning to commodity are referred to by Williamson as *referent systems*. They constitute the body of knowledge from which both advertisers and audiences draw their materials. Mass media advertising, therefore, plays the role of mediator. "For the audience properly to decode the message (transfer meaning), advertisers have to draw their materials from the social knowledge of the audience, then transform this material into messages (encode), developing appropriate formats and shaping the content in order that the process of communication from audience be completed" (Jhally 1987, 132). It is this point which separates the advertising image from other forms of artistic visual images. Unlike a portrait or a driver's license photograph, the advertising image is not the thing it represents, but is instead a part of a referent system, dependent on the viewer's understanding and interpretation of the codes of advertising in general. Understanding this referent system requires an understanding of the larger cultural codes that the spectator brings to the viewing.

Ads have the ability to signify to us when we know the cultural codes that allow us to reference what the signs replace. We, by bringing our own referent systems to the viewing, complete the transfer of meaning to the commodity. Images of gender are highly structured cultural codes in this society. The codes of sexuality transferred to products are probably more widely accessible to more people than other cultural codes and are therefore continually recycled in the symbolic world of image production. It is not unusual to us to see a woman's sexuality signifying the value of cars, stereos, beer, cologne, jeans and so on.

This method of decoding advertisements is based on the work of Swiss linguist Ferdinand de Saussure. Saussure (1956) tells us that in the English language we know the meaning of a thing by knowing what it is *not*. We know that C-A-T is not D-O-G. It is through the *difference* between the sound image of C-A-T and the sound image of D-O-G that each has meaning for us (Hawkes 1977). Based on this concept from Saussure, Williamson concludes that for the viewer, the value of a product depends as much on what it is *not* as on what it *is*.

For example, types of colognes, jeans, paper towels, and so on have very little significance of their own. Advertisements invest products with a value by relating the product to a person, object, emotion, or image which already has value for us. Products not invested with such value through advertising are "generic." For instance, Hanes underwear is invested with value when it is differentiated from Jockey underwear. An advertisement of Michael Jordan in Hanes underwear is a sign which invests the underwear with the image associated with Michael Jordan. What is possibly signified is that highly successful, rich, nice athletes wear Hanes underwear; Michael Jordan becomes the signifier.

It follows, therefore, that viewers give signs value through the recognition of what they replace. By transferring the significance of Michael Jordan to Hanes underwear we are acknowledging a value we place on the image of Michael Jordan. Of course, advertisers hope this is a positive value. However, whether positive or negative, this value differentiates Hanes underwear from Jockey or Fruit of the Loom underwear.

In order for this system of currency to have meaning for the viewer, he or she must be able to associate the image of the product with a value which is in turn based on his or her own cultural codes. "Recognition" is the viewer's first level of involvement with the meaning of advertisements. The second level of involvement is the advertisement's ability to signify the viewer to her- or himself. Advertising insists that we differentiate what kind of person we "are" in relation to a specific product. The product can then be exchanged for the quality of the person(s), as exemplified with "the Pepsi generation." If we drink Pepsi we are signified as qualitatively different from those who drink Coke (Shields 1990); if we wear Gap khakis we are signified as being a different kind of person from someone who wears Levis 501 jeans.

Differentiation cannot be interpreted as a wholly overt and cognitively conscious process, however. Differentiation is often emotional and sensual. Many fashion advertisements, for example, operate at a level of social significance that is once removed from the utility of the product being advertised. The sensuality of the image does not define the commodity so much as it differentiates the sensuousness of one commodity from the sensuousness of another. Calvin Klein uses differentiation to market colognes to different age groups. Ads for CK1 use black and white, gritty photography of a variety of young "looks" in the 16 to 22 age group. While ads for "Eternity" cologne also use black and white photography, the situations pictured are more mature, dreamlike fantasies — suggesting participants who have achieved a certain status in life. It is doubtful that the actual scents of these colognes signify what age group should wear them. Through marketing, however, Calvin Klein attempts to capture two lucrative markets.

Cultural Ways of Seeing

Annette Kuhn tells us that our cultural way of seeing the female form as the object of visual sexualization has very material and historical roots. She points out that "whenever we look at painted, drawn, sculpted or photographed images of women, it is important for us to remind ourselves that images of women have traditionally been the province and property of men" (1985, 10–11). The definitions of good photography and beautiful art have been conceived, owned, managed, and produced by males. Therefore, it is important to remember that the repetitious presentation of gender that we are so familiar with is the historical result of the male gender's choices and tastes.

The transfer of codes of sexuality to commodities in this culture is widely accessible to both males and females because the transfer has become "naturalized" in our popular iconography. More specifically, the transfer of codes of ideal female beauty or attractiveness to commodities has become common sense, even though the relationship between, say, a woman in a swim suit and a can of beer is in itself arbitrary:

I mentioned a beer commercial earlier where you have the beautiful women and the good-looking guys who are with the women and having a lot of fun and whatever else is going on. And I think they take advantage of that. I think it kind of makes it seem like, with them flooding the media or whatever, when you see these kinds of commercials, they make you think that's the normal, that it's normal to have these kinds of feelings. And it's normal to expect to have a beer commercial with beautiful women in it. Basically, what's normal—kind of like a mass consent thing. (Art, 30)

The sign of the ideal female body, in this culturally naturalized state, then, takes on an exchange value all its own. It is an ambiguous discourse that can be visually attached to virtually any commodity in order to lend the commodity value. Therefore, when the woman in the swimsuit appears in an advertisement for beer, the relationship between the sexuality of the female body and the commodity (beer) does not appear to be arbitrary. The sexuality of the female body has lent its general exchange value in this case to the value of beer, but it could just as easily be lent to the value of an automobile or cigarettes.

Although the naturalness of highly sexualized images of women standing for commodities like beer goes largely unquestioned in our culture, this doesn't mean that women do not have a lot to say about the perfect bodies continuously displayed in the marketing relationship. The repetitive nature of particular signs associated with the idealized female body are sources of anxiety. The bathing suit is one such sign. "The Swedish Bikini Team" beer marketing strategy of the 1980s represented the ultimate bimbo-beer-bikini combination. However, a woman in a bathing suit is a common sign attached to a wide variety of products at any given time—vodka, suntan lotion, weight-loss products, hair-removal products, and on and on. When I teach my "Women, Mass Media and Culture" class I always ask the students, "Who in the room feels comfortable in a swimsuit?" Generally no hands are raised. One semester I had a swimmer on the university swim team raise her hand. She said she feels comfortable in her competition suit when at practice or at a meet, because there the swimsuit is almost like an athletic uniform. In semiotic terms, then, her swimsuit is an index of her sport, which is swimming. Another semester a graduate student said she felt comfortable in her one-piece Speedo competitive suit, because she is fairly tall and slim and just feels "athletic" in it. She was quick to add, "however, I would never be caught dead in a two-piece, especially a bikini. I'm not that brave."

More common than the two responses above are "I haven't been seen in a bathing suit in five years! I never feel skinny enough" or "It makes me so self-conscious I can't be myself at all" or "I'm always the only one all wrapped up in a towel or a cover-up. I feel as freaky as when I'm in a bathing suit. I just try to avoid the situation altogether." When I ask why they don't like to wear swimsuits, the criticism immediately goes to their own bodies. "I just feel fat in a swimsuit" or "Even when I'm feeling ok about my body in clothes, like feeling pretty slim, a swimsuit is a whole different story, I feel flabby and jiggly." Why in the world would a little piece of cloth unleash this kind of anxiety? The bathing suit in this culture is for women a "full sign." That is, it is packed with cultural connotation.

Nowhere was this better illustrated than in two "Cathy" cartoons by Cathy Guisewite that appeared in the spring many years ago. The first one shows Cathy entering the dressing room of the department store carrying a swimsuit. Along the way she is trying to build up her confidence, telling herself, "I'm attractive, I'm intelligent, I'm talented." Upon seeing herself in the mirror donning the swimsuit she says, "AACK!" She gets dressed and grabs more suits, once again trying to build up her self-esteem, "I'm bright, I'm charming, I'm thoughtful, I'm kind." Again, upon seeing herself in the mirror, this time in a bikini, she shrieks, "AAACK!" By this time, anxiety, panic, and frustration are setting in. As she looks for other suits, she says to herself, "I'm an upstanding citizen! A hard worker! A wonderful daughter! A fabulous friend! I am an incredible person! I'm a proud, confident, perfectly incredible person! AAAAACKK!!" As she throws the swimsuits into the saleswoman's arms unpurchased, she thinks to herself, "How can something that makes me feel so fat make me feel so puny?" In a second cartoon, appearing the next day, the "Cathy" strip simply shows two bathing suits, a man's and a woman's. Across the top the caption reads: "Swimwear: A Microcosm of Life's Extra Little Expectations for Women." The small picture of the man's swimsuit has an arrow pointing to the drawstring and it simply says, "holds up suit." The woman's suit has arrows pointing to every conceivable part of it, saying things like, "shapes bust," "lengthens torso," "draws attention away from thighs," "draws attention away from arms," "minimizes hips."

For most women the cultural artifact "bathing suit" makes no immediate referent to swimming but instead is a sign for body imperfection, a sign of vulnerability—the naked truth. Not only does the bathing suit reveal all—unlike lingerie or even clingy sportswear—concealing none, its function is to display in public (see Valdivia 1997). The bathing suit as a sign is a repository of female anxieties about their public bodies—the one displayed in public in a society that is well-trained in defining female perfection in minute detail, from head to toe. The skimpiness of the bathing suit allows for this kind of full body inspection, whether real or imagined. In a culture where women often choose their clothes as a way of fashionably *concealing* body imperfections, the bathing suit, if it is to perform as swimming apparel at all, is not designed to conceal, but to reveal the true contours of the body. As the twenty-first century begins, the perfect beauty ideal is not only slim but incredibly toned, tan, and firm. Any flesh that jiggles is unsightly. The *"Baywatch* body" deserves its rightful space on the beach. Anything less (or in most cases, more) is a waste of space, an eyesore.

Susan Bordo in *Unbearable Weight* recalls watching the episode of *20/20* that solicited young boys' impressions of fashion models. The boys called the models "fat." She recalled being appalled by the reactions of the young boys, but at the same time taken aback by her own reactions to images of women in the '70s that once seemed slim and now seem overweight and flabby. The expectation now is not so much of a thinner body, but of a tighter, smoother one. Along these same lines, when Nancy Sinatra was being interviewed after posing for *Playboy* in the late 1980s all the interviews centered around how good her body looked for a woman in her fifties. She said to a reporter that she thanked God for aerobics and the awareness of fitness. Looking back now at her TV appearances in the 1960s, singing "These Boots Were Made for Walking," she described herself as "flabby, and jiggly." She was embarrassed to look at herself in her twenties, not because of the flip hairstyle or the go-go boots, but because she was not perfectly tight and toned. "We thought we looked pretty good back then, I guess we didn't know any better."

Finally, there was a movie review by Rex Reed on the film *Working Girl*, starring Melanie Griffith. There are at least two scenes in the film where Tess McGill (Griffith's character) is trying on clothes in front of a mirror and the audience gets to view her body as voyeur. In the first scene she is trying on the lingerie her fiancé gave her for her birthday. The camera moves up and down her body as she shows her dislike of his gift. She explains that it is not "practical." For once she wished he'd give her a gift she could really wear. So, while the message in the dialogue of the film suggests that Tess is fed up with being dressed up only to be objectified by her fiancé, the overriding visual effect of the camera moving up and down her body is to objectify her for *us*, the viewers.

The second scene in *Working Girl* where the viewer, as voyeur, looks at Tess's body in the mirror is in the female boss's apartment. Tess is planning to attend a party in her boss's absence and, since she is stuck taking care of the boss's apartment, she decides to borrow a dress. Again, we as the audience watch her disrobe and robe in the mirror. In reference to these shots in the film, Rex Reed referred to Griffith's body as "bloated and puffy." He used the words with disdain, as if she owed us a perfectly tight body to look at. How dare she offer up to us a body to stare at with a slight appearance of fleshiness and womanly roundness!

As we can see from the examples above this general exchange-value of the ideal female body reaches far beyond advertising in this culture. This exchange value is what Berger calls a cultural way of seeing. Ways of seeing the female body are culturally imbued codes which are consistent across not only advertising images but other visual images as well, such as film, television programs, music videos, and even portraiture. This consistency in representation helps define what is "natural" to be seen and enjoyed—what is ideal. A photograph or an advertising image is a selective view of reality. In this culture, advertising images of females frequently contain an invisible yet implicit man who approves of and defines the feminine ideal. Thus the point of view in advertisements featuring the perfect female body is almost always that of an implied male spectator. This implied approval by an often invisible male spectator is referred to by feminist scholars as the "male gaze," Seen through the lens of the "male gaze" females are the objects as opposed to the subjects of the gaze.

The male gaze connotes significantly more than mere voyeurism. It is a controlling gaze. "To possess the image of a woman's sexuality is, however mass-produced the image, also in some way to possess, to maintain a degree of control over the woman in general" (Kuhn 1985, 11). Laura Mulvey further explains the concept of the gendered gaze.

In a world ordered by sexual imbalance, pleasure in looking has been split between active/male and passive/female. the determining male gaze projects its fantasy onto the female figure, which is styled accordingly. In their traditional exhibitionist role women are simultaneously looked at and displayed, with their appearance coded for strong visual and erotic impact so that they can be said to connote *to-be-looked-at-ness*. (1975, 366)

For Rosiland Coward (1985), the male gaze encoded in photographic images is an extension of how men view women in the streets. The naturalness of this way of seeing the female body follows from its pervasiveness in all arenas of female representation as well as experience. As Berger puts it simply, " 'men act' and 'women appear.' Men look at women. Women watch themselves being looked at. . . . The surveyor of women in herself is male: the surveyed female. Thus she turns herself into an object—and most particularly an object of vision: a 'sight' " (Berger 1973, 47). In this schema, the female looking at an image is always a "split-subject." Women in patriarchal cultures are placed in a position of always being the embodiment of the object of the sight for someone else's pleasure and simultaneously being aware that she is this object of the sight. It also allows for a way of seeing that seems natural in appeal to both male and female spectators. If aesthetic appeal of the female body is naturalized for both males and females, it also seems natural that the female body is represented as sexualized more often than the male body.

Patricia Mellencamp explains the phenomenon is this way:

It is precisely this misrecognition [the split between a woman's self-image and her mirror image], a real alienation effect—woman divided against her inadequate self, body versus mind, mother versus daughter or son, woman versus woman—that must be overcome. After all, the body is an image and a sack of flesh; it is a historical, personal fiction or style as much as a reality. Certainly, the body is neither self nor identity nor value; we are much more, much greater, than our bodies. Sex and the body don't grant identity, as Michel Foucault said over a decade ago, yet we keep looking there for answers. (Mellencamp 1995, 3)

Many of the definitions, or signs, of ideal femininity offered up by advertisers are enduring, such as thinness, youth, and flawlessness, while other definitions are refined and recirculated cyclically, like body type (e.g., curvaceous versus muscular versus ultra-thin), skin tone (tan versus pale) and style and adornment (natural versus made-up, long hair versus short hair, curly hair versus straight hair), and so on. For those who collaborated in this research the enduring definitions of ideal femininity—thinness, flawlessness, and youthfulness—were seen as the pivotal point of influence by the advertising industry. Further, men and women also were more likely to link these enduring definitions of ideal femininity in advertising to individuals' struggles to "measure up" to these externally imposed prescriptions:

The first thing that struck me about every one of the ads is they sort of depict somebody's idea—maybe a fashion creator's or fashion photographer's idea of what human beauty is. And most of them are female and I think there's the idea, preconception, that the slim, trim, often blonde—not always, but often—is the ideal. I don't know what the percentage is but I wouldn't think a majority of women in this country or society fit that. In that sense it's sort of an unreachable ideal for most. . . . I think there's a conception that, among advertisers, this type of body, this type of image, is the one they want to project for their product. In a sense, that may be in presenting it so frequently, people will strive to be that way, whether or not they can or they really want to. (Kevin, 33)

Yeah, it's perverted, after all, making people into a few salable types. It makes them like cars that are sold for a "look." You get the idea that some powerful king or something decided how he wants his women to be and they serve him up what he wants, it's hard to believe that people would choose some of these parts on their own, more like these women are pimpled. (Mike, 40)

There's an ideal, that's almost, that's being set that's almost unreachable. Rarely do you see females—or else a male also depicted in advertising—rarely do you "see" these people [in real life]. I mean, they're almost out of reach. You wonder, and now everyone gets so stressed out about trying to live up to these ideals and you wonder whether, one, anyone can live up to these ideals and whether the ideal is worth living up to. (Greg, 19)

I just find it a quality that persists through advertisements. . . . I also know that the photographs are touched up and air-brushed and stuff. So they are perpetuating an image that even the super-models can't achieve, let alone the average woman. So, I think it creates this unnecessary pressure to be something that you can never be. It's pointless. . . . It bothers me because maybe women will look at this ad [Jordache ad, fig. 3] and think that they can only be assertive and independent if they have the looks to do that, the certain dress, or style or body. Maybe I can only have that personality trait if I go along with it. (Camron, 22)

It is important to observe here that these men and women do not see these definitions of ideal female beauty as predetermined or unchangeable. Instead, the underlying assumption in their responses was that advertising does not simply offer a mirror of what people would innately find attractive; they were conscious of the fact that advertisers educate consumers as to what is attractive by offering consistent and ubiquitous images of beauty.

However, although both men and women recognized that ways of seeing the ideal female body are culturally defined and recirculated through particular social structures, women gave responses suggesting that they were critical of the arbitrary nature of the implied male spectator across the spectrum of advertising. Women deconstructed the "naturalness" of the male address of the female body across all advertising forums, finding some forums more inappropriate, or more arbitrary, than others. For example, women found the use of the overt male gaze in advertisements in women's magazines particularly offensive, stating that these advertisements suggest to women that if they are not the recipient of this same type of male attention, there is something wrong with them.

Well, the majority of these ads are in female magazines. They are directed toward a male audience but women are only going to see them. So it kind of makes us feel bad about ourselves as women because we don't look like them. That is why I put them in pile number one because these don't appeal to me at all. . . . It disturbs because of the fact that they are selling to women but they are really selling to men. They are in women's magazines and they are selling to men. (Nicole, 22)

So many of them [ads] are images, society's ideals that have been conjured up by men and what they want to see. They are unattainable, these thin bodies, perfect hair, fine clothes, faces. This is the cause of so much distress and poor self-images of women today. At the same time I do rather envy them, their bodies, despite my better judgment, I do. (Rachel, 20)

Further, women suggested that the pervasive male gaze in advertising perpetuates a male fantasy of women styled on a vision of femininity that is one-dimensional. They argued that the mass media's continual perpetuation of one-dimensional images of women based solely on appearance serves to prevent men from seeing, and therefore valuing, women as multidimensional beings. According to these women, the pervasiveness and consistency of images of the one-dimensional female, which are generally coded for strong visual and erotic impact, contribute in a significant way to males' stereotypical visions of femininity. They suggested that such images perpetuate the belief that women should be judged foremost on appearance and sex-appeal.

This concept of women being sold the male-defined, ideal image of themselves is what has been described in cultural studies literature as the "split consciousness" of the surveyed female. In this split consciousness women are aware that they are seeing male-defined images of themselves, and yet still find themselves influenced by these images. As Berger notes, women become aware of viewing themselves as well as other women as the objects of sight.

I think [advertising] helps to contribute to people, and how they think about women. I think it is harmful, what we are seeing is one dimensional things and we are not, men aren't trained to deal with us like regular human beings. Not a lot of them. I mean some of them are. But, everybody including women and including myself, who thinks I'm sort of aware of this, [is] still influenced to see woman as one dimensional things. (Laura, 33)

Women almost always, and men very rarely, possessed the ability to theorize how advertising works to further encourage women to view themselves as objects to be improved upon for the male other, rather than to view themselves as subjects of their own femaleness.

I just feel like I know what is attractive to men. All these pictures fit that category, skinny people are more accepted and attractive people are more accepted in society. . . . Other than the fact that I would like to be built perfect, it doesn't really have that much affect on me. . . I mean, if you are attracted to a man and he doesn't think you're attractive then there is nothing you can do about it. I don't think it is that important to me. . . . I think it would help if I looked more like they do. It would help me because people like to be around attractive people. Not everybody is like that. Attractive people are more well-liked and popular. That could help you in the future. In that way it could help me. . . . It hurts me because if I don't look like this I won't be looked well upon society. Especially as I get older and I don't have the body and the face I think it will hurt more too. Women are supposed to be young looking and your skin is supposed to be nice but men don't have to worry about it because they get better looking as they get older.

She [woman in Obsession cologne ad] just seems like perfect. She's got the perfect body. She's got blond hair. She just seems like she would be really conceited. . . . No, I don't have to worry about being too attractive. It makes me sort of jealous. It is like a ping of jealousy. (Claire, 22)

However, awareness (conscientization, see Freire 1974) or understanding of the process does very little to alleviate inner conflicts experienced by these women as a result of split consciousness. If anything, a heightened awareness of the fact that women turn themselves into the objects of vision (sight) instead of substance, and that they actively participate in surveying themselves for and from a male perspective, adds to a sense of anxiety.

I see this over and over again in my female graduate students who are aspiring media scholars. They have seen Jean Kilbourne's *Still Killing Us Softly* a hundred times, have taught media literacy on issues of the body and feminism to their own students in courses like Introduction to Women's Studies or Introduction to Popular Culture and have written numerous feminist critiques of television, film, and advertising for classes and academic conferences. However, all this knowledge does not easily translate into self-empowerment over these idealized media images, although it certainly helps place some distance between oneself and the air-brushed perfection of women in ads. My graduate students, like myself, are not inoculated, only more conscious. Sometimes this heightened consciousness means simply a heightened sense of guilt: guilt for enjoying the seductive pleasure of the scented *Vogue* pages, guilt for loving it when the soap-opera heroine gets swept off her feet, but mainly guilt for feeling bad about our bodies, when we *know* the bad feelings are being produced not by some internal standard, but an ideal standard perpetuated through the media and by our peers.

For many women the awareness of a split consciousness of the female signified a kind of "loss." They suggested that this overdetermined preoccupation with one's own sense of being a sight for others robs women of the ability to look at other women and appreciate beauty for its own sake. Instead, feelings of appreciation are generally mixed with envy or jealousy, and these women ended up feeling a deep-seated need to emulate, displace, or even eclipse the beauty of other women.

Physical appearances are too important. It has become too important and it shouldn't be. And yet it is, I can't avoid it. I wouldn't mind looking at things from the artist's sense, and saying, oh, this is beautiful or this is natural. But, I don't know, I don't look at it that way. . . . You have a physical appearance, which is whatever it is and you can't do anything about it. You can brush your teeth, brush your hair, and take a bath or something, but to worry about it is misery inducing because you have so little control over it. In the end it is just a stupid thing, it bothers me a lot. . . . I mean just because its not an ideal world and everybody can't be perfect. So then, it's very hurtful to wish that it were or expect that it is—just causing you misery. (Laura, 33)

Well, it is the kind of figure you would want—most women want. We'd all like to have long legs and flat stomachs and just that overall perfection—no spotty skin. . . . I would just like to be that way. Probably eating anything you want as well. . . . [It's] pleasing because it seems so easy to them but they are probably watching everything they eat, so it may not be so easy. . . . It's displeasing in the way that you don't look like that. (Jeannette, 22)

Williamson suggests that advertising feeds off our desire for coherence and meaning. She argues that advertisements attempt to represent to us the central object of our desire, the unified and perfect self, an "Ego-Ideal." Ads suggest that one can become the perfect person in the ad if we only use the right kind of shampoo or deodorant, use the right toilet cleaner or drive the right car. However, despite constantly offering us a vision of a complete, "perfect" self, advertising is not designed to bolster our egos. If we truly felt complete, we would have no need for their products that are aimed at self-improvement. Thus, the major objectives of advertising are to make the person feel she is not a unified being, a complete entity unto herself, but instead a work in progress made up of separate parts, each in need of continual improvement.

Part of advertising's magic, though, is that it offers a continual hope that we *can* move closer to the ideal if we just purchase this one necessary item. Even though advertising may make the viewer feel bad about herself as a person, as incomplete or lacking because her hair doesn't bounce or her teeth aren't quite white, the magic of advertising is that it offers the viewer the promise of redemption. Advertising offers itself as a solution to our problems. It promises that if we buy the product we will move closer to the unified self, and as a consequence be happy. If you feel bad about your hair, your relationships, or your job, it is easy to think that it is because you are lacking something, a something that the product provides. Buying the product will move us closer to our goal of self-perfection.

Seeing these things in the magazines, you tend to think—say you come from a background where there is not a lot of money and you can't get these things, and then when you do get a bit of money, you see these things and you tend to think you can go out and buy these things and you feel a lot better about yourself. I guess it's always in the back of your mind that you can be this perfect-like person and you can have this perfect life, happy every after, the idea that everything seems the way it should be, socially acceptable. (Jeannette, 22)

In reality, however, although a new antiperspirant might make you feel better about yourself for awhile, it does little to really change you or your circumstances. Thus every product purchased with the hope of a magical transformation is doomed to failure. The result can be the intensification of self-doubt.

You want something and you still drive to get it. When you don't it's a feeling of failure. You feel that failure when you don't lose that ten pounds or you don't have blue eyes. (Rachel, 20)

The consumer is linked in a vicious cycle in which she sees herself as a work in process, continually needing to refine herself, working toward the distant goal of a perfect self. An ominous consequence to this process is that with every exchange comes a change to self until the desire to change becomes an end in itself.

Probably the sadness I see in the effort and time women put in to make themselves the supposedly ideal woman. Too many times I think it backfires on them because it makes them even more unattractive 'cause it's not what they really are. (Rachel, 20)

I think it is very counterproductive and destructive to women to be kind of forced into trying to change who and what they are based on the need of a company to sell products. (Megan, 25)

Women talked at length about their desires to change themselves. As stated earlier, an awareness (conscientization) of the processes at work to make them want to change themselves was of little consolation, but was instead a source of frustration and guilt. Interestingly, awareness often resulted in anger toward other women, more than men. Women often saw themselves and other women as perpetuating the problems of split consciousness far more than men. Through their full participation in this culture's demands that females are judged foremost on appearance and should spend considerable personal and financial resources succumbing to "self-improvement," many women discussed how they and other women are implicated in perpetuating their own exploitation.

All my life people have told me, even my friends, that "Oh, you'll look better if you only did this, or that," stuff like that. Of course I would listen to them, most of the time. I was trying to be the best I could be, looks wise. . . . We all characterize ourselves and others by the outer appearance. Women more so than men. Women spend more time in the mirror, we buy things to enhance ourselves to be that perfect woman. What do men buy? Not that much. I don't see too many men in tight clothing. Yet you see women all the time. People will do what is best for them, I guess, and not realize what they are doing to society at large. Women continue to exploit themselves, therefore it is easy for men to exploit them too. If women stop the madness and stop obsessing about the physical side of them, then I think men will change their own attitude towards women. (Jamie, 22)

Rosiland Coward contends that "narcissism" is extremely inadequate as an explanation for women's obsessions with surveying themselves and other women (1985). A theory of narcissism holds that woman are innately vain, finding pleasure in scrutinizing and assessing their outer images. The result of these assessments is the need to masque the appearance in order to improve upon personal beauty. One of the by-products of the pleasure of self-adoration is the need to gauge one's own beauty by assessing the beauty of others critically. The "others" referred to here are not only other real women, but also the women in the mass media.

Coward suggests that it is not self-love that leads to a woman's obsession with her own image, it is actually a form of *self-hate*. Coward calls this form of feminine self-hate "narcissistic damage." In Coward's view, women are fascinated with their own images not so much out of a sense of desire or pleasure as out of a sense of anxiety and urgency to change and to improve.

Yeah, women are not as self-centered as you think they are. We care about other things in life. I care about my health and my well-being, my family, and my friends, things like that. We are more well-rounded than the media, magazines give us credit for. . . .
. . . We are not on this earth to be casted as a piece of meat, or somebody's play toy. We are more than just a piece of flesh. We have a mind and depth to us, all that stuff is overlooked by people who just buy into stereotypes of women. Well, before we had this women's movement, we didn't reveal much of ourselves. Not our minds or abilities and especially not our bodies. Now we have freedom and men and women abuse it. They try to dictate what is good and bad and what's wrong or right. I don't think we should let people like advertisers decide what is right for us. Let us decide what to wear because we like it or feel comfortable. Not pressured into a dress that you can't fit into then starve yourself trying. We need to think for ourselves, then we can help others, not dictate, but help them be themselves. (Jamie, 22)

Coward argues that in a highly visual and image-conscious society such as ours, a woman learns at a very early age that physical appearance is probably the most crucial way in which men form opinions about her worth. However, the image of the flawless magazine cover girls and Hollywood screen goddesses set the standard for this assessment of feminine beauty, not flesh-and-blood women. In real life, women work toward this standard as a goal of achievement, measuring their success by the reflection in the mirror and more importantly, the attention gained by men as well as other women out in public.

Therefore, feelings about appearance and self-image easily get mingled with feelings about security and comfort. Absorption in the world of one's own image can be seen as a means of cultural survival, a bid for acceptance. Women did not so readily identify with the images they consumed, but they sometimes desired them, not as an object of possession, but rather an object of emulation. For these women, the visual image presented clues for proper conduct which can open doors to happiness and fulfillment.

Classic beauty? You grow up in this society wishing that you were one. Right? I mean it's hard to avoid, comparing yourself. I don't know, I always fell kind of short, in that sense. You are always looking around and trying to judge people by appearance or best on the scale is a classic beauty, so yeah it figures that in my life I'm that way. It inter-feres. It's problematic and it bothers me a lot that I even worry about something like that. I wish I could just look and appreciate some things, whatever, for what it was, and not always judgmental against it or something. . . . I mean, I spend too many of my waking hours worrying about classical beauty or looking beautiful and that's the standard on which you judge things. It's a drag. . . . Well, I just know that about myself. Other things matter to me—that I can carry on an intelligent conversation and that I can do well in school. But the thing that eats me away—maybe because I have no control over it, right?—well, it's that you are judging yourself on this physical standard that women are really beautiful. "Well, at least I look better than that one," or whatever. Or "Gee, I can't go out tonight because I look like a piece of shit." And I know that's the case. I hate to admit it, but it is. I find it extremely disturbing and I don't like it at all, but it is part of me. . . . Well, I judge myself by that and other people but in a way, unfortunately—it's an ideal that I don't think everybody is going to have to be. On one side logically you think about it—everybody doesn't have to look like that. Not everybody has to spend four hours a day in a gym. And yet I feel bad because I don't— because I have lumps in my thighs. That's how it relates to my life. . . . I mean I have this reaction. I wish I didn't have this reaction. But it is a part of you. You know what I'm saying? And I do judge people on and if I look at somebody who looks like they are physically in shape then I find it appealing, in that sense. It's a pleasing reaction, but in another sense, I wish it weren't what you judged somebody on, having a bad reaction. (Laura, 33)

Narcissistic damage, therefore, can be seen as the consequence of the per-vasive male gaze, a kind of trap where cultural ways of seeing define what is beautiful and women are thereby attracted to those images. At the same time the women were often repulsed by these same images. It was not so much the image of other beautiful women that was repulsive, but the surge of envy that such images evoked.

They are unattainable, these thin bodies, perfect hair, fine clothes, faces. This is the cause of so much distress and poor self-images of women today. At the same time I do rather envy them, their bodies, despite my better judgment, I do. . . . In the past I envied every single woman I saw in these magazines—her hair, her eyes. I'm slowly realizing I don't have to envy them but just look at them, admire them as well as admire myself. I think it's just a realization that I do envy them, that I can look at them and admire them without having to be them. (Rachel, 20)

I look and I see a beautiful woman walking across the screen or in a car or something and I go look at this crap [ads]. And me I think that's a beautiful-looking woman and then at the same time I'm complaining about this use of woman and then I see the beautiful woman and all this gunk goes into play. "Oh, wouldn't I like to be like that." So, that's what I mean. It must subconsciously reinforce, those images are there in front of your face and I guess if I only saw women here, I'd see that 10% look really beautiful, lots of them look fine or a few of them are disfigured. The only thing is it would be a lot more perspective or something. But on TV it's just like beautiful women on the TV all the time and that must reinforce the dumb notion that [we] have—beauty counts. (Laura, 33)

How We Learn to "Look"

Cultural theorists have shown that our culture privileges male looking. Jacques Lacan (1968, 1977) argues that the right to control others through the look, even the stare, is a cultural logic of patriarchy. An undeniable source of male power and privilege in a patriarchal society is the right not only to define female attractiveness, but also to render the female spectator absent in the defining process. In other words, men may look openly, while women's perspective or sight, if it exists at all, is hidden. Female looking, on the other hand, is generally relegated to private viewing, such as at magazines, television, and the cinema. The stories of men and women I talked with support these arguments. While both men and women discussed the pleasure of looking at attractive females, men tended to make their comments within the larger context of the way they look at women in general, not confining their comments to the advertisements in front of them.

I focused on the sexual aspect of [the ads]. They're good looking. . . . The way I was brought up in society from my interactions, watching TV, and everything else, looking at *Playboy* magazines. I just kind of equate a nice-looking woman with a pleasurable response. The sex and the pictures does that for me. It just makes me feel good. . . . From all the TV advertising, magazine advertising, record albums or whatever it is, you know someone is trying to attract you to their product. . . .
   I guess just looking at good-looking women, really. Whether it be on TV, magazines, or newspapers, or on the street. If I would see someone attractive of the opposite sex, it catches my eye. Not that it's that big of a deal—it would be just like "Wow!"

you know? "That's a nice-looking woman." . . . It does please. How it pleases me is this visual stimuli kind of thing. I find women attractive and it makes me feel good to look at them. Basically, that's it. It's a pretty quick thing that I don't have to linger on with. . . . I guess I equated that with having a lot of fun. You know, being at a party . . . kind of like being on a beer commercial. (Art, 30)

They're good-looking. These girls here—something I would—I definitely wouldn't mind having a girlfriend that enjoyed being outside in the sun and drinking beer. . . . They're hot! Just by what I see—these are women that obviously make money by being good-looking. They probably make lots of it. . . . I wish I was on the blanket too. (Craig, 26)

Reality. Like if you are walking down the street and you see a girl with a hot body, what's behind it comes next. . . . I guess it hinders me because you don't get to meet people who are different and beautiful in their own ways. (Shawn, 20)

I think I'm like any other guy. If a pretty girl walks by, there, I'm gonna look. But, I don't know, I hope, that. . . I could look past that and try to at least, because it's only skin-deep. . . . But, I do admit, a pretty girl walks by, it's almost hard to not just look at them. . . I guess every guy likes to look at a pretty girl. So in that way it pleases you. (Greg, 19)

Female pleasures in looking, in contrast, were confined to the immediate viewing object, in this case, advertisements. Furthermore, women rarely focused on the body when discussing pleasures in looking at women. Instead, women reported finding pleasure in things like facial features and fashion apparel.

[Naomi Campbell's] just a gorgeous girl. End of discussion. She's plain Jane gorgeous. I see her in all the TV ads, magazines, videos, that type of thing. . . . She has a pretty face, she has a very pretty skin tone, unblemished. . . . She's borderline perfect, which is hard to come by. (Collette, 21)

I do find [Isabella Rossellini, fig. 7] personally appealing because she has a really beautiful face. She's pretty. I guess some people would find that [referring to Budweiser ad, fig. 1] pretty too, but I don't find it appealing. She doesn't have too much make-up on. I wouldn't wear that much make-up, but she doesn't look overly made-up to me. . . . She is looking right at the viewer. So she looks like she is on equal footing and her eyes look kind to me. (Ginger, 28)

Well, I like her dress, something about it. I guess I would wear it to a nice affair or something. Her face is pretty to me, she has on all the right shades of make-up. . . . She's dressed in the latest style with big costume jewelry on, and a pretty dress. Something about her, I don't know. She's confident and happy in her outfit. . . . I would love to dress like that and have nice clothes in my closet. But of course I am a poor college student who has no money to spend it on clothing. But when I do graduate and get a nice job I hope to have stuff that's nice. (Jamie, 22)

The naturalness of this way of seeing the female body, that places men as the controllers of the look and women as the recipients of the look, follows from its pervasiveness in all arenas of female representation as well as experience. As mentioned earlier, Jacques Lacan argued that the right to control others through the look, even the stare, is a cultural logic of patriarchy. Possession of the phallus thus allows direct identification with "the Law," while nonpossession does not. For Lacan, the phallus is a socially organized symbol (sign) of the difference between male and female; in patriarchal societies it is a symbol of male power and privilege. An undeniable source of male power and privilege is the right not only to define female attractiveness but also to render the female spectator absent in the defining process.

Our culture, therefore, privileges male looking. Men offered comments concerning not only the consensual nature of looking at female bodies, but the importance of learning *how* to look at female bodies:

I remember reading magazines when I was younger and they didn't really have ads like these, if you wanted to see pictures of women you looked in *Playboy*. I guess those weren't really ads either but they did affect my idea of what it is to be male, to be able to look, but, that was one of those things you could only do pretty much in private. . . . I don't think men really look at pictures of men in the same way as women look at pictures of women. . . . Well, there isn't any way to say anything politically correct about *Playboy*, is there? I mean, that's what pisses me off about the whole thing, with those ads in the piles. . . . You can't talk to a woman about it. It's just grosser to have women posing with clothes on than with clothes off. . . . *Playboy* at some point in growing up helps you see through the bullshit, not to be funny, I don't know why I mentioned it, but every teenage boy has been taught to fear a woman's body it seems, and then they get to stare and they have to get over it, and learn to handle it or they'll never be a mature male — can't relate to a woman if you can't look at her, can you? (Mike, 40)

In sharp contrast, women's stories offered no counterpart notion that females had a right to look openly at men. Further, their stories reflected no recounting of learning *how* to look at men in any similar way to Mike's recounting above. However, speaking as the continual recipients of male looking, women discussed the phenomenon of male looking extensively, never in terms of the artful subtleties of looking at women, but mostly in terms of the degradation they often felt under the male stare. Women often expressed a certain impatience and a profound annoyance at being the recipients of male looking:

I hate having to go places, like events and guys stare at me. Yeah, I'm not a piece of meat. They act like they are starving for affections. I wish people would grow up and stop acting like sex and good looks is all that counts. That's b.s. Dressing in skimpy outfits really wouldn't make me happy. Not at all. That's not the meaning of life, to look good. What about my personality, my mind? People forget about that. (Jamie, 22)

It's not personally appealing to me to gawk at women. . . . All through my life I've never liked people who gawk. If you're paying attention to someone or listening to someone, you're not gawking at them. But if you're just staring at them for the way they look, good or bad, that takes no intelligence. That's just dumb and ignorant and, once again, I have no time for ignorance. (Collette, 21)

What bothers me is that it is a cologne for men and they have three naked women. I guess it represents society in a way because women are men's obsession. And they are naked so they are more of men's obsession. . . . It hurts because this ad is trying to show that we are supposed to be there for men. We are men's obsession. We are just lying there, waiting for them. (Nicole, 22)

Yeah, they are making women appear to be objects which people look at this, men and women, and it hurts women's image to men. They'll look at this and think what silly women with their dresses being blown up and they will think that is how women are. It does hurt women who are serious and aren't floosies. (Claire, 22)

Although the amount of discourse was limited, distinct differences emerged between lesbian and gay male "ways of looking" expressed in this research. Lesbians rarely if ever discussed their attraction to other women in terms of pure objectification of female bodies. As for other women interviewed, this form of objectifying female bodies was seen as a male way of looking. Gay men, however, often described how they felt prone to objectify other men in terms of their outer appearances. Body perfection in male images has a heightened importance among gay men in contrast to lesbian discussions, where other attributes were featured. Although described in the form of a personal struggle, Camron confesses an overriding male way of looking that in some ways transcends sexual orientation.

Just because I am gay, I guess. I don't really consider myself as masculine or macho and so it is a stress factor in my life because I am not what society is telling me to be. Yet, it feels a little empowering because this is who I want to be regardless of what others are telling me. It makes me feel strong because I have the strength to say this what I want to do, no matter what. . . . Especially now, I have a real contradiction inside me about the things I should do now and the kinds of men I should be attracted to rather than who I am really attracted to. It's just like this internal conflict that really gets to me. Politically and socially I know that looks shouldn't matter, but the gay male subculture, that's the way it works. . . . It pleases me because I like seeing macho men in the advertisements. To be honest, I enjoy objectifying men who are attractive even though I know I shouldn't. That pleases me. . . . It make me feel a sense of loss that I can't be objective without objectifying. It does hurt me because I do participate in those kinds of behaviors, what society sets to be the masculine qualities that are more valued. So that really bugs me and hurts me that it is an ongoing internal conflict. If I have a relationship with a man that doesn't fit society's ideals, yet, I'm in love with him, the relationship probably wouldn't work because sexually he wouldn't be as arousing to me. (Camron, 22)

Lesbian ways of looking, however, were more focused on the relational aspects of the image and the ability of the image to facilitate a sense of romantic fantasy and play. Individual body parts were not the focus, but rather the romantic potential implied in the image.

I had to pause because at first this was very appealing to me because I thought this was two women and my chosen lifestyle is represented in an ad for a change. But when I saw that they were speaking of a man, I knew it was actually heterosexual and not as personally appealing. But it's not unappealing. The pros outweigh the cons. . . .There is sort of a subtle message at times. I think there is something very sexual about these two women running, half-naked together on the beach, and there is power. . . . If you showed two women looking intimate in the way that you see a man and a woman looking intimate. (Ginger, 28)

This chapter has explored a way of understanding gender and advertising through the lens of "semiotics" and "structuralism." Ads or images in ads are signs, units of meaning-making which are culturally and ideologically bound. We experience advertising as a code—a currency of signs. The female body in ads is coded in very particular ways; the objectification of the female body in ads has a long cultural history. The idealized female image is a naturalized way of seeing in this culture.

Both men and women agreed that the codes of ideal female beauty and sexuality are both ubiquitous and consistent in this culture, and that advertising does not simply mirror what people find attractive. Instead, advertisers define attractiveness in terms of male fetishes of individual body parts. Only women, however, commented on the arbitrary nature of the male gaze across all advertising. Women suggested that the pervasive male gaze in advertising perpetuates a male fantasy of women styled according to a one-dimensional vision of femininity, to be judged foremost on appearance.

5. Weighing In and Measuring Up

Being overweight is so looked down upon. If you're overweight you must be a slob, you must not like or care about yourself. We never see overweight women . . . in a positive light. . . . In the past I was over-weight when I was young and I remember always being told I needed to diet. I needed to lose weight. So many times I think people attrib-uted my weight to not having tons of friends. . . . I think it made me unhappy. (Rachel, 20)

Fat women and me just don't—I don't find them at all that appealing when I look at them. Fat women to me just portray laziness, and they're not willing to do enough about their appearance to worry about it, they don't care about their appearance so I don't bother to care about them either. (Craig, 26)

I have a friend who is fat and whenever I talk to her my roommates make fun of me. (Shawn, 20)

Overweight people always get the short end of the stick. To society you are just not attractive and you are missing something. You may be nice but that's not good enough. You have to be cute and slim. You see it in all the ads, just cute women with slim bodies. . . . They all are thin and shapely, that's what you have to be in society. That's the ideal woman. . . . I don't show off my body at all. I'm overweight and I've been like this for a long time. I'm very self-conscious about what I wear. I often compare myself to other people, then get mad at myself. Stupid, yeah? My mother tells me never compare yourself to others 'cause you'll always come up short. So I try not to do it. But I wish at times I was not so big. . . . It hurts because these women show off everything. What if you don't want to? Or have the right equipment. I mean your body's not in shape. What about handicapped people? How do you think they feel? It's unfair. (Jamie, 22)

Weight and Discipline

Just as the female body is the site of idealization and spec-tacle for the male gaze, it is also the site of anxiety and in-security for women, who, constrained by the gaze, feel less embodied than objectified and reach out for ways to transform the body into the ideal, or as close to it as possible. Women are made to feel, especially through advertising and other mass mediated images, that embodiment is achieved through striving for the ideal feminine form. This idealized feminine form, of course, has been predefined through the male gaze. Fulfilling the potential of ideal femininity in this culture involves a constant focusing on the body as the site of improvement and as the object of judgment. Without question, the overriding factor in achieving idealized femininity in this culture is the control and discipline of one's weight.

All those who collaborated in this research alluded to one or more ways in which weight plays a pivotal role in society's judgments of individuals and our judgments of one another, especially of women. In response to the question, "What could make the females in these ads unattractive by society's standards?" every respondent mentioned weight or fat in some way. Discussions of weight and fat showed up in other places also, of course, but a distinct pattern existed in response to that particular question. There was a very strong consensus among this group of individuals that this culture despises fat. Their major indication of the truth of this claim was the rare, if not absent, depictions of overweight persons as idealized objects in popular iconography. Furthermore, according to both men and women, fat people are discriminated against interpersonally and in the work place in this culture. They saw fat as iconic for "unattractive."

These strong statements about society's loathing of fat were often riddled with anxieties that point out a striking gender similarity in responses. For men and women anxiety about weight was rooted in personal experiential knowledge. Those who were happy with their weight at the time were fearful of gaining weight as they get older. Those who were overweight at the time feared that they would never be thin, and so on. For these men and women fat was a "devil term." Being overweight was often described as a burden, or a problem. Those not overweight counted themselves lucky, feeling grateful to be thin in a culture where thinness is held at such a premium.

Society's view of fat people being unsuccessful has hindered me, whether it be conscious or subconscious as a constant pressure that I have to maintain some type of physical image in order to be accepted. Even though I don't really worry about the feelings of other people in the general sense, it [being overweight] still would be a burden I wouldn't want to be around. (Richard, 24)

[Overweight] is what society considers unattractive especially today with health conscious as people tend to be. Exercise constantly, trying to be a little more healthy, in shape. I guess society always, especially for the drink ads, would think more of people drinking and having parties with better looking women than somebody way overweight or something, I don't know. I know that's why they use women that look like that. (Jim, 37)

It is important now as I'm getting older that I start watching things like my weight. Because if I don't then I will start to look like people who are not wanted by society. . . . It helps you because it keeps you motivated and on the right track. . . . It is really disturbing because it is impossible to be the people that you see in the ads. It is frustrating because you can't. (Nicole, 22)

One thing I'd have to say right off the bat is if they weighed more, if they were heavier set or something that would make them unattractive. If this one didn't have the attractive face . . . I'd probably have to stick with the weight one. I think that's what society looks at as most important. (Mario, 28)

I think it [thinness] is the prevalent characteristic of women depicted in advertising. . . . None of the women are overweight. I can't think of any advertisements that I have seen with overweight women. I really can't. Unless it was an advertisement for a store that sells clothes for larger women. . . . I guess, whether I should feel this way or not, I feel lucky because I'm not overweight. And that is a characteristic about me, but that is also a characteristic that crosses gender lines. Men that are overweight aren't attractive. I guess it makes me feel lucky that I don't really have to try to keep my weight down. It's not something I worry about. It's a huge burden that I am glad that I am free of. (Camron, 22)

There was complete agreement by men and women that fat people are discriminated against, persecuted, and unwanted by Western society. The evidence men and women cited for this was the utter lack of positive images of fat women, or for that matter, aging women, and often women of color. This is an example of "symbolic annihilation," a way of denying existence by excluding groups of people from the representational or symbolic world (Gerbner and Gross, 1976; Tuchman et al. 1978). An example can be observed in the writing of history.

Until very recently, women's roles and activities were virtually ignored by history books, which were written by men to reflect their own interests and values. It was therefore quite common to go through college, receive a history degree, and still have no idea of the accomplishments of women on both the global and local scales. One result is that women, like other underrepresented groups, are unanchored from the past and have few historically recognized role models to emulate. Symbolic annihilation therefore, helps train individuals to think that members of their own group, and consequently, they themselves, are insignificant, "different" and outside the "norm" from those who *are* written about.

In terms of the body, the symbolic annihilation of body fat within the realm of the media means that we rarely ever see role models of fat women looking attractive, receiving love or attention, particularly from handsome men. Moreover, when we do see rare images of heavier women, they tend to be negative images—jealous, angry villains like Ursula of Disney's *The Little Mermaid*, Sally Struthers in *South Park*, Mimi of *The Drew Carey Show*, or child-like pathetic creatures (the suicidal girl of *Heathers*, the mother of *What's Eating Gilbert Grape?*, participants of Richard Simmons's infomercials and every ad for excercise and/or diet products). The result of this is that we conceive of fat as being something outside the norm or linked to socially unacceptable behavior. When the vast percentage of media stars, actresses, and models we see are extraordinarily thin, we begin to lose perspective on what really is the average weight of most women, and get a sense of the norm as being accurately represented on TV. And of course, the "normal" weight of actresses and models is far below what is actually the average weight of everyday women (Women's Action Coalition 1993).

What might be the result of the way that heavier female bodies are symbolically annihilated? Several of those interviewed equated the difficulties of being overweight with being handicapped, at least in the eyes of society. When asked what might make any of models unattractive, Ginger replied:

Make one overweight, make one woman have a prosthetic arm. Maybe she is, quote, disabled. (Ginger, 28)

They all are thin and shapely, that's what you have to be in society. That's the ideal woman. . . . I don't show off my body at all. I'm overweight and I've been like this for a long time. I'm very self-conscious about what I wear. . . . It hurts because these women show off everything. What if you don't want to? Or have the right equipment. I mean your body's not in shape. What about handicap people? How do you think they feel? It's unfair. (Jamie, 22)

Jamie notes that both the overweight individual and the handicapped person would be unable to "show off" their bodies. In other words, fat or disability prevents women from being seen as objects of sexual desire for others. If part of being a woman is based on being a pleasurable spectacle for the male gaze, then fat becomes a way of signifying a lack of femininity. Thus it is perhaps not surprising that Jamie's words suggest a certain amount of ambivalence. On one hand she maintains a derogatory tone about the societal requirement to "show off" her body as she says the thinner women do. Yet her response lacks a consequent feeling of happiness about the fact that her heavier body might free her from societal demands to make herself into an object of the gaze.

Here we need to differentiate between two seemingly contradictory ideas. First is the idea of woman as object, as spectacle of the sight. The position of woman as object has traditionally been thought to be negative, a sign of women's subordinate social status. However, the idea of the spectacle is not as simple as it seems. Kathleen Rowe (1995) observes that to hold any form of public power or high status within society, as men traditionally have, means that one must be a spectacle. Men regularly make spectacles of themselves as politicians, athletes, and heroes, roles which welcome the gaze of others. This blurs the lines between subject and object. Part of what differentiates the two is the level of knowingness. A politician giving a speech holds real power and his body represents that to us, while a model can be read simply as existing *for us*. Thus, Rowe has written about the power of the "unruly woman," a woman who makes a spectacle of herself. By *making herself* spectacle, in control of her own images, she retains her subjecthood. She thus turns the table on the traditional power relationships and blurs the lines between subject and object.

It appears that Jamie's ambivalence about her situation reiterates the feelings of many women. As women, we do not want to be seen as objects and don't want to participate in objectifying ourselves; yet if our bodies are deemed "invisible" how do we get recognition? Making a spectacle of ourselves is one way to get people to pay attention to the person and spirit within the body. It is also a way to focus on the body, which need not necessarily be an example of female objectification. At some point, it must be argued, we are all sexual beings with sexual urges, who have a need to display ourselves to others. What does it mean when, like Jamie, both heavier and lighter women feel unable to "show off" their bodies because they are not measuring up to the ideal? The unspoken message behind Jamie's response is the idea that fat women (like minority women and those with disabilities), should not and can not make spectacles of themselves because, as outside the ideal, they are "nonwomen" and have no right to claim a sexual identity (or their sexuality is seen as dangerous, and in need of censorship).

The dilemma for these women, as it is for other over-weight women, minority women, and disabled women, is what to do with a body that does not conform. In terms of weight, Jamie's response, to cover her body in bulky clothes, is certainly common. The nonconforming body, the body that doesn't match the pattern, must be denied or hidden. Jamie denies her body by covering herself, unconsciously participating in society's dictates that the body needs to be symbolically removed. But while small amounts of fat may be hidden for a time, what should the response be of those who are so outside the boundaries their difference cannot be hidden with a sweater?

There were several ways that these women, in particular, dealt with the discrepancy between idealized bodies and the reality of unruly bodies. Most made the choice not to spectacalize the body and thereby own it, recognize it, and acknowledge its desires and hungers. Instead, like Jamie, the most frequent impulse seemed to be the urge to hide it or disavow it. The women interviewed verbally affirmed two kinds of "vanishing" acts, in which the unruly body was made either to disappear or to reorder itself into a more aesthetically pleasing (smaller) mold.

The Disappearing Body

The first response was to focus on the mind and spirit while ignoring the body; the second was to discipline the body through diet and fitness, to make the body "vanish" by shrinking it closer to the norm. Although most thought the stigmatization of fat was unfair, it is important to observe that few thought the answer to anti-fat biases lay in changing the attitudes of society, societal standards, or the kinds of images offered for consumption. Rather, the focus of all the men and women was in how they could change *themselves* to fit society.

One of the main solutions was to change the way they themselves reacted to the unfairness of the situation. The general responses were that people had to "get above" the demands, not to focus on them, to learn to value ourselves for ourselves. Most were actively engaged in a disavowal of the pain and effects of cultural restrictions on them, by arguing that you can't let other people's attitudes "get to you," that happiness and self-satisfaction must be found within the self rather than in others. This response will be discussed later in this chapter. The second solution that most men and women found to deal with this hostile environment was to endorse the idea of "fitness." They argued that even if a person doesn't have a perfect body, he or she can still move closer to the ideal by working out and focusing on health rather than appearance.

On the surface, these seem like healthy ways of dealing with an impossible situation—do what you can and don't worry about what others are thinking. However, the rhetoric used by the collaborators in this research needs to be examined further because it points to the ways some elements of ancient cultural discourses are absorbed, reinforced, and continually reintroduced as men and women negotiate the meaning of ads. When we take into account the ways that cultural discourses are continually recirculated and reintroduced, it becomes possible to connect such statements back to these discourses, which have existed for so long in our culture that we have a hard time even noticing them. The idea is to uncover some ideas and assumptions that lie behind the surface meaning of words. What we see is that both methods of dealing with the anti-fat culture—either focusing on the mind or improving the body—

are similar in that they are both ways in which women, in particular, separate themselves from their bodies.

In *Unbearable Weight* (1993), Susan Bordo convincingly shows how narcissism, the self-directed gaze, is a logical extension of a long tradition of Western thought: the epistemological and philosophical obsession with dualism. Dualism is the splitting of the head (the self, the "me," the part that thinks and reasons, the spiritual self) from the body. Bordo observes that the "self" in dualist thought is identified as that which has control, while the body has historically been conceived of as the enemy. The body is subject to disease and distracts the mind from thinking or spiritual activity because of its need for food, warmth, rest and other bodily functions. Importantly, women, as "irrational" and representative of nature, have been depicted as being closer to the body, while men, who have been depicted as the rational architects of society, are seen to be closer to "the mind."

Bordo shows how contemporary views on the virtues of slenderness simply reiterate the way that the "self" is expected to control and discipline the body. Just as today we make assumptions about an individual's worth, self-liking, or laziness based on their weight, in the past the ascetic values of fasting monks and saints were represented by their wasted flesh. The saints' ability to fast, to deny the needs of their body, was a way of demonstrating their control, and thus the superiority of their mind and spirit, over the unholy body. The spirit was seen as separated from the body. In other words, one measure of our mental and spiritual control, indeed, our morality, is through how well we control our bodies. Slenderness thus not only becomes a sign of our mental health, but represents our status as a good person.

As Bordo reveals, this theme reappears today as thin people are likewise popularly represented as having mental control (will power and self-discipline). In contrast, fat is associated with the lack of will—the inability to control the needs and processes of one's body and hunger. Fat is seen as a demonstration of the person's inside lack of control over the demanding body. So, in addition to being symbolically annihilated, when they do appear in the media or in literature, fat people are characterized as out of control, greedy, childish, or even mentally unwell. Carole Spitzack (1990) has likewise observed that fat people are seen as even disliking themselves.

While men as well as women have certainly been stigmatized by the war against fat, it is no coincidence that women feel the threat of fat most strongly. Bodies and fat become even more terrifying if the appetite that is out of control belongs to women. As noted, it is the female body which has most often been associated with the body and natural processes. And it is female bodies who are most often used to represent the body out of control. A variety of reasons have been suggested for this fear of fat female bodies. One is the primeval fear we all have of the maternal body—the body who at one point was our sole source of nourishment, warmth, and love. But the abundance represented by the fleshiness of our mother's female bodies could just as easily remove itself—mother could ignore our cries, punish us, or abandon us. Thus, hatred of the female may be a backlash against those days when we were all in the thrall of our mothers.

Moreover, fat, female flesh has always been linked to maternity. Maternity, like aging, has been linked to a state of liminality in our culture (Rowe 1995). Liminality is a position of boundary crossing—not as being in one or the other stage—such as life or death—but as possessing a mix of the two. Such liminal states have been sources of power and wonder, but they are also perceived as threatening because liminality tends to foreground the material quality of bodies. The foregrounding of materiality reveals our mortality: no matter what we achieve, whether we are president, celebrity, or scientist, we *are* flesh and blood and we *will* die. Living in and with the body makes death an ever-present specter. In our individual-obsessed culture, death is looked upon most often as a source of horror and fear. Suppressing the body is a way of hiding from that fear. Yet the female, maternal body refuses to be diminished, with excess flesh bursting from our breasts, bellies, and hips. Female bodies, like aging bodies, are in a constant process of change and serve as reminders of the processes of nature bringing us closer and closer to the end.

However, other reasons exist for the hatred of female fat. As Susie Orbach (1977) has noted, fat is a particularly sensitive issue for women not only because of the historical association between women and the body, but because of women's position in the cultural pecking order and access to resources. Cultural and feminist scholars like Orbach, Bordo, Spitzack, and Naomi Wolf (1991) have all examined the ways that female consumption—of food and other resources—for both nourishment and pleasure has been suppressed throughout history. Consequently, female hunger for food, like female desire for sex or knowledge, has been derided and suppressed.

Even now women are not free of the virgin/whore dichotomy. The sexual pleasure women take is still supposed to be less than that they give to others, while in some cultures women are not supposed to experience sexual pleasure at all. Female sexuality must be kept strictly in control for the patriarchy to maintain the status quo. It is not coincidental that female sexual desire has been linked to female hunger. A woman who "breaks the rules" and eats a lot signals her sexual availability. A woman who eats so much she gets fat signals not only sexual availability, but a deviant morality.

In *The Unruly Woman*, Kathleen Rowe uses the idea of bodily looseness to connect issues of bodily appearance to issues of body behavior and morality. Rowe writes,

Body language conveys the individual's relation to the social group along a continuum of control, from strong to weak, from total relaxation to total self-control. Among the socially powerful, relaxation signifies "ease." Among those deemed in need of social control, it signifies "looseness" or "sloppiness." (Rowe, 1995, 62)

Thus, she observes that sexually active women, regardless of their level of fat or thin, are perceived as loose with their bodies and their sexuality is portrayed as being out of control. Similarly, round and fleshly women, who "let themselves go," whose bodies are "loose" rather than "tight," are considered unfeminine, rebellious and sexually deviant—either getting too much or too little sex.

Following Michel Foucault (1977), Rowe, like Bordo and Spitzack (1990), describes how social groups maintain control over their members by setting standards of normalcy. In a famous example, Foucault describes the idea of the panopticon in which prisoners are so used to being observed by the prison guards that they begin to police their own behavior to conform to the set standards of the prison (or society). The body that refuses to follow the aesthetic standards of its culture whether in bodily beauty or behavior can thus "communicate resistance to social discipline" (Rowe 1995, 65). Women whose bodies show their willingness to eat, to have sex, or who break the rules of femininity in other ways are perceived as transgressing against the social bounds of propriety. At some level they are refusing to limit themselves, refusing to pretend that their hunger and desires do not exist—and thereby posing an unspoken threat to patriarchy. Thus, Rowe argues that female fat is hated in part because "it signifies a disturbing unresponsiveness to social control" (1995, 61). In today's culture, body fat may be read, albeit unconsciously, as a sign of women rebelling against the male gaze by refusing to conform to standards of beauty. Female fat also signifies a woman's ability and desire to consume for herself as subject—rather than to merely exist as object and for the pleasures of others.

An excellent example of how female fat is equated with transgression while slenderness is equated with being socially and morally acceptable is the 2000 Jenny Craig campaign by former Presidential girlfriend Monica Lewinsky. In the media coverage surrounding "Lewinskygate," it was often unclear what was more offensive, Lewinsky's liason with the President, or the fact that she was having sexual relations without being stick thin. Ridiculed for her sexual behavior and weight, Monica was a pariah in the media until she became spokesperson for Jenny Craig in January 2000. In her ad, she links losing weight with her attempts to start over in her life, presumably leaving her older, sexual, and "bad girl" persona behind with her unwanted flesh.

That is why for women like Jamie the body must be carefully hidden behind baggy clothes, an apology to the patriarchy for the transgressive self. As earlier observed, a woman who flaunts her heavy body—who makes a spectacle of herself, as the performer Roseanne did in earlier years—makes a spectacle of her unwillingness to conform and by doing so performs a critique of the status quo (Rowe 1995). Yet, as a result of flaunting the body, these woman may become the target of intense vilification and hatred from others. And women whose bodies are spectacles simply by virtue of being overweight or outside the thin, white, ablebodied norm are subject to unwelcome comments and criticisms from others:

Now that I am active presently and like to lift . . . one person said the other day that I was such a brute, that I wasn't feminine enough because I had certain mannerisms. . . . I was overweight when I was young and I remember always being told I needed to diet, I needed to lose weight. So many times I think people attributed my weigh to not having tons of friends. . . . In the past, I wanted one of those (thin) bodies because I thought it would make me happy. I thought it would make me a better person and that more people would like me. (Rachel, 20)

All my life people have told me, even my friends, that "Oh, you'll look better if you only did this, or that." Of course I was listening to them, most of the time. I was trying to be the best I could be, looks wise. . . . In Junior High School guys said about me, "Oh she's cute but fat." This guy would always tease me about it. (Jamie, 22)

I think it is just when you see the way people act toward people who are slightly disfigured, how people can be quite nasty. (Jeannette, 22)

We see it being preached constantly. Being overweight, you have to lose weight because of your blood pressure and cholesterol. (Jane, 32)

Every time you read a magazine or you turn on the television or see someone walking on the street it is always there. It also shows you the people who are overweight or who are fat as people who are not looked at as positive as some other people. (Nicole, 22)

I mean I have this reaction. I wish I didn't have this reaction. But it is part of you, you know what I'm saying? And I do judge people on and if I look at someone who looks like they are physically in shape then I find it appealing . . . people have to be perfect. Even physically, right, and also just in terms of activity that they should be working out a lot and they look real good . . . those are silly kinds of ideas that I have and wish I didn't have. (Laura, 33)

Just as criticism is the reward for transgression, the rewards for conforming also come in increased attention and social approval. Jamie, for example, reported that after she lost weight the same guy who had always teased her wanted to date her.

Thus, the male gaze built into photography and evidenced on the streets is absorbed and reinforced by others in everyday practices. People who mean well and care about us, including family members, friends, and significant others, believe that fat is bad and reinforce the messages gleaned from the media through their comments and reactions to physical appearance. It is no wonder that the penetrating male gaze throughout this culture incites women to impose discipline on themselves, especially their bodies. Women in this culture internalize the panoptic logic of split consciousness that insists that the woman must identify herself as the principle of her own subjection, playing the roles of tower guard and prisoner simultaneously. She is spectator and spectacle, one who sees and is seen at the same time. Panoptic logic, of course, means that few people will step outside the norm, since the specter of punishment, both verbal and physical, is ever present.

Certainly, the individual's desire to be free of the specter of fat and all the societal disapproval it brings is understandable. Yet again, it is interesting that, while many interviewed were quite articulate about the ways that society had shaped their attitudes, and could perform critiques of the way anti-fat messages were propagated, it is also noticeable that most men and women displayed a level of acceptance about the ubiquity of these ads. It was as if the beliefs represented within the ads, such as fat being iconic for unattractive, were inevitable, based on unquestionable standards that will never change, no matter what humans wish. Thus, despite frequent criticisms about how society is cruel and unfair, the "natural" state of our anti-fat culture was reinforced by the majority of men and women who focused, not on the need for ads or societal standards to change, but on the need to change themselves. This is evidenced, for example, by Nicole's growing concern with her weight.

It is important now as I'm getting older that I start watching things like my weight. Because if I don't then I will start to look like people who are not wanted by society. (Nicole, 22)

The fact that she is able to articulate the damage this has for people and then in the next breath reinforce the very same viewpoints she has just critiqued is an example of the cultural hegemony at work. At the same time that she is aware of how advertisements have shaped her, she also follows their dictates.

I had to be thin, in shape, attractive. Not only thin but physically fit. I think I got those ideals from ads and women on television. I have learned how to eat right and stay thin. It constantly reinforces the importance of physical beauty. (Nicole, 22)

Nicole even found anti-fat advertisements helpful, because they kept "you motivated and on the right track." The questions that Nicole fails to ask are "What is this track and who is guiding it?" and "Why is it important that we follow this particular track and not another?"

Health and Disease

Of course, one rationale given by many people, including doctors and the government, is that fat is seen as unattractive because it is unhealthy. Keeping in shape is a way of keeping fit for ourselves and for our loved ones. In fact, the new discourse of the diet industry seems to stress the happy alignment of body and mind. It is quite usual in common discourse to hear the mantra repeated that it isn't fat that makes a person unhealthy, but a lack of exercise and fitness. Yet the work of feminist scholars shows us how the newly created fitness industry and the rhetoric of health often obscure the disciplinary nature of exercise and the equation of fat and the natural female body with disease. Women suggested that they are not always conscious of where the drive to self-discipline comes from, as if an unconscious force propels them into working on the body:

I'm always dieting and different times I get on an exercise kick and I don't know why. See, that's a good question, why? That's just because personally, that would make me feel better and maybe if my attitude was, "that's the way you should look," that would be good—but it's a hindrance, because that's not my attitude. (Collette, 21)

There are some times that I would rather be doing some other things but I say, no I have to go to aerobics tonight. No, I ate too much, I have to go to aerobics today where I would rather have been out doing something else. (Jane, 32)

In *Confessing Excess* (1990), Carole Spitzack suggests that this arrangement is aided by an ideology of women's health that condones policing the body in order to reap the reward of "freedom" or "release" from the unhealthy fat body. In order to maintain the healthy liberated body, one must continuously discipline it, police its cravings and excesses, and reprimand the self when discipline falters. Nicole, for example, has learned how to "eat right and stay thin" and "stay on the right track," while Jane says that "weight has always been important to me, fitness and weight. I watch what I eat and do fitness. I try to keep it under control."

Aerobic exercise helped introduce the ideal of the "female physique." Like the other beauty industries, aerobics offers a solution to the disjuncture between the image of fashion models' bodies and real women's bodies by disciplining the body in the name of fitness—the triumph of culture over nature. The 1980s ushered in a new female physique complementary to aerobic exercise and activity. This curvaceous, muscular look, which is now most closely associated in its ideal form with super model Heidi Klum, is a combination of cultural antitheses: thin and muscular, hard and curvaceous, it suggests power and yet a slender boyishness; furthermore, those very muscles which empower are also the material of feminine curves.

Achieving this combination of attributes is difficult, involving an investment of large amounts of time, money, and effort on "body work." As Susan Bordo (1993) has observed, the ultra-thin look of the 1960s and 1970s could be achieved through starvation diets alone, but today thinness without muscle tone falls short of the ideal feminine physique. The ideal must be achieved through a regimen of diet plus exercise. Women exhibited exasperation with the acknowledgment of this extra cultural pressure to be not only thin, but also muscular and fit. For women this added requirement for ideal femininity simply widens the chasm between idealized female bodies and the flesh of their own bodies:

I think that if you aren't body beautiful it doesn't matter. You have to be beautiful or look 100% in shape or have the world's best shape to be in any ads . . . I guess it is something I strive for, to maintain health and stay well and stay in shape so I think that's a goal for me and I think that's why I relate well to these articles and advertisements. . . . It helps me maintain that goal, to go after and reach that goal. . . . Sometimes you want to do things and you feel like you have to be very disciplined because it would be a lot easier to take off and not do it. I find myself saying I could go do this. I do give myself breaks when I don't want to do things. It's not like I do these things constantly. I take breaks. It does help. You know, that aspect of everyone expecting you to look 100%. Sometimes you think I could just go with them and forget this whole thing. (Jane, 32)

Tellingly, most men and women discussed the role of fitness in their own lives. For example, aerobic exercise has become a magic tonic for women, staving off the processes of aging, under the guise of physical and emotional health. "Health food" has replaced "diet food" in common parlance, and being physically fit is preferable to being simply thin. Both men and women showed some ambivalence here, on one hand being critical of the demand to be perfectly thin, yet at the same time uncritically accepting the general and larger cultural discourse of the time, in which health is equated with working out, feeling good about ourselves, and eating products like Weight Watchers. Evident in their response is the ideal that to be healthy is to be fit, and thus the opposite of fat.

Men and women, therefore, often couched their discussions of anxiety-ridden weight loss in terms of health, suggesting that some of the most positive images in advertising today emphasize exercise and fitness, as a societal ideal and a personal ideal. However, many men and women admitted that these ads showed only a slight and subtle shift from presenting the aesthetically perfect body for mere appearance, to presenting the perfect body as representative of health and fitness. Nonetheless, men and women regarded this as a positive shift in representation. A distinction men and women made between perfection for the sake of appearance and perfection for the sake of health and fitness was that achieving perfection in appearance targets the outside world. However, perfection for health and fitness is something the individual does for herself or himself. In this slight shift in representation, then, mere "appearance" becomes secondary to the "pleasure of discipline."

Once again, that spills over into my own life and what I do. . . . She's staying physically fit, healthy. That's probably the best thing. She's staying healthy for herself. She's able to run on her [own] two legs. Not everyone in America can say that they are healthy and run on their [own] two legs. I think that's nice. . . . It's like a catalyst. Just do it. (Collette, 21)

I associate exercise with a healthy lifestyle of getting out and around and doing things. I personally feel a lot better about myself when I'm able to exercise and go out and do things, especially when I'm able to exercise outside. (Mario, 28)

I think it is definitely an ideal because society is really health conscious. The ads on television are constantly talking about eating right and keeping fit. This [Johnnie Walker ad, fig. 2] is a perfect example. Two women running on the beach. It kind of gives you the impression that it could be fun to go running with your friend. It has nothing to do with the ad. I mean, when I look at the ad I didn't know what it was for. . . . I think the focus on society, right now, is being fit and eating right and they are concrete things for Jenny Craig or Weight Watchers. That is what society really looks for. Not only do you have to be attractive and make a lot of money, but you have to be thin and in good shape. (Nicole, 22)

The woman looks healthy, she's all in healthy pursuits, and I think society — that's what society is interested in. . . . Well, I guess everyone wants to be in shape even though obviously I'm not. (Dean, 32)

It pleases me in some way that people should be more aware of their bodies. . . . It hurts because everybody is not going to have a perfect body even if they work out for hours everyday, they are not going to look like the people in the ads. I think that is bad because people shouldn't worry about what they should be. (Nicole, 22)

As Spitzack argues, "Women are socialized to view the ongoing surveillance of their bodies as a form of empowerment that arises from self-love. The newly slender woman purchases a new wardrobe, presumably, because she likes herself now that she is thin: when fat, she did not like herself and consequently did not give adequate attention to appearance" (35). Spitzack observes that these competing discourses surrounding body reduction help to position the discourse of thinness with that of health, thereby placing weightiness or fatness in binary opposition with health, as "disease." These discourses work with numerous other institutions and practices to encourage self-correction and, therefore, "liberation" from the disease of fat, especially for women. Thus, women, whose bodies are made to put on weight, find their natural bodies represented as diseased and abnormal. The possession of fat itself—of femaleness itself—is a sign of disease.

This type of self-surveillance and discipline, however, can often exceed societal parameters of health or even beauty. For some women the self-surveying gaze becomes overwhelming and, in turn, distorted. For example, the anorexic can no longer gauge the image in the mirror against the ideal with any objectivity. No matter how thin the anorexic becomes, she still sees a fat and therefore powerless body in the mirror. In time, any plumpness of flesh on the body looks like unwanted fat and must be excised from the body through starvation and exercise.

Both men and women cited societal pressures for women to conform to ideal body images, presented throughout society, as a prominent contributor to the epidemic of eating disorders in this society, such as anorexia nervosa (self-starvation) and bulimia (binging and purging). These men and women considered advertising images, especially in fashion magazines, major contributors to the problem of eating disorders. Although most popular and academic literatures on anorexia nervosa and bulimia present these eating disorders as complex psychological pathologies, the collaborators in this research did not discuss the phenomenon of eating disorders in terms of psychological problems generated from within particular individuals. Instead, both men and women characterized eating disorders as a societal or sociological problem being generated by cultural pressures to conform to the ideals of thinness and attractiveness.

Just in a general sense I think that that's [weight] what women are preoccupied with for looking good. There seems to be quite an emphasis on exercise and diet and all that. . . . I know women who are concerned, if not obsessed with not being overweight. I know people who have eating disorders probably because of the feeling society gives them—that they must be overweight. I know one person in particular who's had a very traumatic experience probably somewhat directly due to society's ideal. . . . I find it disturbing that society has this ideal and that it leads women to hurt themselves. (Bill, 26)

I'm of an age where it was just growing up past the Twiggy sort of thing, idealizing women who were not necessarily tall but who had bodies like boys. For the generation of women who came before me and during my time and somewhat afterwards, it was an objectification of bodies, but not in this way [current ads], but little boy bodies. That affected all of us females in thinking you could never be too thin. I can't help but think that contributed to the whole burgeoning of the anorexic behavior. This real need to just be as skinny as you could possibly be and this is healthy. (Christi, 35)

It hurts me to see people who I think are, have absolutely no weight problem at all, and to me, you don't have to be a model in order to be of ideal weight. To me, I think there's nothing wrong with having a little chubbiness, to be not necessarily of a model's proportions. But I see people that I think are of good, average, healthy weight do nothing but worry about losing more weight. I've known friends of mine that weigh 110 pounds, they're 5'8" and weigh 110 pounds. And they always talk about, "Oh, I got to lose another 10 pounds, oh, I got to lose another 10 pounds." . . . I've actually known people with bulimia and anorexia and it really, really hurts . . . to think that people, I don't know if it's a self-image problem or what, that people think that. So people think that the only way they can be attractive is if they lose more weight, more weight, more weight? (Mario, 28)

I guess because being overweight is so looked down upon. If you're overweight you must be a slob, you must not like or care about yourself. We never see overweight women shed in a positive light. . . . In the past I was overweight when I was young and I remember always being told I needed to diet. I needed to lose weight. So many times I think people attributed my weight to not having tons of friends. . . . I think it made me unhappy. It held me back in being what I wanted to be in school. . . . It doesn't please me. I see these women [in the ads] and say I'm not them. I don't have to be them to be happy. It disturbs me because these images are so harmful to women. They become bulimic and anorexic. That disturbs me and makes me angry. (Rachel, 20)

For many women the pathology of eating disorders has touched their lives very personally. Either they have suffered from the disorder themselves at some point in their lives or they have known other women, sometimes family members, who suffered from it. Although a few men commented on how eating disorders had affected women they knew, none of the men had ever been afflicted with an eating disorder. Consistent with national statistics, those interviewed characterize eating disorders as a woman's disease. Women contextualized their own experience with eating disorders as symptomatic of societal pressures to conform to an unattainable physical ideal. Eating disorders were seen as a killer of women's spirits.

I have gone through a lot of conflicts with other people and with myself. There was a time in which I would have starved myself to get a slimmer body, but not now I know that is not the right way of going about it . . . In junior high school guys said about me, "Oh, she's cute but fat." This one guy would always tease me about it, then when I lost weight in 12th grade, he asked me for a date. He claimed that he got to know me and now he likes me as a person. That's b.s. I know all he cares about is my looks. I got a lot of that. I wish it didn't happen, but it did. . . .

It hurts every woman with a weight problem. Some women will starve to death just to achieve a look. I think that is horrible. What has society come to? Allowing women and men, I guess, to starve their bodies. I have friends who have done this. It's crazy. We need to change, if we don't we will have people dying of malnutrition. I don't want my children to go through all the things I did. They will learn that the body is a machine and without proper tools and nutrition the machine malfunctions and dies. I hope they won't be stressed out over material things like I was when I was young. (Jamie, 22)

Although many men and women have been touched by the eating disorders of their friends, family, or themselves, it is important to recognize differences between women. Studies have shown that individuals who come from groups considered "outside the norm," like African American women, are less likely to feel negatively about their weight (Parker et al. 1995). African American women, for example, are far less likely than whites to suffer from eating disorders, although that is beginning to change. A suggested reason for this is the different culture of black America, in which racism and economics forced many women to assume a more "masculine" role as the breadwinner and head of the home. In addition, African American women, by virtue of their skin color, have been considered farther from the "Barbie" ideal than white women, and until recently have not had many thin black women presented to them by the media. Yet precisely because of this unequal presentation, it must be remembered that the relationship of black, and other women of color, to the beauty myth in Western culture may be even more painful than that experienced by whites in a culture in which the norm is based upon ideal, *white* beauty. Women of color may suffer less from eating disorders, but experience equally intense pain over beauty issues.

Cultural studies theorists like Stuart Hall (1996) and David Morley (1986, 1989) have said that those who are most separated or isolated from a text by virtue of their different life experiences are those most likely to be resistant to it and perform oppositional, critical readings. Thus, while the limited racial mix of collaborators in this research makes it impossible to discuss racial differences in how women evaluated their body against the media, it is interesting that, as the women aged and moved farther from the ideal body, they began to evidence not only a greater awareness of media messages, but a greater ability to distance themselves from the messages with critical readings and a stronger sense of self. Such negotiations will be discussed at length in Chapter six.

Focusing on Self

A few individuals expressed that they were personally unaffected by the imagery in ads. Most of these were men, but a few were women. They saw the weight and appearance obsessed culture as problems within society, but a problem that they themselves were distanced from.

I don't find these images personally attached to me enough so that what they do or don't do, [is] personally painful. I think it's a shame that there is such an emphasis on these women's bodies . . . it's a shame that that's the way the world works, but I don't find it personally painful. I dismiss it because I realize its not appealing to me. I don't see myself in it. I don't say, oh woe is me, I'll never be in a Budwesier ad. (Heather, 29)

Heather's comments reflect a competing discourse in which people focus on their personalities and downplay judgements based on looks alone. The person "inside" is what matters. While such attitudes are undoubtedly reinforcing to the individual psyche, it may also be seen as a second example of cultural discourses that make the body disappear. Just as the fitness industry and anorexia are ways in which the body is policed and shrunken, focusing on one's personality, or "the mind," is a way of denying the body. It is a return to the dualist school in which the mind and spirit are beautiful and eternal, yet the body is unholy and dirty. The problem with this logic is that to deny the body and the reality the body plays in our lives may merely replicate traditional masculinist ways of thinking in which the body is seen as unimportant. It asks us to be split within ourselves.

Nomy Lamm eloquently sums up the problem with ignoring the powerful effects of the beauty myth in our lives.

It's not good enough for you to tell me that you "don't judge by appearances" — so fat doesn't bother you. Ignoring our bodies and "judging only by what's on the inside" is not the answer. This seems to be along the same line of thinking as the brilliant school of thought called "humanism": "We are all just people, so let's ignore trivialities such as race, class, gender, sexual preference, body type and so on." Bullshit! The more we ignore these aspects of ourselves, the more shameful they become and the more we are expected to be what is generally applied when these qualifiers are not given—white, straight, thin, rich, male. It's unrealistic to try to overlook these exterior (and hence meaningless, right?) differences because we're still being brainwashed with the same shit as everyone else. This way we're just not talking about it. And I don't want to be told, "Yes you're fat, but you're beautiful on the inside." That's just another way of telling me that I'm ugly, that there's no way that I'm beautiful on the outside. . . . My body *is* me. I want you to see my body, acknowledge my body. True revolution comes not when we learn to ignore our fat and pretend we're no different, but when we learn to use it to our advantage, when we learn to deconstuct all the myths that propagate fat hate. (Lamm 1995, 90–91)

The split consciousness of the surveyed female is consistent with the concept of the "male gaze." The split consciousness of the self-surveyed female is her embodiment of the object of the sight and simultaneously her awareness of being the object of the sight. Women, it seems, have the ability to theorize how advertising works to further encourage them to view themselves as objects to be improved upon for the male other, rather than to view themselves as subjects of their own femaleness. However, awareness (conscientization) or understanding of the process is rarely consolation.

Fulfilling the potential of ideal femininity in this culture involves a constant focusing on the body as the site of improvement and as the object of judgment. Without question, the overriding factor in achieving idealized femininity in this culture is the control and discipline of one's weight. All the men and women interviewed alluded to one or a number of ways in which weight plays a pivotal role in society's judgments of individuals, and our judgments of one another, especially of women. In order to maintain the fit, healthy body, liberated from fat, one must continuously discipline the body, policing its cravings and excesses, reprimanding self when discipline falters. This ideal must be achieved through a regimen of diet plus exercise. For women this added requirement for ideal femininity, of being not only thin but fit, simply widens the chasm between idealized female bodies and the flesh of their own bodies.

For some women, the self-surveying gaze becomes overwhelming and, in turn, distorted. The anorexic can no longer gauge the image in the mirror against the ideal with any objectivity. Both men and women cite societal pressures for women to conform to ideal body images presented throughout society as a prominent contributor to the onset of eating disorders in women such as anorexia nervosa and bulimia. Consistent with national statistics, men and women considered eating disorders a woman's disease. Women contextualized their own experience with eating disorders as symptomatic of societal pressures to conform to an unattainable physical ideal.

6. Elizabeth's Story

Elizabeth's personal story is a typical example of the journey many women take with media images of ideal femaleness. Although there are similarities in accounts, each woman's story is highly personal and unique to her circumstances and experiences. Elizabeth's is a case study of one individual who illustrates the journey from a "female" relationship with advertising to a "feminist" consciousness. In Elizabeth's story the dynamics between social experiences and textual negotiations figure prominently. Elizabeth finds meaning in her own life through ads; at the same time her reading of ads is always influenced by her real life experiences. She negotiates with the culturally imposed rules of femininity learned through the media and elsewhere to arrive at a strong sense of personal identity and personal desires. Her reading of ads also has changed depending on her realization of how well these roles served her.

The story is taken from an account written by Elizabeth herself. The self-interview, using Sense-Making questions and techniques, was a major course assignment in a gender and communication class. Students first were asked to do a library search of ads that had meaning for them across their life span. They were then asked to perform self-interviews about the following time periods of their lives: childhood, preteens, teens, adulthood, and across time. Within each time period they were asked to address the following broad questions (follow-up questions were included in the assignment, but are not included here): Can you recall a time during this time period when you were aware of "lessons" from society (parents, school, media, etc.) on how to be female? Did you spontaneously recall any ads from this time period that stood out as portraying ways to be female? Think about the specific ads you found in your historical search. Describe them. To the best of your recollection, what did these ads say to you in that time period about being female? The final self-interview section asks: Looking back over your life, what do you think advertising has had to do with your thoughts about and actions relating to being female?

The students in Elizabeth's class were then asked to take their self-interviews and their ads and write an analysis of their findings.

In 1993 Elizabeth was twenty-nine years old and returning to college to complete the undergraduate degree that had eluded her thus far. Set back by a strained relationship with her parents, an unhappy marriage, and then divorce, Elizabeth had reached a point where she was beginning to call her own shots. She had also reached a point in her life where she could clearly reflect upon how media images of gender had played an integral role in shaping her feelings and actions regarding herself and others. Elizabeth put these thoughts down on paper for an assignment in her Gender and Communication class.

Elizabeth's Story

During each time period of my life the decisions which I made about how to live my life were greatly influenced by what I was learning from society. Sometimes I would wholeheartedly accept what society was saying, while at other times I would totally reject it. Regardless of my reactions, there was a constant flow of information from society regarding "proper" and "improper" behavior for females. One of the characteristics of this information was that, because it came from so many sources, there were many contradictory views about female behavioral norms. The information which I was receiving from the media and my peers was usually in complete contrast to what I was receiving from my parents. For example, my parents said that I should remain a virgin until I got married, while the media told me to be sexy and appealing to men. While some girls at school told me to have sex at fourteen, others felt that it was better to wait until age seventeen. To further complicate matters, there were often contradictions within individual messages, such as the media's portrayal of women as both sexy and pure. The conflicting messages were a source of confusion for me during early periods of my life, at least up until the point when I obtained a more critical way of viewing society's evaluations of women.

During my preteen and teenage years, I experienced an overwhelming sense of being "different." This sense of being different was a source of self-criticism and self-hatred because of my wanting to fit in. Beginning somewhere after my teenage years, this sense of being different became a source of self-identification and eventually a positive outlet for change in my life. One source which provided me with information on how to be female during each time period was my parents. They were consistently providing me with what could be labeled 'traditional' beliefs concerning the role of women in society.

During the earlier years, their opinions, attitudes and actions were a source of conflict and confusion for me, and it is only now that I seem to have developed a better understanding of the dynamics which were shaping these beliefs and also alternative ways to deal with them.

Furthermore, the information I was receiving during those early periods of my life about how to deal with men and boys had an effect on my actual behavior concerning men and boys. The fact that I expressed my interest in boys at all seems to have been integrally connected to the fact that I felt like I was *supposed* to like them. My unrealistic expectations of boys and men was a direct result of what I had been taught about how relationships *ought* to be by the media and especially by soap operas. Once I was actually in these relationships my behavior was often dictated by how I was expected to act as a woman.

The media, and advertising in particular, had an effect on how I viewed myself as a girl/woman during each period of my life. Not only were these ads shaping the way that everyone else was evaluating me and my behavior, but they also had a significant impact on my own personal beliefs and actions. During the early time periods of my life I placed much more confidence in what the ads were telling me because I was concerned about what society thought of me and my femininity. As time went on I became less interested in what advertisements were saying to me about being a woman. When I was less confident about myself and very confused about where I fit into society, I accepted what these ads were telling me and used them as a way to formulate guidelines for my life so that I could become more acceptable. As I grew to be more confident in myself, I began to reject what the ads were telling me because I realized I no longer needed society's approval. Another reason that I began to reject advertising was my growing realization that I had personally been affected by the portrayal of women in advertising and that some of my self-destructive behavior had been a result of such portrayals.

Pre-Teens (8–12 Years), 1972–76

My fifth grade year was really influential. I was ten years old and just beginning to realize what was going on—before then I was totally oblivious, and as a matter of fact I barely remember anything from before this time. I remember being really concerned with how overweight I was, how awful my clothes were, and how gross I felt in general compared to everyone else. The lesson that stands out in my mind for this time period just happens to be one of the worst memories I have from my childhood. I was a cheerleader for midget league football.

My brother had played football for the same team that I was cheerleading for, but this year he was too old. In the years that my brother had been playing and I had been cheering, my parents had religiously attended the games. During my fifth grade year, when it was just me, my parents hardly ever came to the games and would usually just drop me off before the game and pick me up afterward. I don't remember if that part bothered me much. I think it might have but I suppose I just figured that since cheerleading *obviously* wasn't as important as playing football, that *obviously* they wouldn't want to come.

Anyway, this particular year our cheerleading squad was excellent and we ended up getting the Spirit Award—basically a big deal. I remember feeling very proud and excited. At the end of each season there was always a big banquet for each team and all the parents and kids would come and eat and get trophies. Every other year, my parents would go to the banquet with my brother and me, but this year they didn't want to go. I guess it was understood that it was no big deal that they weren't going. I remember feeling bad, but of course I didn't say anything because I knew it would seem silly if I made a big deal out of cheerleading. So I went to the banquet and all of us cheerleaders got extra trophies and neat things because we had gotten the Spirit Award. My mom came to pick me up and on the way home I began to feel really horrible because she didn't really seem to care about the neat trophies I had gotten. When we got home I just went to my room and cried and cried. I didn't let my parents hear me or anything because I must have been embarrassed. And I hid all my cheerleading things and the trophies. I still get upset when I think about it. The lesson I learned from this situation was very simple – girls, and the activities which they pursue, do not deserve as much attention as boys and their activities.

The other important lesson I learned during this time period had to do with "boys." For some reason, almost every girl in my fifth grade class liked this boy named Joel who was in the sixth grade. I said that I liked him too but I really didn't even know what that meant. I was just kind of going along with what everyone else was saying because I wanted to fit in. From that time on there was always someone that I "liked" even though I don't remember having a real interest in any of the boys that I had crushes on. These crushes usually involved spending time talking about the boy to my girlfriends and acting really silly when he was around. This lesson about girls always putting their energy into thinking about boys was reinforced by all my encounters with girls my age, not only at school but also at church. What it taught me was that, as a girl, I was expected to always be interested in a boy and that I was supposed to focus almost all of my attention on obtaining a boyfriend.

The lessons which I learned from the media during this time period mostly came from soap operas, which I had been watching since I was very young. My mother always had them on and so I watched them quite a bit, especially in the summertime. I based a lot of my ideas about relationships, beauty, and love on the characters and their lives. I remember loving to watch soap operas and desperately wanting my life to be like the lives of the characters. The lessons which soap operas taught me had to do with how women should behave and what their concerns ought to be. Basically the women on soap operas spent most of their time getting boyfriends and, once they got them, life was unrealistically happy and exciting.

I would be really pushing it to say that any of these lessons helped. The only thing that I can think of is indirect help. At the time these lessons took place I was aware that I was hurt and confused and this made me very aware that I was "different." Feeling different was bad because it made me feel like a freak and made me want to conform even more, but I think that feeling different was good for me too. When I was finally old enough to figure myself out I actually began to feel good about being "different" and therefore unique.

These lessons definitely hurt me. The cheerleading one hurt me emotionally because it made me feel bad that my parents weren't interested in what I was doing and that they thought my brother was more important. In a broader sense, I think it helped to bring my level of self-esteem down even more. It made me feel like nothing I did was important. The "boyfriend" situation, which was actually more like a "crush situation" since nothing ever became of my infatuations, was equally hurtful. Not only did I have to constantly fake interest in these boys, I also had to deal with bad feelings when none of the boys liked me. This was usually due to the fact that I always liked boys who were the most popular and who already had girlfriends. It was also really hurtful because so much of my attention was being focused on other people and not my own interests. Unfortunately, this type of behavior continued throughout my teenage years and also into college.

These "lessons" definitely impacted my thoughts on being female and how my life was going to turn out. The cheerleading situation and the message that girl activities were not as important as boy activities had an impact on my sense of self and on my sense of my future. I never thought of what type of career I wanted for myself, at least not seriously. The emphasis on finding a boyfriend really worked with this fact to create my visions for my future—I thought mostly of marriage and children and love. I had very unrealistic expectations concerning how blissfully happy my life would someday be.

Thoughts about love and blissful relationships had a great impact on my actions. I began to daydream constantly and eventually I came to have a whole other world constructed in which everything went just according to plan—just

Figure 9. Tampax.

like on soap operas. Because my life was so inadequate compared to how it was *supposed* to be, I constructed an alternative place to go where everything was perfect.

I found some ads that I remember from that time period. For example, Tampax tampons. Half the page is a photo of a smiling young woman who is playing tennis. The other half of the page is all text with an insert close-up photo of the young woman. The focus of the text is on the product itself—the applicator, whether it's disposable or not, how it is made, whether it is deodorant or not, etc. Some of the more interesting phrases are "internal protection"; "embarrassing odor"; and "individual vaginal contours." The word "blood" is not mentioned once.

This ad told me that women should be concerned about "embarrassing odors" and that tampons were thus the better choice over pads. Tampon ads always stress that you can do more and be more when you wear tampons instead of pads. Because of the ambiguity of the language in some areas of this ad it also told me that girls shouldn't talk about what *really* happens during menstruation (like bleeding), although you could talk for days about tampons themselves.

I got my period when I was ten, and I had absolutely no idea what was going on. I found some things to read about menstruating and figured a few things out on my own. At any rate, I still didn't understand many things about menstruation. My mother was always opposed to me using tampons because of the whole "valuable hymen" approach and also out of a general fear of the unknown since tampons weren't a common thing when she was menstruating. The impacts of this ad were helpful insofar that it gave me at least *some* information about tampons and menstruation. When I got to the point where I really felt that I needed to use tampons—the beach—then at least I had heard about them and knew some of the facts. When I saw this ad and other tampon ads I always felt really bad because I could tell that they were something that I *should* use, but that I wasn't allowed to. I definitely bought into the idea that tampons were more sanitary and better for you than pads.

The impacts of this ad also hurt in a very broad sense because it reinforced all of the general notions surrounding menstruation—that you couldn't really talk about it openly and that there were things to be embarrassed about. It also gave me another opportunity to feel inadequate since I wasn't allowed to use tampons. This ad basically reinforced my thoughts about how one of my main concerns as a female was the concealment of my period from the rest of the world.

Another is Secret antiperspirant. This is the "strong-enough-for-a-man-but-made-for-a-woman" campaign. The woman is soft but sexy in her strapless evening gown while the construction worker man is sweaty and rough. The text is somewhat confusing. First it states that Secret is putting an end to the "feminine weakness myth." Second, it states that Secret is an effective antiperspirant, effective even for a "he-man." Then it states that Secret is for women because its scent is soft and gentle and beautiful. The conclusion is that Secret is strong enough for a man but made for a woman. It never talks about women *needing* an antiperspirant that is strong and effective. It would therefore seem that the only reason that Secret is made for a woman is because of its soft, gentle, and beautiful fragrance.

This ad basically told me that being female meant being tall, thin, and stylish. It also implies that every woman had a "he-man" in her life and that all women want an antiperspirant that is "soft, gentle, and beautiful." This ad and other ads about women and antiperspirants had a huge effect on my beliefs about women and sweating. Since all these ads stressed that women didn't perspire much, especially not as much as men, I believed that this was true. Certainly no one else was talking about perspiring except for the antiperspirant and deodorant ads, and I had no other information to go on. This ad always made me feel bad because I always perspired a lot and I felt like there was something wrong with me because women weren't suppose to perspire.

A third ad is Nuance by Coty. "If you want to capture someone's atten-

Figure 10. Secret.

tion, whisper." The photograph of the woman is very "soft" and very close-up. Her nails and lips are glossy and mushy looking. The look that the woman is giving the viewer is somewhat seductive, especially since her eyes are also very glossy and mushy looking. The text points out the fact that Nuance, like a whisper, is hard to resist.

This ad told me that to be female is to be quiet and delicate and soft. It also told me that whispering, which is seen as seductive, is something which women can utilize to capture someone's attention. This is perhaps based on the fact that women can't get attention otherwise or even on the fact that a woman who is loud and forward is unladylike. This ad reinforced my image of what the ideal woman is like and how I should be—more quiet and demure and soft. Since I was always very loud and talkative, I don't know how seriously I took this ad. I think that I probably laughed at the silliness of whispering, especially since I was young at this time. I think that it did have some hurtful implications in that it made me feel different or inadequate because I wasn't quiet and I didn't even know what might be sexy about whispering.

Finally, I found an ad for Hanes pantyhose, "Gentlemen Prefer Hanes." Two male/female couples are shown on a yacht. While one woman looks out at the sea her male partner eyes the legs of the other woman. Her legs are long

Figure 11. Hanes.

and toothpick-like in shape, and she looks very cool and comfortable in her sundress. In contrast, the woman who is looking out to sea is totally covered by pants and a jacket and seems oblivious to her partner's admiring glance at the other woman's legs. This ad told me that to be female is to have long skinny legs as well as a long skinny body. It also told me that a really sexy woman is able to attract attention from men who are with other women. This ad made me believe that having a man who was with another woman look at you and your body was a good thing.

This ad was really hurtful to me in the long run because it added to my distorted views about men and women in general. I know that this affected my later thoughts on married men and the fact that I always wanted to be involved with one. It helped to make me feel more comfortable with the idea of infidelity. I remember incorporating ideas about married men or "already-taken" men into my daydreams and fantasies. At a later age I would always get a kick out of men who would check me out when they were already with their girlfriends or wives. It seemed like a good thing and I think that this ad really reinforced that idea.

Teens (12–18 Years), 1976–82

The situation at school focused mostly on how girls should look and act. Some of the basic messages from my peers were that I should be very concerned about how I dressed and how I wore my make-up (I began wearing make-up and lots of it, when I was fourteen). The standards varied from clique to clique, but within each clique girls strictly abided by what was proper and improper behavior and appearance. For example, if you were preppy you could never wear Levis and a heavy metal T-shirt, and if you were a burn-out (a druggie) you couldn't wear plaid skirts with penny loafers. Such behavior would lead to ostracism. Although there was a lot of variation from group to group, the one message that was the same in each group was that being overweight was not a good thing—everyone was always on diets and concerned about how much they weighed.

The idea of always having a crush on a boy or an actual boyfriend was also one of each group's criteria. Most girls spent all their time talking about boys—which ones were cute, which ones liked them, etc. Around the time I was fourteen I started meeting lots of girls who were having sex regularly. Being sexually active signified that you were attractive to boys or men, and this was stressed as very important to the group I was associated with—mostly burn-outs and "alternative" people—throughout high school. To some of the other groups of girls—the preppy ones—being sexually active was considered sleazy before a certain age—around sixteen or seventeen maybe. There were definitely girls at school who were considered "sluts" and others who were considered "prissy."

The messages from TV, magazines, and other media sources basically reiterated what I was experiencing at school. These messages stressed that teenage girls were always concerned with how they looked and about boys. The whole sexuality thing was also presented in a similar fashion, with sex being shown as both good and bad—depending on what "type" of a girl you were.

Also during this time period I encountered a number of teachers who had an impact on my sense of being female. This was mostly because they helped me to raise my self-esteem and also because their evaluations of me were based on something other than how I looked and whether I had a boyfriend. The fact that I got praise from some teachers about being a good student or the fact that I could have conversations with these teachers really helped counter some of the other experiences that I was having during high school

The lessons that I learned from the teachers that I was friends with were really priceless. I was so confused all through this period that it helped to know adults who liked me and supported me. Even though I was constantly changing through this period and there were times when I felt really horrible about myself, there was always a part of me that felt good about who I was underneath it all and I think this had a lot to do with teachers. They never mentioned I couldn't become whatever I wanted to because I was a girl.

The most hurtful lessons at this time were about identity and individuality. Because I never fit into any group, I ended up trying out almost all of them and not liking any of them. In junior high I was very preppy but the other girls in the crowd were really stupid and vain and I couldn't stand them any more so I stopped talking to all of them. Then, from age fourteen to sixteen, I was a burn-out. But all those people led such crazy lives that I usually couldn't relate to them, especially since I was never allowed out of the house and they were always on the streets because their parents never paid any attention to them. At seventeen I became a born-again Christian and I lost an incredible amount of weight by fasting for religious purposes. Finally, just as high school was ending, I found a group of "alternative" people who were artsy and intelligent who were actually good for me. The point to all this is that I was constantly taking on different identities and I was constantly confused. I never knew what was right because of all of the conflicting information I was getting

I remember I always felt that when I got older I would be independent and do what I wanted to do. Although I was always buying into everything that society was feeding me, there was a part of me that knew that it wasn't right because it didn't *feel* right. I always argued and fought back with my parents and with people who bothered me at school, even when I didn't know what I was really fighting about. I always knew that being a girl was a big part of what was making all of these awful things happen to me.

On the other hand, the part of me that was buying into what society was telling me was thinking along different lines. I also really wanted to get married and be normal and traditional during this time period. I always hated myself for not fitting in and I was always attempting to fit in somewhere. It was a weird combination of wanting to be liked and accepted but not always being willing to conform totally.

My thoughts about wanting something different from what I was experiencing eventually led me to start hanging around with people who were really progressive. These thoughts led me to go to college and get away from my parents and all of the people in my hometown. My feelings of self-hatred led me to do some self-destructive things during this time period. When I went on my near-starvation diet I was responding to ten years of being made to feel like I was disgusting because I was overweight. The few times when I had semi-sexual encounters with boys I was never motivated by the fact that I actually liked the boys, but rather because I felt pressure to have a boyfriend. These

Figure 12. Bain de Soleil.

experiences were all traumatic. I was basically always doing things to myself to improve how I looked and acted. I never really liked myself too much and I was always confused.

I found some ads from this time period I want to talk about. The first is for Bain de Soleil. A very, very thin European woman in a black bikini is lounging in the sun and is looking away from the viewer. The only text is "Bain de Soleil for the St. Tropez Tan." The mention of St. Tropez, combined with the French newspaper she has, gives the ad a very definite "jet set" feel. What this ad said to me about being female was that if I got a dark tan, was really skinny, and wore a black bikini, then I would look beautiful and travel to tropical lands too. I thought that this woman was just stunning and I really felt some sort of a connection to her because I always tanned very easily and I knew that I could get that dark. I was also impressed by her very classy look and the whole "jet-set" appeal of the ad. This was one of the rare occasions when I somehow felt like I had something in common with a model in an ad. Even though I was overweight, I knew I could match her on the tan. It was helpful then to feel good about myself in any way possible. Even though I felt like I could compare with this woman's tan, I think that it only made me more aware of the fact that I didn't have the "right" kind of body to make the tan look good. This ad definitely had an impact on the importance I placed on getting an incredible tan every summer. Each summer when I was in Greece I would spend innumerable hours in the sun, even during the hottest parts of the day when everyone else would leave the beach. I never used any type of sunscreen, but I did use Bain de Soleil tanning oil. Sometimes people would mention skin cancer but I would just laugh it off like it was the most unrealistic thing to think of. I loved the way my skin felt when it was tanned and I liked the way I looked. Being darker made me look thinner and I would usually lose weight in the summer because of the heat and loss of appetite. Everyone would always be really envious about my tan and I enjoyed that.

Another important ad at the time was for Marathon mascara. "It looks just put on. . . . until you take it off." The photo is of a woman's eye with long, thick lashes. The text takes up most of the ad and the main focus is on the fact that Marathon is waterproof, making it different from other mascaras. There is also an insert photo of a model – although we don't really know if that is *her* eye up there or not. According to the text, "Big beautiful eyes begin with big beautiful lashes"; in order for my eyes to be beautiful, my eyelashes had to be longer and thicker than they were naturally.

I used to get pleasure from the ritual of make-up, and mascara, which I did in fact use, was really exciting for me because it was new and different. It was also fun to talk with my friends about make-up and I distinctly remember talking about Marathon mascara with them. I think it helped to feel a part of something "normal" because longer, thicker lashes were something I could obtain. I really believed what this ad (and other mascara/make-up ads) was telling me. Mascara was a large part of my make-up ritual.

After I would put tons of make-up on just like they showed it in *Seventeen* magazine, I still didn't look like the models. This ad, and all other make-up ads, made me feel like it was the most natural thing in the world to be obsessed with how long and thick my eyelashes could be. During this time period, I never really questioned the whole notion of women spending all their time "fixing" themselves. Wearing make-up was something which I expected to do for the rest of my life.

I bought Marathon mascara and I used it. It was impossible to remove because it was waterproof and I had to buy a special solution to get it off totally. To get my lashes to curl upward like they were "supposed" to (like they do in the ad), I got one of those eyelash curlers that look like surgical instruments. I lost many eyelashes this way. Once again, I just accepted this as part of the ritual and I really enjoyed another toy to play with.

I found another ad from this period that had an impact on me. The ad is for

Figure 13. Marathon (Cover Girl).

Kissing Slicks: "I'm not as innocent as I seem." "Forbidden Fruits." There is a half-page photo of a woman applying the product onto her lips. She is wearing a very tight T-shirt and is surrounded by leaves and fruit. She is staring right at the viewer with a very seductive look in her eyes. The text talks about the fruit flavors that Kissing Slicks comes in and states that, with Kissing Slicks Lip Gloss and T-shirt, "You're ready for anything." I believed what the ad was telling me, especially since lip gloss was a very big deal during most of this time period.

It reinforced my notion that women should be both innocent and seductive at the same time, and that women should have shiny, glossy lips and wear tight tops so their breasts stick out. I think that the impact was hurtful because I was basically wearing lip gloss to make me look more attractive and essentially the goal was to be kissed wearing this stuff. Lots of my friends were getting kissed when wearing it and the boys they were kissing would comment on the flavors, but I never got kissed while wearing it and so I always had this feeling that I was wasting my time with lip gloss. This ad and my feelings surrounding my use of the product really heightened my sense of wanting to be older and more sexually attractive. I figured that someday my life would include some "forbidden" experiences.

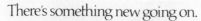

Figure 14. Kissing Slicks (Maybelline).

Finally, there were ads for Wind Song perfume. A very handsome man is wistfully looking at the viewer as he rests his chin on his wrist. "I can't seem to forget you. Your Wind Song stays on my mind," is the only text for the ad. This is what all of the other ads in the magazine are leading up to! Men like this are the reason why women wear make-up and look sexy. He is the goal. I thought that this man was just beautiful. Since he was "perfection," I began to judge the appearance of other men according to his looks.

Using this man as a guideline for evaluating other men had some really hurtful impacts on how I felt about myself and the boys and men that I was encountering. Because I wasn't attracting anyone who looked like this I felt bad about myself. In addition, I would totally disregard boys or men that would like me that didn't look "good" enough, regardless of their personalities. I thought that getting a man like this would be the ultimate achievement possible for myself and any woman. Because I was evaluating all men and boys according to the standards which I set based on the man in this ad and other ones like it, I really limited the number of encounters I had with men and boys as platonic and romantic friends. This also led me into relationships which were based on looks, so that I often ended up in relationships with boys with whom I was incompatible.

Twenties, 1983–93

During this time period I became very aware of feminism and eventually came to label myself a feminist. I have gotten to the point where I am very aware of the lessons I am being taught about being female *as they are occurring*, so that I have more control now over what I let affect me. In the earlier years of this time period, though, I was still not very confident in my own beliefs so I had the dual experience of feeling somewhat in control of my life as a woman, while at the same time feeling totally out of control. For example, any time I would have a relationship or brief encounter with a man, I would usually turn into an emotional weakling, becoming very clingy and dependent. This was what I had been taught to do and it was so easy just to lapse into it, even though I always felt really powerless as a result. What also influenced this type of behavior was the fact that whenever I would act strong and independent it would turn off whoever I was involved with, so that I learned that if I wanted to be accepted by some men I would have to act more "feminine."

Another lesson which I learned was something which I knew from a very young age but that I had never really formulated into a concept. My parents always encouraged me to go to college, but it didn't occur to me until I was there that they didn't expect "great" things from me. They certainly encouraged me and supported me, but it was always understood that it was OK if I couldn't handle things or if I messed up. This lesson revolved around my status in our family as the daughter, or the "non-son." The only thing which was really expected of me was to get married and have a family.

The lessons that I learned in my relationships with men helped me because they forced me to encounter some inconsistencies in my life. Even though I was always very independent in other areas of my life, when it came to my relationship with men I would become dependent on them in very unhealthy ways. After getting hurt too many times in such situations, I finally began to learn how to treat myself better, and in this way these relationships were helpful. The message I got from my parents was really helpful in that I felt much more free to explore myself than I think my brother did. I was able to choose to do unconventional things because, as a woman, there was less riding on my future.

The lessons that I learned in my relationships with men during this period were very hurtful emotionally. Not only did I always feel degraded in these relationships, but the fact that I knew that I was being degraded and yet I let it happen to me was the most hurtful part. I never felt like I could blame how awful I felt on anyone but myself because I knew that these relationships and interactions were not good for me *while* I was participating in them.

My parents' expectations for me were also hurtful. Even though it's wonderful not to feel any pressures about career choices, I get a lot of pressure about my personal choices. The fact that I am expected to get married and make babies really hurts me because I feel like that is a very personal choice and not something on which they should base their evaluations of me. However, I grew to be much more conscious of the roles that women take on in relationships and I vowed that I wouldn't compromise myself to please anyone else. I also began to encourage myself to become more serious about what career choices I was making, because I realized that, since women are often not expected to do much, we need to motivate ourselves and take control of our lives. I began to do better in school and I used better judgment when dealing with men. Basically, I began to have more control over my own life and focus on *my* needs.

Some of the ads I have chosen are recent and some are from a few years earlier. The first is a six-page ad for Armani. The first page shows a man in a suit with the text: "One Suit leads six different lives." This page and the next four feature this same man utilizing the same suit to have five different outfits. The sixth page features the last of the "six different lives." There is a blond woman wearing a purple stained dress and the jacket from the man's suit with the text: "And don't forget who's wearing the trousers." She is looking at the man on the opposite page with a grin on her face. He is looking in her direction with a very stern look on his face and is wearing gloves and sunglasses. The photo of the woman is closer up, so that most of her legs are cut out of the picture, while the other five photos of the man were total body shots.

This ad's message about women was really hard for me to figure out. I knew that by using the comment "And don't forget who's wearing the trousers," they were saying that men shouldn't forget the place of women in relation to men. What I couldn't figure out was what this meant for this ad in particular. Did it mean that she shouldn't be wearing his jacket? Is that why he's looking at her in anger? In that case, maybe the expression "don't forget who's wearing the trousers" is directed to the woman, telling her to remember her place and to quit wearing his jacket. What it could also mean is that he shouldn't forget about her presence and the fact that she is indeed *not* wearing trousers. Apart from this confusion, I think the main thing that this ad says about being female is that women have a certain place and role in relation to men.

When I first saw this ad I was mostly confused because I couldn't figure out what *exactly* they were saying about men and women. I also thought that it was one of the silliest ads I had ever seen just because the man looks so dumb as he acts out each of his new personalities through his different outfits. I ended up talking with a friend about what the meaning might be and we decided that

Figure 15. Guess? jeans (first page).

the basic point is that she shouldn't be wearing the jacket because it is his jacket and she is emasculating him and has usurped his power. It was the way that they are looking at each other that really disturbed me — he looks so angry, like a daddy, and she looks so rebellious and mischievous, like a little girl.

I think that it was really helpful that this ad confused me because it forced me to actually *look* at the ad. During this time period I began ignoring ads because they became useless and bothersome to me. Being so confused about this ad really made me think about all of the possible messages it was putting out. The impact of this ad hurt because I was very angry at the ignorance and sexism in it. It bothered me that the woman in this ad was used in such an abusive way. What bothered me the most was the confusion I felt about what the ad was saying – I felt really stupid and helpless.

What can you say about those Guess? jeans ads! The one I've chosen is a two-page ad. The first page shows a man and a woman sitting on a wooden cart which is being pulled by an animal. The woman is holding the reins but the man is actually controlling the animal by holding onto the reins also. The woman has her legs crossed, is wearing high heels, is sitting very ladylike and sexy, and has her eyes closed. The man has a concentrated and happy look on his face. The second page is a photo of the woman alone. She is playing with a lock of her hair and looking dreamily off camera.

This ad told me that being female means looking sexy and letting the man take control. Even if you have the ability to do something or the chance to learn how to do something, just close your eyes and let the man take over. The message is to be passive and attractive. I was really disgusted by this ad, not only because of the blatant sexism of the first page but also because of the ridiculous expression on the woman's face on the second page. I felt really helpless and very sad for the woman—I just wanted to shake her and tell her to quit acting so powerless. It just really upset me and made me feel really gross and dirty and angry.

My next choice is a three-page ad for Reebok. The first page shows a woman in a black dress and high heels sitting on a chair with her head turned away from the viewer so that her face is shadowed. The text reads "In the 50s the pump restricted women's movement . . ." The second page shows a woman exercising with her back to the viewer. Her back muscles are flexed and her hair is wispy and wet and there are sweat stains on her outfit. The text reads "In the 90s The Pump liberates us." A photo of the Pump appears below the text. The third page shows a woman who is also exercising. The lower half of her face is shown and she has an expression of physical stress as she is jumping and extending her arms back. The text on this page explains in detail what was said on the previous two pages—that the Pump is liberating women in the '90s, unlike the pump of the '50s. The last line explains that the Pump is "strong support for the women's movement."

This ad is saying that women are more liberated now because they can wear sneakers instead of high-heeled pumps. It also says that women can be sexy even when they sweat and exercise as long as their bodies are muscular and just the right size. This ad really made me angry because I felt that it totally exploited the women's movement theme. By saying that women were restricted by the pump in the '50s they are implying that women in the '90s are not restricted by the pump, which in fact they still are. Women are only allowed to wear the Pump when they exercise or for very casual occasions. They still need to wear high heels when they want to look sexy or authoritative. I also didn't like the way that there are no faces on these women. Even though the ad is trying to emphasize how strong and liberated these women are by showing their fuller bodies and muscle, they are still objectifying them by only giving us "parts" of them. It made me more aware of yet another twisted approach to women's bodies and how this ad went about utilizing the women's movement to promote their product.

The ad also bothers me because I know that some people think that it's really great these days that female models are "allowed" to be more muscular and not just toothpick thin. I feel like it's the same thing as before. These

Figure 16. Norelco Ladyshave.

same people would feel this ad was showing "strong" women because they are shown exercising and sweating, but I feel that this type of look has become sexually attractive and that is why they use it.

Finally, there is this ad for Norelco Ladyshave: "Baby Your Legs." A woman in shorts holds a naked baby across her legs so that the viewer gets a side view of both of them. The baby is looking at the viewer with a pleasant face while the woman smiles at the baby. The text below the photo explains why "Norelco can shave grown-up legs baby soft and silky smooth." The main thing which this ad immediately tells me about being female is that women need to remove the hair on their legs. It also says that because women's legs can be as soft as a baby's, that women are *like* babies in some way.

I found this ad very interesting in that it came right out and said that women become like babies when they shave the hair of their legs. When I first became aware of some of the implications of women removing body hair, one of the first discussions which I participated in focused on the idea that when women don't have body hair, they seem more like adolescent girls and are therefore less threatening to men. It was therefore really interesting to see this connection presented in an ad promoting leg-shaving. I found this very disturbing because obviously people must think that its fine that women are being compared to babies.

It was helpful for me to realize that some people do not find it disturbing for women to be compared to babies. I think that it was useful to my understanding of the perception of women in terms of their body hair. It was also helpful in that it made me feel even more thankful that I'm not as obsessed as I used to be about removing my own body hair.

It hurt me to realize that women are being told to do something as useless as shaving their legs—something that wastes their time and money. And the whole idea of expecting women to want to be soft and smooth like a baby made my skin crawl. It is so obviously motivated by the fact that someone will somehow get pleasure from touching a woman's legs because they're as soft as baby skin. The more I thought about it, the more obscene it became.

Discussion

It is very clear that Elizabeth's life experiences influenced her readings of these ads; at the same time the messages encoded in the ads helped Elizabeth define herself at certain times. In the earlier half of her narrative Elizabeth recalls how her lack of self-identity led to her seeking an identity from ads. At the same time, the fact that she did not fit the images of femininity portrayed in advertisements affected her sense of self, making her feel as if she was different, abnormal. As she grew into possessing a stronger sense of self, Elizabeth consequently developed a more critical relationship to ads. Elizabeth's developing sense of self was influenced by a range of life experiences that in turn influenced her textual negotiations

Some of these experiences were positive, like her interactions with caring, concerned teachers. Other experiences, such as bad relationships, seem to have been painful. However, all these experiences ultimately helped Elizabeth in her journey to a critical relationship with ads because they highlighted the disparity between the images of femininity found in advertising and the practicality and usefulness of those images in real life. For example, Elizabeth notes that early messages of femininity, as sexually alluring yet innocent, affected her relationships to men, perhaps leading her into destructive affairs. Advertising influenced her evaluations of others, such as men who did not live up to her ideal. The consistent way in which heterosexuality and the need for a man in her life was stressed by Elizabeth's friends and family was reinforced through advertising. Elizabeth thus found herself entering into sexual encounters based not on her own desire for the act or for the person, but because of a sense that this was what it means to be a woman.

Elizabeth's story also illuminates the way that female pleasure plays a role in negotiating texts. At the same time that ads both reinforced and defined un-helpful messages about femininity, it is also important to note that in the early part of Elizabeth's narrative, her relationship with ads was not all negative. For example, she mentions enjoying the mascara ads because of the pleasure she got from the make-up ritual. As part of this ritual she would talk to other women and had a new "toy" to play with, in the form of eyelash curlers. She was also able to feel "normal," because she could participate in this ritual of girl culture and bond with other women (see Lewis 1990). This sense of plea-sure in her normalcy, however, was later disrupted by the fact that she did not look like the models in *Seventeen*. Elizabeth describes a similar process in re-lation to the Bain de Soleil ad; she liked the ad because she could identify with the woman's dark tan, but was once again distanced by the fact that her body did not conform.

Eventually, it was the clashing of the fantasy and idealized images with reality which helped Elizabeth move to resistant, "feminist" readings of ads. Elizabeth's experience of what it is to be a woman in this culture, a role learned through culture and advertising, similarly shapes her later readings of texts. She is quite clear about the power relations embedded within advertising. It would be unfair to say that Elizabeth is "free" now that she can perform resis-tant readings. Elizabeth repeatedly expressed disgust and frustration over the ways women are represented. And this frustration undoubtedly comes from her personal knowledge that advertising does not occur in a vacuum, but is representative of the way culture views women, and that it will undoubtedly influence future women in turn.

For Elizabeth, advertising provided clues for what was normal and so-cially acceptable when she was growing up. Yet it is important to note that many of these clues were reinforced on many levels by her culture, including family and friends. What is clear from her narrative is the fact that she grew up in an environment in which girls were second class citizens. Elizabeth's par-ents, for example, valued the achievements of their son but gave Elizabeth the sense that, as a girl, she was unimportant. Even as an adult, Elizabeth received similar messages from her parents, who continued to base their evaluations of her on whether or not she fit socially approved roles. Her narrative also reveals that it is not only women who suffer from these gender imbalances. While Elizabeth was certainly hurt by the lack of importance attached to her achievements, she believes she was consequently granted the time and space to explore herself—a flexibility denied to her brother, who was immediately shunted into the high pressure world of masculine achievement.

Elizabeth's experiences in this regard are quite similar to those of many girls and women. Women grow up in a culture in which girls, their activities and achievements and girl culture are devalued. This devaluation occurs in many contexts: the family, schools, and media, which consistently preach a well-defined, limited range of options for appropriate feminine behavior, including appearance, career choice, and sexual preference. The devaluation is even more severe for those whose differences set them apart, like minority women. And advertising plays an important role in both reinforcing old standards and creating new ones — like the new thin, muscular look. Once again, we see a process of symbolic annihilation, in which the full range of what girls can be is symbolically killed off by the lack of representations. Girls, who begin life possessing limitless possibilities of being, are told again and again that their unique qualities don't fit the mold. As such, they waste energy, time, and money trying, like Cinderella's stepsisters, to cram their unruly personalities, bodies and thoughts into constricting glass slippers.

In her journey growing up and moving through the dangerous terrain of advertising, Elizabeth found a strategy for navigating the relationship between femininity, media and self. She, like others interviewed, learned to apply critical analysis to ads that in the past may have hurt their psyches. However, the challenge remains for many females, particularly girls. As Mary Pipher says in *Reviving Ophelia*, girls today are much more oppressed. They are coming of age in a more dangerous, sexualized, and media-saturated culture. They face incredible pressures to be beautiful and sophisticated.

As I looked at the culture that girls enter as they come of age, I was struck by what a girl-poisoning culture it was. The more I looked around, the more I listened to today's music, watched television and movies and looked at sexist advertising, the more convinced I became that we were on the wrong path with our daughters. America today limits girls' development, truncates their wholeness and leaves many of them traumatized. (Pipher 1994, 12)

Elizabeth's story describes the journey of one individual through this dangerous terrain. What are other possibilities for women and girls to learn to resist those images which may be harmful to them? The need is to discover ways in which to encourage and foster women's and girls' healthy development as individuals in a media obsessed society.

7. Differences Within Gender: Manufacturing Distance

I have always been aware of how I look when I enter a room, taking into account the lighting, who can see which side of me, and how my clothes are hanging. When I catch myself doing this it angers me because I have no reason to be so concerned; it all boils down to being female. (Barbara, 30)

It is one thing to want to look nice, but to want to totally alter my present lifestyle to offer a new me—forget it! I've learned my lessons and they are not from commercials. (Ann, 38)

I try to be evaluated according to my actions rather than my looks. This is one issue that I am constantly faced with in that others expect me to look in a certain way, to fit the image of a professional worker and portray this feminine appeal. I find it difficult to challenge these assumptions and still remain consistent in my message. (Angela, 24)

To this point, we have discussed gender differences found across the discourses of the men and women interviewed. However, feminist critics such as Michelle Barrett (1987) argue that analyses that focus exclusively on gender differences are essentialist in their biases. Barrett argues that the analyst should not assume at the outset that the differences between men and women are the only and most important divisions since individual audience members bring their own experiences, situational constraints, socioeconomic experiences, racial background, and sexual orientation to the viewing. In other words, it is necessary to examine differences *within* gender.

It must be noted that the patterns of difference within gender examined in this research offered less diversity and variety than the differences between genders. This can be explained by the homogeneity of the sample. Because all those interviewed were residents of similar university districts, they share certain educational experiences and fall into similar socioeconomic categories. Most of the men and women are white, come from the American midwest, and are from middle class families. Nevertheless, differences within gender are clearly observable, and the patterns explored below offer considerable insight into the places where decoding strategies break out of both the imposing structures of advertising and the imposing structures of gender.

This chapter focuses on three themes of difference within gender. The first theme that will be addressed is "negotiation and resistance." While women at some point in their lives tend to buy into the dominant images presented by advertising, they often learn to resist the imagery and values represented therein. The first section of this chapter will examine the range of female readings from dominant, or "female" decoding to what feminist scholars call "feminist" reading practices. We will then move on to examine some of the contributing factors in women's lives that enable them to negotiate and even resist societal messages about ideal femininity.

The second difference within gender that will be examined in the chapter involves the symbolic annihilation of certain men and women who belong to marginalized societal groups: gays, lesbians, and African American women. These men and women expressed that "who they are," either in definition of lifestyle or in appearance, is not represented in the dominant images of what is supposedly attractive and normal. Finally, we will examine differences between *men*. Some male responses revealed a heightened sense of feminist consciousness compared with other men. This feminist consciousness most often manifested itself in terms of genuine empathy for female experiences with dominant images.

The Female Gaze: Negotiation and Resistance

The findings of this study thus far have strongly supported the conceptual frame that the conventions of the "male gaze" in popular mediated images and the "split consciousness of the self-surveyed female" as a socially constructed response to those images *are* strongly evidenced in female, and even male, responses to advertising. However, one of the problems for feminist scholars is that because the influence of the male gaze is so huge, it is often hard to see how women can look at anything without participating in their own oppression. Might there be a "female gaze"? If so, how does a "female gaze" operate? As many feminist critics of female spectatorship have theorized, there is more to female viewing than can be analyzed within the parameters of the male gaze and the self-surveyed female. Women have developed their own ways of looking that cannot and should not be defined only as the result of seeing representations through a masculine lens. There are dimensions of female spectatorship that do indeed exceed the parameters of the controlling male gaze.

In a well-known article, Christine Gledhill (1988) describes a process called *negotiation* that is very useful for understanding how women might decode texts in ways that do not necessarily buy into oppressive ideologies. The term negotiation implies the holding together of opposite sides in an on-going process of give and take between text and viewer. Gledhill sees the relationship between text and audiences as a process of struggle between the dominant meaning encoded in the text, and the real life experiences, motivations, and ways of thinking of the audience members.

The process of negotiation relies on an understanding of *hegemony*. In the past, cultural scholars tended to think in terms of ideology understood as a way of thinking/being/behaving that is issued in a top-down fashion, as in the chain of military command, in which those in power force their own views upon the powerless. In recent years, a notion of hegemony derived from the work of Antonio Gramsci has replaced this idea. This view assumes that it is not useful to think about power as a set of particular institutions or people "doing" something to others in a premeditated fashion. Instead, this concept of hegemony assumes that in order for ideologies to be reproduced and carry on over time, they must to some extent be internalized by the population. Though people might resist or argue with parts of an idea, overall, people agree with much of it. For example, one hegemonic idea in the United States is that all people are equal. However, how this idea really plays out in practice is defined by a constant process of negotiation. Culturally, this process is evidenced in the debates by people over such issues as affirmative action, the distribution of wealth, and race relations, in which the practical meaning of "equality" in our society is fought over.

It must be noted that because hegemonic ideologies are not imposed upon helpless people, they go through a process of continuous negotiation and renegotiation (Gledhill 1988, 8). In other words, the meaning of "equality" is not static, but will change over time as people constantly renegotiate the idea. Thus we see the change from what was meant by "equality" in the early United States, in which it was interpreted by the revolutionaries as being between landowning, white males, to a conception of equality that includes women and minorities. The notion of hegemony also assumes a level of subjectivity, of power, in the audience; They are not a mass of easily influenced dupes, but have the power to decode and interpret texts in a variety of ways. For example, people have different viewpoints on the idea of "all people are equal" in part because of differences in their life experiences, philosophies and social location. A black man, for example, might have a different interpretation of the meaning of the American flag than a white man because of the different histories and experiences of the two groups. Therefore, texts need to be examined for the multiple and sometimes differing possibilities of meaning that might be found in them by different people.

Thus, as a model of meaning production, negotiation conceives cultural exchange as the intersection of processes of production and reception. Meaning is neither imposed nor passively imbibed, but arises out of a struggle or negotiation between competing frames of reference, motivation, and experience. This is not to say that texts have a *limitless* number of meanings embedded in them and will vary entirely depending upon who is reading them. Indeed, most texts will have a "dominant" or "preferred" meaning, which is the interpretation that most people will understand as the intended message. However, even if people "get" the message encoded in a text, they may choose to resist or reject parts or all of it.

One idea, briefly discussed earlier, is that people will choose to resist, negotiate, or go along with the preferred reading depending on how well the message matches their experiences, beliefs, and values. Those who do not find their experiences or their perceived selves adequately represented will be more likely to critique the message for those gaps in representation. Advertising works hard to appeal to people by touching on internalized values at some level—conscious or unconscious. For example, a lower income single mother named Susan may be drawn to a glamorous advertisement for expensive designer cologne. Although her immediate experience is that she cannot afford such luxuries, she may have internalized the values that as an American she has the right to indulge in such extravagances as designer perfume. Susan is really not resisting the image at all, even if it is impossible to purchase the product.

However, Susan may have a highly resistant reading of an advertisement for a new medical hospital opening soon in her city. She doesn't have good health insurance and when her kids are sick she must take them either to the emergency room or the local clinic. However, she knows that her children would get higher quality health care at the new medical hospital. Unlike the perfume that she feels she deserves but cannot afford, she believes that she and her children, as Americans, deserve good health care *now*. She doesn't agree that good healthcare should be available only for those who can afford it, and she thinks it unfair that she and her children are expected to wait for good health care until she can afford it. Because of her deeply internalized idea that all Americans deserve the best health care available, she "talks back" to her TV when the ad for the new medical facility comes on.

Complicating this idea of negotiation is the question of female pleasure. What are the ways women take pleasure from media texts? How do these pleasures affect the negotiation between their female gaze and the dominantly inscribed texts of mass media? In feminist research the question of female spectatorship emerges in the examination of audience responses to media forms that are actually widely enjoyed by women. Stacey (1994) has said that it is necessary to understand that "popularity and pleasure does not necessarily result in an endorsement of the texts producing it, nor a condemnation of the female spectators watching it" (46). Likewise, studies by Tania Modleski (1982), Ien Ang (1985), and Janice Radway (1984) found that, while women may buy into the preferred readings of such texts, this doesn't mean that women are cultural dupes. These studies underscore how female pleasure in certain cultural forms is negotiated. Pleasure is found in parts, while less pleasing elements are resisted or rejected. Thus female pleasure in texts in which women are objectified does not mean that women are masochistic, but that they are selectively concentrating on those elements which have meaning to them.

For example, in her study of romance novel readers, Radway (1984) found that readers regularly dealt with common aspects of romances they *didn't* like, such as the hero raping the heroine, by ignoring or overlooking them, concentrating on the parts that they did like, such as the hero comforting and cosseting the heroine. Moreover, by analyzing the romance readers' appreciation of romances within the context of their everyday lives, Radway found that romance novel readers often enjoyed the romance as a form of escape from their daily routines. Readers found pleasure in the actions of the male hero, who was seen as a nurturing, caring man—one who would nurture the readers much as they nurtured everyone else in their family on a daily basis. Radway observed that the women's desire to escape and be nurtured contained an implicit critique of the patriarchal status quo in which women are regularly overworked and act as caretakers for everyone but themselves. Thus, understanding female pleasure in the romance points to the ways in which women negotiate with texts. While not necessarily a sign of oppositional or resistant reading, female pleasure may be a sign of women claiming their subjectivity—their particular "female gaze" in which the specificity of women's lives, experience, and points of view work to create a different "way of seeing."

Another example is Angela McRobbie's (1984) study that examined the relationship between dance and female pleasure. She found that young girls' attraction to texts such as the movie *Flashdance* and the TV series *Fame* may not be as simple as females "buying into" sexist representations of women's bodies. In fact, girls may find a real freedom in dancing, a pleasure that is not necessarily directed toward the male partner or spectator, but is in fact a pleasure of experiencing their own movement, their own sensuality. McRobbie argues that while girls are trained to be aware of being watched, sometimes they can use that "way of seeing" to derive pleasure from seeing themselves move and have fun.

One important idea in female spectatorship is the idea of fantasy, which allows women to find pleasure in a variety of images. Ang (1990) argues that it is necessary to examine how texts construct possible modes of femininity. For example, female soap opera characters embody "versions of gendered subjectivity endowed with specific forms of psychical and emotional satisfaction and dissatisfaction, and specific ways of dealing with conflicts and dilemmas" (83). Soap opera women are not seen as role models by female spectators but as "symbolic representations of feminine subject positions with which viewers can identify in fantasy" (83). Fantasy allows women to move beyond the roles and constraints of everyday life and take up different positions. Ang's point is that while in real life women may suffer from negative consequences of certain forms of femininity—such as passivity and dependence—fantasy allows the reader to enjoy the possibilities of taking up a certain identity without experiencing any negative repercussions.

It is important to remember, however, that if female pleasure may be seen as a sign of women claiming their subjectivity, pleasure with an image is not necessarily a sign that women are free of the negative effects such texts may produce on a cultural level. Women may be actively reading and negotiating with ads, while buying into the hegemonic ideas they are circulating (Botta 1999; Radway 1984). The next section will explore how women negotiate with the dominant male gaze in advertising. Do women find pleasure in the male gaze structured within the preferred readings? What kinds of negotiations do they perform? What readings are resistant?

Female Pleasure with Advertising

It is worthwhile to note that women rarely framed their readings in terms of "pleasures." In fact, women expressed mostly extreme displeasure with advertising images:

I guess I'm glad that I notice it, but at the same time, it really makes me so mad, that when I think about pleasure and this reaction the two don't go hand-in-hand. It just makes me so mad that it happens. If I would say I was pleased with this reaction, I wish the thing didn't happen. I wish advertisements weren't like that. (Laura, 33)

"Pleasure" plays a minor role in this analysis, and yet this study provides ample evidence that female spectatorship is not completely confined within the parameters of the male gaze. This suggests that perhaps "pleasure" is actually a sub-process of the larger phenomenon of negotiation.

Rosemary Betterton (1985) argues that a result of the evolving feminist consciousness that has seeped into the popular imagery and discourse of this culture over the past twenty years is the ability of many female spectators to switch points of view between the position of surveyor (active, voyeuristic) and the position of the surveyed (passive, narcissistic). This ability empowers the female spectator with the ability to take up a critical position of looking that is not traditionally masculine or feminine. For example, when looking at a glamorous actress half-nude in a favorite soap opera, it is possible to be fascinated and attracted by the image and at the same time be well aware of the difference between the image and one's experience, and one's body image, for that matter.

This study did find evidence to support Betterton's position. Some women discussed their abilities to glean the positive from dominant representations while at the same time being highly critical of them.

They're strong, they are images of strength and also being feminine because there is no great attempt to hide that. I mean she [Virginia Slims ad, fig. 6] still has the purse and a pink coat but she is in a suit even though she disregards her health completely. This one's [Nike ad, fig. 8] tough. She is not afraid to wear her tights in public and she doesn't care if she is too fat for them. I'm learning to live with that one. Yes, it is emotional. I'm attached to these women who represent me. . . . I haven't always and I'm learning to appreciate myself. . . . I'm excited that I can look at these pictures and actually get excited about saying that these women represent me. . . . I think this is an image that even if society or I don't think society likes it, it doesn't bother me. . . . I think we've all tried on different roles in our life and these are not offensive since I can say that I've lived through them, neither are they pleasing because I am in the process of trying to remold or reshape them, discard them, change them in some way, so they don't look like this anymore. . . . Sure, I've tried all kinds of images on to see which one works. (Patricia, 35)

Although this discussion offers some evidence for Betterton's position, the weight of evidence points to another conception of the two sides of female negotiation with dominant images. This conceptualization of female negotiation most closely resembles the theories of Diane Waldman (1989), who argues that once we begin to theorize about the possibilities of the critical, and at the same time responsive female spectator, it is helpful to distinguish the positions that are "feminist" from those which are strictly "female." This ability to move between culturally defined male and female viewing positions is not the innate province of the female psyche, but is instead the result of a disruption in traditional ways of seeing which can be directly attributed to multiple feminist discourses in society.

The domain of the "female" responses ranged from female spectatorship that was uncritical of the male gaze, helping to perpetuate this cultural way of seeing through beliefs, behaviors and discourses—to spectatorship defined by the beginnings of reflection upon personal experiences with split conscious-ness and resultant narcissistic damage. At one end of the spectrum, a dominant, or uncritical, reading of the male gaze in representation offers a mirror of the dominant themes in advertising depicting idealized female bodies.

I just feel like I know what is attractive to men. All these pictures fit that category, skinny people are more accepted and attractive people are more accepted in society. . . . I think it would help if I looked more like they do. It would help me because people like to be around attractive people. Not everybody is like that. Attractive people are more well-liked and popular. That could help you in the future. In that way it could help me. . . . It hurts me because if I don't look like this I won't be looked well upon society. Especially as I get older and I don't have the body and the face I think it will hurt more too. Women are supposed to be young looking and your skin is supposed to be nice, but men don't have to worry about it because they get better looking as they get older. (Claire, 22)

While an uncritical dominant reading like Claire's is an example of one type of "female" looking, the beginning of self-consciousness about the domi-nant male gaze in advertising and culture is also part of "female" looking, primarily because beginning reflections on, and questioning of, dominant rep-resentations are often based on personal experience and through intuitive rea-soning, rather than formal feminist messages.

I've looked back. I've wondered about that, you know, the fact that we were talking about this ideal beauty that you have so much of your own self-worth [wrapped up in]. I was wondering where on earth that ever came from. Advertising has always been implicated, and I look at advertising and all I do is complain. I criticize and I keep thinking, could it be getting me subconsciously? I'm not really sure, but it certainly must be. I don't know where those things came from and that's the most disturbing, although advertising sometimes is just stupid. That bothers me. And the other thing that bothers me is how women are portrayed and how, it's hard for me to think about all the developmental terms. I can just think about how I feel right now. (Laura, 33)

"Feminist" looking, in Waldman's (1989) conceptual frame, is in no way confined to formal education in feminist theory and politics, which would be considered an advanced stage of conscientization. "Feminist" looking is a conscious awareness not only that the male cultural gaze has the potential for injurious personal and societal consequences, but that as women, we have all actively participated in this system of exploitation and oppression.

Active female negotiations with images reflected the tension women felt between being active participants in an oppressive system and an awareness that they wanted to break free of that system, not only for themselves, but for other women.

> I am fine with myself now, I don't care what others think of me. As long as I'm happy, then that's all that matters. . . . I have to live with it all. I feel it has made me a better person. And also a better, or more aware person of what I want and how I go about and get it. . . . I have been hurt, but I look at it as a growing experience. I can laugh at my actions and previous thoughts. Yet, I am afraid for other women who might buy into the stereotypes. That scares me because they will go through most of the same pain I did, that's really unnecessary. (Jamie, 22)

Gaining this "feminist" awareness is, for most women, an historical journey. As in Elizabeth's story, a common pattern in female responses involves a journey from adolescent years to the present. These women reported that as adolescents they fully and uncritically participated in perpetuating the dominant conventions of the male gaze. However, the repeated attempts to live up to these standards continuously resulted in differing types of personal pain. Through the pain, and often other competing structures such as feminist thought, an awareness grew in them and active negotiations with images began.

> Well, I try to become pretty myself, I mean, I don't try too hard or anything. I just want to look decent. Yet, there was a time in my life that where I couldn't leave the house without looking into the mirror several times, and not leaving until I had the perfect look. I was conscious about everything, shoes and hair. Vanity, I guess one would call it. Yet, now I don't have much time to put much into looking good. I've got school and other things to tend to. I don't have time to worry about my looks as much. I dress kind of casual now, sometimes I don't care how I look, as long as I get my papers in on time and keep up with my responsibilities. I have a boyfriend now and I don't try to impress him because I know he loves me for me. Why should I go out of my way, for who? Certainly not the people on campus. They could care less. But I'm sure they look at me funny cause I don't wear stuff that's flashy or make-up or junk like that. (Jamie, 22)

> In junior high and high school we were supposed to wear so much make-up and get up at six o'clock to make ourselves pretty. Now I think I'm at the point where I don't bother with it as much. . . . I think it's helped me to be more real with people and who I am whereas in the past I was so busy being who they wanted me to be that it made me very unhappy at times. . . . I think it's only helped me in realizing that more natural is more beautiful. It made me more brash to people cause I'm not willing to be fake to people. . . . I think it relates to my life now in realizing that I'm not those things but I'm just as intelligent, just as sexually appealing, I'm just as good. . . . In my past it

[hurt]. It made you think you weren't good enough to be loved but now it's different. (Rachel, 20)

I think, especially being a teenager, this is what everyone was doing. A product would come out, that's what everyone wanted. But, as I started to get older, it's easier to see that not everyone fits into the mold of how advertisers place women in photographs or commercials. Looking at that and saying I don't fit into that or I do. . . . Just as I've matured, I've cared less with trying to identify with the images of women in the materialistic side of advertising. (Megan, 25)

I've almost gotten to the place where I don't try the images on anymore. I just sort of settle into whatever I am or whoever I am. . . . I went through a very awkward, gawky duckling stage as a teenager. It took me a number of years to recognize that I had (a) grown out of it, and (b) wasn't really [an ugly duckling]. But, there is always part of me that remembers that it is a surface characteristic, it's what everybody sees although it may not be important. . . . I think there was a time when I was willing to do anything to be part of that acceptable role including making myself unseen like this woman without the head [Montana ad, fig. 4]. Keeping my thoughts to myself, forgetting that I had a voice. I think I've gotten over that particularly when you speak up and people still pretend that you don't have a head. (Patricia, 35)

For these women, active negotiation with dominant images of femininity involved trying to find comfort in themselves and their bodies when most of the messages in society were telling them that they were not pretty enough or good enough, not close enough to the ideal. It was the search for the embodied unified self beyond what could be gained through the consumption of products. Women reported this as one of the biggest ongoing challenges in their lives: feeling comfortable with themselves in spite of how poorly they fit society's ideal. These women were struggling to truly appreciate "difference" among women while actively fighting the homogeneity of dominant images of representation.

Looking at the pictures, I wasn't sure what they were, so it made me think, well, am I appealing to people? Am I appealing to someone if I'm not that? . . . I still think I question it now, whether I'm appealing or not, but not as much as I did when I was younger. . . . Sadness that so many women don't have confidence because they're not society's ideal. . . . In the past I was incredibly sad because I wasn't this or I wasn't that. It made me doubt myself and I think it makes a lot of other people doubt themselves, but now that I'm older and mature I feel smarter than that in knowing that I am appealing for who I am. . . . It may assist me in knowing that I'll strive even more to be who I am, if that makes sense. To know that I'm not feeding whatever it is that makes other ideals better than me . . . It makes me angry at myself to know that I still feel like that, that I would still feel sad about not being one of those [women in the ads]. . . . In the past I wanted one of these bodies because I thought it would make me happy. I thought it would make me a better person and that more people would like me, although I realize I don't have one of these bodies and I need to put myself in a situation and a mind set where people love me and accept me for what I am, not what society says I should be. . . . It might assist me in that it really drives home how much I need to be thankful for what I really do have and that it's not necessary to be ideal. . . . I think once you realize these women are different from you, that you don't have to be them, you're much more confident. (Rachel, 20)

For most of the women, negotiation with images was a personal and psychological process, a daily affirmation of worth and ability. For others, especially those who were further along on their journeys, active negotiations resulted in conscious behaviors to subvert the male gaze. This active subversion was achieved in a multitude of ways. One way that Jamie described subverting the dominant gaze was through offering an alternative concept of "body size" and appropriate apparel.

Society doesn't think you are at your full potential when you have all your clothes on. . . . Yeah, in my life I've always had big clothes. So I don't look too fat, and people have to guess my weight. I'm not going to easily expose myself. I like going to the amusement parks, cause there is always some guy trying to guess my weight. He never does, so I win a prize. That's the only game I will play. Sometimes I think I look better in clothes that fit me tighter, but I'm still not comfortable wearing those things. So I wear what I'm comfortable in, big clothes. (Jamie, 22)

An advanced stage of negotiation is resistance. Much like Hall's concept of oppositional decoding, resistance to dominant images constructed through the male gaze implies a rejection of the preferred meanings encoded in the text of the image. Women reported that, as they advanced on their journeys negotiating with images, many reached a point where negotiations are fewer and far less difficult and personal. This stage of resistance was reached when a woman finally felt embodied and no longer looked to societal definitions of beauty and attractiveness to define herself. At that point she defined her gender identity by her own criteria and not as the self-surveyed female.

I'm not saying I've known this all along, but at some point you realize how fake these things were and to not let it personally bother you. I suppose it could if you let it. So at some point I reached a stage that stuff was meaningless. It doesn't make me feel bad. It doesn't hurt me anymore. If I wanted to talk about larger things about how it reflects a woman's position in society, that's a whole other question. For me, it wasn't personally upsetting. (Heather, 29)

Just maybe in the past I wouldn't have been so prone to laugh at it, until I started realizing how women are used in ads to be more sexual for their allure than for the actual product. It's just stupid and redundant and completely unnecessary. . . . It pleases me that I can think [the ads] are stupid. In the past I really liked these ads and as I got older and matured I think I realized how unnecessary they are and how faulty they are in the way they portray women. (Rachel, 20)

I suppose if I got into a debate with some guy who really thought this was a neat ad, my high horse might come out. Five years ago it probably would have been worse. Now its more like, "You like the ad? So what do you like about it? Oh, yeah, great, fine." Please me, help me? Nope. Hurt me? Doubtful, unless I had a real militant on my hands and I got real militant back, which I've been known to do on occasion. (Patricia, 35)

Competing Structures

Every female respondent's journey is different through the negotiation of dominant images constructed through the male gaze. Some women did not actively negotiate with images, at least in the "feminist" way suggested by Waldman. However, all women reported some type of engagement with and against dominant conventions of seeing and looking in this culture at some stage in their lives. For women active negotiation resulted from a steady and growing awareness over time of the tension between society's messages about ideal femininity and a desire to be self-defined, embodied individuals.

Some women reported, however, that they have had the ability to negotiate with, and even resist, dominant messages about ideal femininity from a very early age. The explanation that they offer is that their families provided a competing structure for them by encouraging them from early childhood to be happy with their inner abilities and to be comfortable with their bodies.

I'm not sure that I ever found [advertisements] that much of an influence on my own life because I was taught that everything I saw was fake. Those women on there didn't look like my mother or anyone I knew. We always, we had our mother saying to us, a lot of that is garbage. Personally, I can't ever think of myself seeing a woman on TV and saying, "That's what I want to be like or not like." I didn't look at TV that way. . . . Well, that was a good thing. It has saved me a lot of heartache in that sense. I don't let those beer ads bother me, I suppose they could. I know that they bother some people. (Heather, 29)

I guess in college is when I really started—high school and college—is when I really started to deconstruct advertising. But, before that, my Mom and Dad always made me feel valued for what I was as a person, not what I looked like. Although they made me feel good about my body, good self concept about my body. I knew I was valued for the kind of person I was. I was kind. I was sensitive. I was a good listener. I was intelligent. But even if I weren't intelligent, my parents always valued me. No matter if I failed or succeeded, as long as I tried. So I grew up with a good self-concept. So when I saw pictures like this even at a young age, I didn't see this as pictures of myself. I saw it as the twins up the street. . . . They valued what clothes you wore to school rather than how you treated them. . . . I had shorter hair, I didn't wear make-up, and I was seen as sort of the smart kid in class, sometimes teacher's pet. I was also athletic and so I was known as super jock. I was not the antithesis, but I didn't fit this role, even though my Mom offered to show me how to put make-up on and buy me clothes like this, I wasn't interested in this type of thing. So, I knew at an early age that there were different paths that girls could follow and were allowed to follow. This is not the one I chose. . . . If I had grown up in a different atmosphere, my view of images would be different. If I grew up in a house where it was extremely important to go out looking a certain way, then my weighting of what is appealing and what is ideal would be different. So, I see that sort of socialization tied very directly to the way I view the world. Even though my parents would rate these very different than I do, I grew up with support that allows me to question critically things. (Ginger, 28)

Women discussed how the family was a young girl's only real defense against the overwhelming pressures to conform to society's ideals of femininity based foremost on appearance. As young girls, women needed constant reinforcement that they were valuable as multidimensional beings. Central to the competing family message on femininity was this: a clear and consistent definition of "appearance" as only one attribute among many that make a person who she is. Parents cited in the examples above were careful to ensure a balance between emphasis on abilities and other attributes and on appearance whenever supporting or praising their children. For the children, their girlhood self-esteem was not built on the fragile veil of outer beauty, but on a strong foundation of inner worth and ability. Unfortunately, in many families, female appearance is placed at a premium above all other attributes, if not consciously, then subconsciously, through casual remarks and criticisms. These conscious and unconscious family messages, therefore, serve to reinforce, rather than counter, larger societal messages about female worth based on appearance.

Symbolic Annihilation

In Chapter 4 the underrepresentation of women in history was discussed briefly. In media theory, a conspicuous and serious underrepresentation of certain social groups has been coined *symbolic annihilation* (Gerbner and Gross 1976; Gross 1991; Tuchman et al. 1978). A second pattern of differences within gender involves the symbolic invisibility felt by certain men and women who belong to marginalized social groups: lesbians, African American women, and gay males. These individuals offer their own answers to the questions posed in Chapter 1: What if one rarely sees representations of oneself in mass media to emulate? What if one's identity is deemed unworthy of representation in the dominant ideology of images?

The core interview group included two lesbians and one gay male who specifically identified themselves as such. I believe there were other gay men or lesbians in the core study who chose not to overtly identify themselves. Furthermore, the observations below are also based on classroom conversations with gay and lesbian students. Recent gay and lesbian film criticism on looking and spectatorship suggests that not only do lesbian women find different pleasures in looking at women than straight women, there are also differences between lesbian pleasures in looking and gay male pleasures in looking. This study found support for these statements, although more similarities were found between the responses of lesbians and gay males than differences. In fact, one male respondent explicitly defined the link he saw between women's oppression and gay oppression:

A lot of the work I do is combating the oppression of women. I find that very much intertwined with my identity as a gay male. A lot of the things I have suffered from and been hurt from have been because of heterosexism and homophobia and I think hatred of gay men is the perception of men as weak or feminine. So I respect anyone who combats that kind of notion and mentality. (Camron, 22)

Camron's words support the writings of theorists, like Suzanne Pharr, who link homophobia to misogyny. Pharr writes:

When gay men break ranks with male roles through bonding and affection outside the arenas of war and sport, they are perceived as not being "real men," that is, as being identified with women, the weaker sex that must be dominated and that over the centuries has been the object of male hatred and abuse. Misogyny gets transferred to gay men with a vengeance and is increased by the fear that their sexual identity and behavior will bring down the entire system of male dominance and compulsory heterosexuality. (1995, 283)

The overarching theme that bound the lesbian and gay male responses together and differentiated them from responses of their straight counterparts was the fact that their chosen lifestyle was symbolically annihilated from popular representation in a continuous and systematic fashion. Not seeing themselves in representation was painful and these individuals felt that this lack of any positive representation of homosexuality in the mass media helps to fuel societal prejudices against gays, often resulting in negative personal consequences.

Part of the frustration is that I don't look like any of these people [in the ads]. I'm not a person, my image isn't used to advertise a product and that's frustrating. . . . It hinders my choices, the choices I have available. My frustration can lead to feeling excluded from the market. . . .

. . . that some would look at me and say, "you don't fit the norm," and then attack me in a number of ways whether through discrimination or verbal assault or something like that. That might not be the case because that hasn't really happened, but that people in general are judged by these kinds of rules. It has nothing to do with who they are except maybe what they look like. And consequently how they do live their life. So, maybe a woman who isn't married but, you know, that really isn't a reason to have problems based solely on that. That bothers me when people make those kinds of judgments and then base their feelings strictly on those kinds of criteria. (Megan, 25)

They described trying to manufacture their own meanings from these dominant representations that they knew were not meant for them. For one of the women this meant finding pleasure in images that may have subtle, but never overt, references to intimate female relationships.

I guess I would say that seeing these two women [Johnny Walker ad] intimate like this is a positive image for me. Because my partner and I have gone running on the beach, although she or I don't wear underwear when we go. . . . I had to pause because at first this was very appealing to me because I thought this was two women and my chosen lifestyle is represented in an ad for a change. But when I realized that they were speaking of a man, I knew it was actually heterosexual and not as personally appealing. But it's not unappealing. The pros outweigh the cons. . . . There is sort of a subtle message at times. I think there is something very sexual about these two women running, half-naked together on the beach, and there is power. . . . If you showed two women looking intimate in the way that you see a man and a woman looking intimate, perhaps more than weight, that would not be society's ideal. Lesbianism wouldn't be allowed, I think, in these photographs. (Ginger, 28)

Camron, however, combats symbolic annihilation of his chosen lifestyle by adopting a "homocentric" way of seeing, as opposed to the heterocentric ways of seeing that dominate popular representation.

I guess I have just become a little homocentric, if you want to call it that. I've been bombarded by images of heterosexuality, Caucasian people, and the family structure that I just don't pay attention to them any more. I've just become desensitized to them, like oh, there is another ad like that. It is kind of good that I've become a little more gay-centric and I don't pay that much attention to [the ads]. That is what the advertisement wants. Pier 1 wants me to looks at this ad and they want me to take a second glance at it. I think that for me not to pay attention to it, at least on a conscious level, that is good because if I did pay attention to it than I would be supporting the country. I would be buying into Pier 1 the way they want me to and I don't really want to buy into Pier 1 if they aren't going to have an ad that appeals to me—for gay reasons or feminist reasons. Again it just goes along with the lack of advertisement with women of color or lesbians or overweight or elderly women. It bothers me that is lacking in this and that if those things were present than I would take a second glance at it and I would take an interest in it. It's something I would like to see visualized. (Camron, 22)

One major difference was found between lesbian and gay male discussions, more closely mirroring gender differences in the larger sample. Lesbians never discussed their attraction to other women in terms of pure objectification of female bodies. Like other females in the study, they saw this form of objectifying female bodies as a domain of male ways of looking. Gay males however, often described the objectifying of other males in terms of their outer appearances. Although described in the form of a personal struggle, Camron's response still suggests an overriding male way of looking that transcends, in some ways, sexual orientation.

Just because I am gay, I guess. I don't really consider myself as masculine or macho and so it is a stress factor in my life because I am not what society is telling me to be. Yet, it feels a little empowering because this is who I want to be regardless of what others are telling me. It makes me feel strong because I have the strength to say this what I want to do, no matter what. . . . Especially now, I have a real contradiction inside me about the things I should do now and the kinds of men I should be attracted to rather than who I am really attracted to. It's just like this internal conflict that really gets to me. Politically and socially I know that looks shouldn't matter, but the gay male subculture, that's the way it works. . . . It pleases me because I like seeing macho men in the advertisements. To be honest, I enjoy objectifying men who are attractive even though I know I shouldn't. That pleases me. . . . It make me feel a sense of loss that I can't be objective without objectifying. It does hurt me because I do participate in those kinds of behaviors, what society sets to be the masculine qualities that are more valued. So that really bugs me and hurts me that it is an ongoing internal conflict. If I have a relationship with a man that doesn't fit society's ideals, yet, I'm in love with him, the relationship probably wouldn't work because sexually he wouldn't be as arousing to me. (Camron, 22)

Another marginalized cultural group had representation in this group of participants. Two African American women were interviewed in the core study, with many more represented in the larger study. Again, the observations below are also informed by African American women I have had in my classes. Feminist scholars such as Jacqui Roach and Petal Felix (1989) suggest that we live in a culture where the dominant gaze is not only male, but white, and therefore, the gaze of the African American woman is doubly constrained.

Up until the last decade or so, representations of blacks were not only excluded from dominant media, but also stereotyped and ghettoized, presenting a spectrum from negative representation to no representation. Currently, blacks are placed outside "natural" and "beautiful" representation in advertising and positioned as "other." However, unlike the "exotic other" of the Hawaiian or Asian girls (see Williamson 1986), blacks are society's mundane other (Fredrickson 1988; Miles 1989; Omi and Winant 1986), "a blot on the cultural landscape" (Roach and Felix 1989, 130). This is changing, but very slowly.

Critics like bell hooks (1992) explain that blacks have come to understand that in order to enter the mainstream media, one must look and sound as "white" as possible, altering voice, diction, and most importantly, appearance, to present a close ideological fit with the white status quo.

Blacks in commercials and on news programs may be perceived as "Exotic Primitives," blacks with "white" talents. They are non-threatening to the white community while providing assimilationist role models to the Black community. They have successfully conformed, in the eyes of the white culture. (hooks 1992, 163)

This conformity helps maintain a black invisibility. However, gender was the overriding concern for most of these women. In fact, only one of the two women included in the core study made reference to race in her responses. The observation she makes, however, is a powerful one. Like the gay man and lesbians interviewed, Jamie saw women of color as symbolically annihilated from popular representation. Jamie saw this lack of positive representation as contributing to a profound desire of African American women to change themselves. Further, she felt it was important to deconstruct the concept of representation by observing that when a group is represented, those doing the representing are not always fair or just.

Because you see people changing their lifestyles according to what the fashion magazines say. Or that we buy this product because of this or that. We see white women as more beautiful than other women of color, not because they are, because they are depicted more in ads. They are represented more. So we start to buy into that type of thought. . . . I feel that all types of women from black to white have beauty, but society mainly pinpoints on the white women especially if they are thin. What about women of color? Who represents them? It's true we do have a lot of Black magazines out to promote Black fashion and beauty but what about Asians and Indians who are Americans? Who represents them? And do they do it fairly? (Jamie, 22)

Jacqueline Bobo's (1988) study of the viewers of *The Color Purple* revealed that black female viewers found a positive connection to the film, even though it had been seriously criticized in both the popular and academic press for showing a negative and stereotypical view of blacks, especially black males. Utilizing Stuart Hall's concept of articulation, Bobo concluded that the ability of the black women viewers to not only enjoy but gain positive messages from this film was a result in part of these women's awareness of and connection to another set of discourses, that of "the renaissance of black women writers" (93). This set of discourses has given voice to black female experience, an area habitually absent from dominant writing and representation. *The Color Purple*, although considered dubious in many of its representations, had something to say about black women and black female experience. For the women in Bobo's study, the messages of the writings of black women and the messages of the film formed a particular type of cultural connection, an articulation. It was important to them that the image of black women's experience was present at all, and much less important that the images were not perfect.

Male Empathy

Finally, difference within gender categories showed that males are not monolithic in their responses, nor do they always decode images of females through the dominant male gaze. Some men possessed a heightened sense of feminist consciousness and thereby showed genuine empathy for female experiences with dominant images.

This type of male empathy is most closely akin to Waldman's concept of "feminist looking." Feminist looking is a conscious awareness not only that the male cultural gaze has the potential for injurious personal and societal consequences, but that men and women both actively participate in this system of exploitation and oppression. A feminist consciousness by men was rarely achieved through formal educational channels, but instead through popular discourses and informal education from female family members, girlfriends, and wives.

Well, it upsets me, the fact that I personally am very glad that I'm male now, now in society, because there is emphasis on male, both male and female to be attractive, but I think it's ten times worse for females. I hate to have to see my sisters growing up with this, because I know that this is how they're going to be judged, unless things radically are altered. In the near future, they're going to be judged, number one, on their appearance. And then, if they pull, pass the test, then they'll be looked at for whether they're intelligent, athletic, you know, like determined, hard working, things along that [line]. So it does upset me. (Greg, 19)

Friends of mine, and especially female friends of mine, come across discrimination from time to time, because they might not necessarily be the most beautiful or most attractive. I mean, they might have what it takes upstairs to—intelligence-wise—to perform on a job or do anything that really needs to be done, but because they're not the most beautiful or the most attractive, I mean, they necessarily didn't get the job or they didn't get a position or even a lot of times it's a lot more covert than that. It's just, you know, they don't feel that they get the respect from society or from male coworkers or just from people in general, that someone who is very attractive gets. . . . So, I would consider incredible people of substance that have been, not had all the advantages of life, because they didn't necessarily have the aesthetics to go along with it. (Mario, 28)

Like women whose families provided a competing structure for the dominant view of women in this culture, conscientized males often confided that their families not only instilled in them competing values from those of advertising, but that the gender relations they witnessed in their families, in their homes, also contradicted the dominating, active male/submissive, passive female dichotomy:

The fact that I have values. It helps me decide what I like. The values that I grew up with and that I got from my family helps me make judgments in life and I appreciate that. . . . Our family, I thought, worked pretty well together as a unit. While we could all come together and make decisions, we also all had the freedom to go our individual ways and everything. There was no strong, dominating type force that said, "You do this or else." . . . Yeah, my father was certainly the provider of the family, and he was certainly the breadwinner, [but] it was never like it was in the TV commercials. Heck! If Dad would've come home and said to Mom, "Get me this, or get me that," Mom would have showed Dad the door [laughs]. It was never anything like that at all. (Mario, 28)

I think there is a big contradiction between what advertisers are telling me and what my parents—especially my father—is telling me about [things]. Advertising in a lot of ways is presenting these sexual images things along the line that males must be, must have this macho, there's this macho mystique about it. . . . It's gotta be this big, burly, mountain man type of guy. That's the image the media presents. Then, there's my parents, who are telling me to be very respectful of women, very respectful to elders, thoughtful, hard working, this and that. At least in my life there's a large gap between what I'm being told. . . . It may just have been that I wasn't raised to think that way. I'm manly no matter what everyone else is telling me, I know I'm not going to do it. I tried, and I think successfully, to stay away from acting in that manner. So, I see this image as kind of a negative image, something to stay clear of, those actions. (Greg, 19)

Like femininity, masculinity is a socially constructed ideal (Kaufman 1998). Like women, one way that men may learn a sense of their own gender identity is through the media (Bordo 1999; Faludi 1999). Myths of masculinity and proper masculine behavior are communicated in media (Craig 1992), as, for example, in beer commercials (Strate 1992) and TV shows (Garfinkle 1985).

Traditional conceptions of masculinity which embrace domination, power, and pain have been much critiqued by feminists. Donald Sabo (1980, 1998) has compared patriarchy to the game of football, rooted in an idea of competition and hierarchy in which the winners dominate the losers and which is dominated by an ethos of pain. In this model, pain is a necessary component of winning—as in "no pain no gain." Patriarchy thus requires men to adopt a self-identity rooted in dominating others: women, children. and other men. This model requires men also to dominate themselves—repress those parts of themselves that do not fit into the structure. Michael Kaufman says:

Masculinity requires a suppression of a whole range of human needs, aims, feelings, and forms of expression. Masculinity is one-half of the narrow, surplus-repressive shape of the adult human psyche . . . boys and men harbor great insecurity about their male credentials. . . . In a patriarchal society being male is highly valued, and men value their masculinity. But everywhere there are ambivalent feelings. (1998, 8)

This conception of masculinity, it has been argued, is responsible for harming both women and men (Connell 1987; Kimmel and Messner 1998). Not only because it has been linked to great violences, like war, domestic violence, child abuse, and rape, but because of the great psychic violence it does to men and women. As Susan Bordo says of patriarchy, "A culture that idealizes, that fetishizes, is addicted to the hard and impenetrable, is a cold and unforgiving place to be" (1999, 59). Similarly, while men certainly have a privileged position in patriarchy, there is an increasing awareness that it is as impossible for a man to live up to standards of masculinity as it is a for a woman to live up to standards of femininity.

In fact, it is clear that much male violence is performed by those who feel the impossibility of living up to their male gender roles (Faludi 1999; Kaufman 1998). For example, Kaufman writes that "In the testimonies of rapists we hear over and over again expression of inferiority, powerlessness, anger. But who can these men feel superior to? Rape is a crime that not only demonstrates physical power, but does so in the language of male-female sex-gender relations" (1998, 9). In a sense, they are demonstrating a Napoleonic complex, overperforming masculinity in order to gain a sense of identity that they lack.

Like women interviewed, those men who possessed the more feminist inspired readings of advertising images were those who, like Camron, a gay male, were outside the dominant framework of heterosexual masculinity, or those whose families stressed a mode of masculinity critical of domination. In the case of Mario and Greg, fathers were important in teaching an alternate masculine viewpoint, as expressed in Kaufman's framework. For example, Mario's father modeled a nondominating, nonaggressive version of masculinity that was respectful of women, while his mother modeled a nonsubmissive version of femininity, regardless of the fact that they held the traditional social roles of masculine provider and female nurturer. Greg's father similarly articulated a masculinity based on maintaining respect and empathy for those around him. Like the women who were told by their families that they were lovable and important no matter what their appearance, Greg possesses a sense of assurance about his own masculine worth—a feeling he is manly no matter what he does. He therefore does not need to engage in or identify with those "masculine" behaviors that might be harmful to either himself or those around him.

Certainly, what stands out is the distinction between Mario, who expresses a more empathetic readings of ads, and Shawn. When asked what would make the women in an ad unattractive, Shawn stated "ugly, fat, bitchy." In his reading of ads featuring what he deemed to be attractive women, Shawn linked his reaction to the ad with his daily life, saying, "I hate when girls are attractive and they treat guys like shit. . . . Girls are bitches." Shawn displays a contradictory attitude towards the women in ads which he consistently linked to his experiences with women in his own life: desiring them if they fulfilled the conventions of attractive femininity, but at the same time despising them for looking down on him.

Why should they think that they are so much better than everybody else? I am not asking a girl to go home and sleep with me. I am just asking her to be friendly. There is a girl that works at the bar I go to. She works at the door. I mean, I am in there almost every night, like three or four times a week. I don't ask her to go home with me or anything and she always looks at me like, "Who the fuck are you?" I'm like, "Fuck you, I spend money here. Go to hell." (Shawn, 20)

Shawn's anger and fear over his own sense of *lack* of masculinity and self-worth seems to be transformed into rage against women, whom he desires sexually yet at the same time labels "bitches." Shawn clearly considers himself to be inadequate, yet at the same time he projects his anger and frustration outward. Shawn's comments echo the sentiments of the rapists referenced by Kaufman. This is not to say that Shawn is a rapist, but rather to point out that standards of masculinity create feelings of inadequacy and pain for men, feelings that have repercussions for others in turn, especially women.

In contrast, men like Mario and Greg have been encouraged to embrace those sides of themselves not necessarily considered "masculine," such as concern for and respect for others. They have been encouraged to be empathetic in their relations with others and as a consequence have a sense of themselves as essentially masculine, an identity independent of the perceptions, behaviors, or attitudes of others.

While it is important to acknowledge that masculinity, like femininity, takes different forms in different cultures or contexts, there has been a growing awareness in recent years of how rigid conceptions of masculinity work to perpetuate injustices in our world. Kaufman says, "There is a need to promote the personal strength and equity necessary to allow men to make more fundamental personal changes and to confront sexism and heterosexim in our society at large" (1998, 15). Kaufman argues for the need to develop "a strong powerful man who does not need to operate in an oppressive and violent fashion in relation to women, to other men, or to himself. And that . . . will play some part in the challenge to the oppressive reality of patriarchal, authoritarian, and class societies" (15). What may result from such empathetic attitudes is a greater sense of self esteem among men in which "feminine" qualities like caring and concern are welcomed, and, consequently, a greater respect for and concern about women by men.

The concept of the male gaze and the self-surveyed female does not tell us everything about gendered viewing. Women, for example, actively negotiate with these dominant conventions and in some cases learn to resist them altogether. However, this study suggests that, contrary to much feminist literature, female pleasure in looking is not the primary place where breaks with the male gaze occur. Pleasure is actually a subprocess of the larger phenomenon of negotiation. A more fruitful division in analyzing female responses beyond the male gaze is the difference between "female" and "feminist" viewing.

Feminist viewing regards advertisements from outside the dominant cultural framework. For example, lesbians and gay men often work to manufacture their own meanings from dominant heterosexual representations. Gaining a feminist awareness is for most women a historical journey, beginning in adolescence when they attempted to construct themselves for the male gaze. For most women, like Elizabeth, active negotiation involves trying to find comfort in themselves and their bodies when all the messages in society told them they are not pretty enough, not good enough, not close enough to the ideal. Active negotiation is the search for the embodied unified self beyond the mere consumption of products. Women who had a sense of themselves as embodied had experienced supportive family and personal relationships at an early age. The next chapter will address other possibilities for women and girls to find this embodied self.

8. Interventions and Changes

These ads make me angry. This is an ad that is typical of a lot of advertising where women are shown in these passive positions, eyes closed, head drawn back or bowed. So I wasn't angry when I saw this ad. I've seen so many of these ads. They also make me laugh. They are so stereotypical. I don't think these are very realistic of the way most woman act: lips pouted out, head drawn back . . . the man is never shown this submissive. So, I think it is unfair. And I wouldn't agree that anyone should be submissive, so in either case I wouldn't like the submission or the power that is shown. (Ginger, 28)

This is like the ultimate depersonalization . . . maybe that is the perfect female [laughs] can't talk back and can't run away. (Christi, 35)

[These] girls look like they are on drugs. "Girls should be seen and not heard," that type of thing. That's not helping me at all. "Just Do It." Don't wait for anyone, just do it. It would be kind of neat if it was the same slogan and she wasn't doing something athletic, but something else that's important. (Collette, 21)

I would say now I'm so tired of seeing ads like this. . . . The whole scenario of woman being made into objects leads you to the question "What's the point?" . . . It doesn't please me but by seeing these ads it helps me continue to realize even more how degraded woman are in advertising . . . it disturbs me definitely because it disgusts me . . . it's so stupidly degrading to our own self-images. . . . Women are not objects and they're continually shown that way. It makes me angry. And the more it continues the harder it is to drive it home to people that women are equal as human beings and not objects. (Rachel, 20)

That's not the meaning of life, to look good. What about my personality, my mind? People forget about that. . . . as long as we buy magazines like [*Cosmo*] then we'll always have the sexy girl mentality and the perfect man mentality. We'll never become ourselves. (Jamie, 22)

Embedded in these comments is the desire to find images of women that project qualities of independence and subjectivity. Such images are important not only for individuals, but also because there is an acknowledged connection between the presence of ads and negative cultural attitudes toward women.

As the previous chapters demonstrate, women raised in environments in which the role of appearance was downplayed while aspects of their personality and individual achievement were praised, acquired the ability to resist the pressures of advertising from a very young age. Similarly, Mary Pipher (1994) has written that in order for girls to be raised with a sense of themselves as embodied, unified subjects they need to be supported in other ways. Obviously advertising does not take place in a vacuum; to a great extent, the liberatory potential of any image is reliant upon the social structures that surround it. To that extent, changing imagery is not enough. The culture itself must change, from being one in which girls and women are devalued to one in which they are cherished. Thus, in education, the unequal treatment of boys and girls from elementary to graduate school must stop (Sadker and Sadker 1994). The glass ceiling in the workplace must be acknowledged and obliterated. Furthermore, equal access to health care, political rights and economic security are a must.

Yet positive imagery will also play a role. Pipher has argued that "Adolescent girls need a more public place in our culture, not as sex objects, but as interesting and complicated human beings" (1994, 289). Similarly, more positive images of women may be central in influencing females' self-perception. More positive reporting on female public figures like politicians, athletes and women in entertainment are necessary. Women's magazines and their advertisements may also play a role.

A Wink Toward Women

In the past fifteen years or so marketers have made a concerted effort to develop ad campaigns that seem to speak directly to female experience. Advertisers have also tried to capitalize on the fact that women are more conscious than ever that blindly striving toward the idealized body in ads, film, and MTV shouldn't be their raison d'être, that the rewards are hollow and the time and effort lost could be put to more meaningful and sustaining use. Advertisers have also picked up on the fact that women are tired of the size-4 body being presented to us as "everywoman." However, most of these ad campaigns offer "a wink" toward women and not a viable alternative to traditional sex-sells campaigns. Advertising scholar Daniel Nicholson describes the wink — or self-referentiality within an ad — when advertisers want the reader to recognize that "we know you know what we're trying to do, but because we're letting you know we know, it makes it okay — because we're so hip to your hippness. Get it?" (1997, 182–83).

Take some advertisements for Special K cereal. A television ad campaign for Special K in the mid-1990s suggested that women shouldn't be taken in by

Figure 17. Special K.

the prescriptions they see in the media, they should accept themselves. This particular campaign doesn't linger visually on any female body, but features a woman, probably in her forties, moving to light music as if in a yoga class. She is shot in soft-focus and no full body shots are revealed and no body fetishes are lingered over. This campaign showed that Special K could provide an intervention if they really wanted to. However, can we as consumers above the age of 35 really forget that it was Special K commercials that got the whole nation obsessing in the 1970s about whether we could "pinch an inch"? Yes, this quickly became another measure of whether one was too fat in the 1970s. I have very clear memories as a teenager latching onto the question of "can you pinch an inch?" and being quite horrified that, indeed, I could. Pinching an inch of flesh was shameful and meant I needed to get right to work on my body. I don't think I was the only teenage girl who took Special K's ad campaign as more of a prescription than an ad slogan. Their campaign tapped completely and directly into a culture of thin-obsessed girls and women who were willing to take advice from almost anywhere, even a cereal commercial, to achieve that "goal" of ultra-thinness.

Furthermore, the marketers of Special K seemed to suffer from a type of schizophrenia in the 1990s. Around the same time they were suggesting that women just relax and accept their bodies and themselves, a print ad in women's magazines featured a small floral bikini simply lying against a white background. The caption reads, "It's not doing any good in your drawer." Again, Special K couldn't resist tapping into one of women's phobias—being seen in a bathing suit. Current ads for Special K seem to be one of the biggest winks toward women yet. The television ads feature supermodel Cindy Crawford first making fun of her/our participation in fashion trends and then suggesting it is just as silly to participate in eating fads, finally suggesting that Special K always has been and remains a sensible diet food, positioned somehow outside of diet trends. A very natural looking and unglamorous Crawford is metaphorically winking at us saying, "I know that you know I've probably done as much as anybody to make you feel paranoid about your body through over two decades of modeling, but when we are all in our jeans and T-shirts we are just the same—responsible grown-ups who can live both in and outside of diet trends and fads—Right?"

"The wink" can also be construed as a postfeminist attitude (Dow 1994), a covert acknowledgment that social equality for women has been achieved and the only politics worth pursuing are the micropolitics of one's own life. This view suggests that gender politics play out at the individual level, political correctness is no longer necessary, and shows like Comedy Central's *The Man Show* aren't backlash but satire. However, when hip new television shows work from these assumptions the result is not always that the audience or especially the advertisers are operating in this idealized postfeminist era at all. For example, when Ellen DeGeneres tried to bring a comical, yet realistic portrait of lesbian relationships to television, she was first hailed as a trailblazer; advertisers who were hip would stand by her, and those who didn't were bigoted establishment creeps. However the show seemed to hit the boundaries of what the audience, advertisers, and network would tolerate when the show began to focus solely on the lesbian relationship between Ellen and girlfriend Lori. *Ellen* offered an expanded landscape of female relationships, but the realism was apparently too much for most.

The situation was rectified by the networks with *Will and Grace*—for all intents and purposes the show is about two male/female pairings. The men happen to be gay and the women happen to be straight, but the two gay main characters are not involved with one another and "gayness" is handled through gestures, jokes, and innuendo. Even the on-air kiss between Will and Jack during February sweeps was handled as a jest between friends. Although we see Grace with men in relationships, we never see Will in a relationship. This seems to be the network compromise for an audience and advertisers who want to construct themselves as hip, but do not want to admit their homophobia.

Then we have *Who Wants to Marry a Millionaire*, in which women competed to be selected as a millionaire's bride. The game show every woman wanted to play—either on stage or at home—but no one wanted to win! For 49 contestants the "dressing up" in dresses, beach wear, and finally a wedding dress, and doing it on national television—*was* the event. Winning became the booby prize—selected bride Darva Conger seemed to realize this the minute she was chosen. The spectacle had us all watching, and for most of the contestants it was a game—a flirtation with fame. The ultra-hipness of the concept was postfeminist and postcourtship, while at the same time retaining the concept of romance as an American ideal. In other words, all participants, including the Fox network, attempted to construct this pageant as a new millennium solution to our crazy, overscheduled lives that leave little room or time for traditional courtship, while at the same time constructing courtship and marriage as a respectable goal for all. For all its construction as a postfeminist spectacle, the fallout landed on two real people in particular, Darva Conger and Rick Rockwell, the real people paired on TV, with no courtship outside it. They didn't just play a married couple on TV, they really were – there's the rub. In an extended fifteen minutes of fame, Darva Conger quickly got an annulment from Rick Rockwell and then parlayed her fleeting celebrity status into a photo spread for *Playboy*.

Positive Interventions

Are there ways that images of girls and women can become more positive? Are there progressive images that do more than merely "wink" at women? Yes. For example, *New Moon* magazine, an ad-free subscription magazine for girls and young teens, is an example of one way the media can become more female-friendly. *New Moon* has structured a magazine in which the voices of a wide range of girls are heard. The magazine is particularly interesting because its editors are composed of girls. A recent publication *New Moon Sports* exemplifies *New Moon's* approach to the media and their attempt to create a more welcoming space for girls. The magazine and books are edited by groups of girls from across the country. They consciously set out to address and refute stereotypes, such as girls not being good at sports, and feature a plurality of voices, often basing their support of girls' sports on examples of, and stories by, real life girls as well as women. Tellingly, however, *New Moon* does not feature advertisements or other visual imagery. The conundrum of representing female subjectivity remains.

Can women be represented in such a way as to break with the traditional objectification of women, particularly when this representation is tied to advertising practices and market economies? The remainder of this chapter discusses some recent advertising campaigns successful in promoting, superficially at least, more positive images of women.

Mode

Like our participants, many women feel pain at the way they are supposed to conform to idealized standards of beauty. In recent years, perhaps linked to the growing awareness of eating disorders as a cultural phenomenon, there has been something of a movement to offer alternative media messages, particularly in regard to size. Several magazines exist which are geared toward larger women. Of these magazines, *Mode* has perhaps received the most publicity for its stated intent to provide attractive images of women that reflect the diversity of women, in relation to both size and race. In fact, unlike *Big, Bold, and Beautiful*, a magazine that caters to larger women, *Mode*'s stated goal is to promote positive self-images of women of all sizes. It presents itself as against not only fat oppression, but also sizism.

For example, in the February 2000 issue under the regular feature "Mode Matters," a story titled "Can't Lick It!" addresses how sizism affects all women, thick or thin:

Size discrimination in Hollywood has taken a new turn. Lara Flynn Boyle, Jennifer Aniston, Calista Flockhart, and others are being referred to as "The Lollipop Girls" (big heads, stick bodies). After our initial snicker, we realized that it's still size discrimination. We believe no one should look to anyone for validation. Give your body what it needs to live a happy life. Oh, and of course, read *Mode* for real inspiration. (Day 2000, 32)

Reflecting the unwillingness to label by size, until January 2000 the cover of *Mode* used to read "*Mode: 12, 14, 16...*" Now it simply reads *Mode: The New Shape in Fashion*.

The slightly knowing, "in with the joke" tone in the last sentence of "Lollipop Girls" cues us into another quality of *Mode*. It presumes and plays upon a high level of media literacy and the fact that its readers are cognizant of the pressures found in mainstream advertising. In other words, its readers are already presumed to be negotiating or resistant readers. This is clearly evidenced in the letters to the editor section, which offers much more interesting and often critical responses to the content of *Mode* than are found in other magazines. For example, in the February 2000 edition, MH writes:

Figure 18. *Mode* magazine.

Regarding your recent query about *Mode* men, please don't go there!!! Virtually every other women's magazine on the market has scores of article on men, sex, dating, etc. The very thing that keeps me hooked on *Mode* is that it helps me (at size 14–16) look the best *I* can. I don't need any more advice on relationships or men or anything else. Please keep your wonderful magazine in its original, fresh, relevant, and helpful state. (*Mode*, February 2000, 21)

MH worries that *Mode* will become too much like other magazines. However, it is clear from many reader and editorial comments, as well as advertising imagery, that part of the appeal of *Mode* is based on how it takes images that are currently outside the dominant frame and attempts to normalize them. Letters to the editor consistently express the relief (and consequently the past pain) experienced by many women at finally recognizing themselves in ads. Part of the appeal of *Mode* is that it makes women feel like they belong, that they, and their size, are "normal," even beautiful, and that they too can indulge in the pleasures of other women, like fashion magazines and style.

"Magic in Manila" writes: Oh my. It was the first time I'd ever seen a glossy magazine that delighted and inspired me! The models on your pages actually have tummies. They are shaped just like me! I've always been full-figured, and my whole life has been a struggle for acceptance. Your magazine has boosted my self-esteem to such a high level that I feel great about my body. Even the Just My Size ad (the one that goes "I am not 100 pounds . . .") brings tears to my eyes. (21)

Other examples:

I read "More is More" and I cried. I was overwhelmed with the knowledge that I am beautiful. As for my belly, which was the main culprit for my thickness, I now think it is a soft, voluptuous part of my body that both my husband and my daughter love. So, thank you *Mode* and [*Mode* model] A.G. for reminding me that I am beautiful (including my belly). (R.G., Houston TX) (*Mode*, March 2000 44)

When looking in *Mode*, I realized something; that you don't have to be thin to be beautiful and sexy! When flipping through your January issue, I saw something that changed my life—a photo of one of your models. I stared at that beautiful woman for a long time with my mouth open. My first thought was, "She is beautiful!" Then I thought, "I am beautiful!" Never in my life have I had these feelings about myself. I could not have asked for a better Christmas gift than this. (A.P., Bloomington, Ind.) (*Mode*, March 2000, 44)

Unlike *Ms.*, *Mode* does not take a "feminist" perspective per se and is not presented as an "alternative" magazine. *Mode*'s glossy paper is like that of any mainstream fashion magazine. The advertisements reflect traditional advertising aesthetics, but also offer more images of "normal" sized women. Indeed, the content, format, and style of *Mode* are much like any other fashion magazine. The articles deal with dating tips, new seasonal styles, a health and fitness section, make-up tips, and bridal pages. The products offered inside are primarily clothing and make-up, with an occasional car or other product ad. *Mode* stresses the fact that all women want to be and can be stylish. The similarity of *Mode* to other magazines means that women can read *Mode* without feeling ostracized from other women. It is not positioned as "other," but as addressing the same concerns other women's magazines have, except for allowing greater diversity of size.

"What a relief" writes: Finally, someone has created a magazine for full-figured women. It has always been a source of great frustration to me that when I shop for clothes for my wife, it's so difficult to find stylish and affordable clothes for her. She is a beautiful woman, and it hurts me to see her agonize over what she can wear. Not anymore! . . . Thanks to your magazine, the "Rubenesque" woman will undoubtedly regain her rightful place. (*Mode*, February 2000, 21)

However, while the rhetoric of anti-sizism is clear and there is a repeated editorial insistence on the dangers of labeling, *Mode* actually does quite a bit of size labeling. Many letters to the editor feature profiles on notable women, and blurbs on the magazine models make some kind of reference to their size, framed usually within a clothing size (14-16 or 22). While, on one hand this reinforces the idea of size as a label, it also projects and speaks what is usually unspoken for women of normal and heavier weights and sizes. Speaking and naming the size as 22 or 18 makes, those sizes seem more acceptable. Yet this also reinforces the idea of women fitting into pre-categorized shapes. This is particularly interesting since the meaning of a "size 14" varies from designer to designer, whose use of different models and cuts when patterning their styles means that a size 14 from one designer may not equal a size 14 from another designer.

However, the tendency to categorize is contradicted by the repeated emphasis on individuality. For example, the cover of *Mode* typically projects the idea that it will offer its readers clothes and products that are designed *for* them, not products that the reader will have to adjust herself to fit. The February 2000 issue features typical headlines: "*Fashion* that fits your *Body* & your *Budget*"; "Bridal Special—Your Wedding, Your Way"; "men we love and men who love us." The *us* implied is either all women or heavy women—note how the distinction between the two is blurred. (The article is actually a two-part story: the first is about popular male stars while the second is about artists whose work depicts heavier models.)

One cover story on *Mode* was on the varying body shapes of *Mode*'s "size 14" models. The article was meant to illustrate the various shapes that bodies can come in even when they wear the same clothing size. However, despite its promotion of diversity, *Mode*'s models are strikingly uniform. The models may be "plus-sized" at a size 14, but they are all well proportioned with long legs and waists, beautiful faces and larger breasts. There are no short squat women, women with short legs, dumpy hips, or large stomachs whose proportions might disrupt the flow of clothing. It is noteworthy that the plus-sized models *Mode* uses, like the 5'10" blond model Emme, are a size 14—a size that is actually average for American women, although the 5'10" height is certainly not. In addition, perhaps as a sign of anti-sizism, or perhaps reflecting old biases, not all the models appearing in *Mode* are plus-sized. A large percentage are standard-sized models. Only a few are heavier than "normal" models. Of these heavier models, none look like what most people would qualify as heavy.

In fact, the March 2000 edition of *Mode* is quite interesting for its lack of thick models. It features profiles on five of the top plus-sized models in the business, including full-page color photos and information and gushing commentary on their good looks. And yet, going through this edition, I was struck that only a very few models look "plus" size. In fact, one of the ads is of Cindy

Crawford for Company by Ellen Tracy. While certainly an anti-sizist campaign means that "normal" models will be included within its pages, it is still questionable why there are so few larger models, and why Crawford, whose presence bespeaks the iron-maiden realm of traditional advertising more thoroughly than any other model ever, should find a home in this particular magazine. While *Mode* features no "waif" models, the vast majority (68) of the ads in this addition featured regular-sized models. Granted, this count is based on my subjective, but not irrational, reading of the definition of "plus" size. It can also be argued that other issues have offered more visions of thicker women. Still, the fact remains that the imagery in *Mode* is not quite as "open" in its presentation of different shapes and sizes as editorial, and reader comments, would initially lead us to believe.

Mode has made efforts to diversify the images of women on its pages in ways other than size. The magazine attempts to incorporate images of women from different races and ethnicities. Many ads feature women of color, predominantly black, but also Asian and Hispanic. Three of the five "supermodels" profiled in the feature article, "Reigning Runway Royalty" were of minority or mixed-ethnic heritage. However, very few ads feature women over 30.

One thing *Mode* does do that sets it apart from other mainstream women's magazines is to run feature articles on real women, many of whom *do* fit into a heavier mold. For example, "Power Movers" (March 2000, 118–22) features five normal to heavier women, in their thirties to fifties, two of whom are minorities. They are photographed in black and white with profiles of their activities. "In the Editor's Seat" likewise features a two-page spread of *Mode*'s editorial staff, standing arm in arm doing a Rockette style kick. The staff photo includes women of varying shapes and ethnicities and even one man, and features blurbs on why they enjoy working at *Mode*. Similarly, "Mode Matters" features photos and blurbs about actresses who are examples that the "*Mode* spirit is spreading." Actresses including Stockard Channing, Sherri Shepard, Kathleen Turner, Drew Barrymore, Kate Winslet, Whoopi Goldberg, Debbie Harry, Aretha Franklin, Marilyn Monroe, and Sophia Loren are depicted. These women were praised either for their heavier appearance or for making public statements supporting weight acceptance. "Mode Matters: Celeb Circuit" features three small photos and blurbs about former *Mode* cover models—Caroline Rhea, Camryn Manheim, Star Jones, Kathy Najimy, and Queen Latifah.

Certainly such articles create a better sense of plurality. However, as our respondent comments and earlier enthusiastic letters to the editor suggest, it is important to note that the actual number of women of different shapes, sizes, and ethnicities may be less important to readers than the fact that *Mode* offers *any* differing images. Given the impassioned reaction by readers, it is worthwhile to examine the codes at play within ads that break with traditional imagery. What is it that causes these ads to stand out and be read in such a positive light?

There is, in fact, little difference between *Mode*'s ads and other mainstream fashion ads. *Mode*'s ads may shift the size of the model used, but otherwise the ads remain the same. The different sizes and shapes of its models remain contextualized within a traditional discourse of individuality and choice.

Mode *and Virginia Slims*

An example of this traditional rhetoric can be found in a Virginia Slims ad appearing in the March 2000 issue of *Mode*. It is a two-page spread featuring an older but thin and noticeably blonde woman, with short-cropped hair and piercingly blue eyes, staring aggressively out at the reader. The copy, placed on the left-hand page, reads: "I look temptation right in the eye and then I make my own decision. Virginia Slims. Find Your Voice." This ad is typical of its kind in that it has coopted the language of feminism, for example, using the feminist image of "voice" as a term of empowerment to sell cigarettes. This woman is so strong that she refuses to run away from her own desires (to smoke), as she looks "temptation" in the eye. She isn't controlled by others (like the medical community or the boring status quo) but makes her own decisions. She doesn't smoke just because it is cool or socially acceptable — she is a rugged individual who is "empowered" enough to *choose* to smoke. Smoking is a sign of her rebellion against those who would silence "her voice," her articulation of her individuality and personal perspective.

The Virginia Slims ad is notable because of the ironic promotion of the use of an addictive drug as a means to achieve female empowerment. However, its rhetoric of individuality and choice is fairly typical of advertising, and, when not contextualized against the selling of cigarettes, seems to connect easily with a "feminist" sensibility.

Just My Size

A series of ads for Just My Size Pantyhose exhibits how *Mode* utilizes similar discourses of individuality and choice associated with the "new woman"

Figure 19. Virginia
Slims.

rhetoric, using standard ideas of femininity, but combining them with alternative body-sizes to create a new discourse of body acceptance.

Many of the newer ads focus on transformation and freedom as meaning not only freedom from others but freedom from the self. Just My Size has created a series of ads that are quite successful in this tactic, titled "Just My Opinion." It's a two-page spread laid out like a magazine poll. The "My" in the title is in bold red, emphasizing the concept of individuality and ownership. The top halves of the two pages feature poll questions and respondent replies, while the bottom sections are an ad for "Lasting Sheer" pantyhose. The lower left shows a color picture of a black woman partially reclining against some pillows with one leg stretched in the air and her hand caressing her leg. She wears a black bra, white pearls, a wedding band on her finger, and pantyhose. She is smiling and looking out at the spectator. Part of her stomach is hidden by her arm and leg, but we can see the fleshy creases around her lower belly, and her legs and partially exposed bottom appear thick. Her skin has a rich brown sheen. Her eyes sparkle. She is glowing. Partially printed across this image are the words "I am the product of a lifetime of learning." The motif of thick red print recurs here, with "I am" printed in larger, bold-faced, red type.

On the right-hand side of the ad the copy continues, reading, "Where I was uptight I am comfortable. Where I was bound I am free. Come on. Loosen up. It's time to change your attitude. It's time to change your pantyhose." The "I am" in all these lines is done in thick red type. "Comfortable" and "pantyhose" are in soft blue and larger type. "Attitude" is in a larger, soft purple type.

The consistent stressing, by size and color, of phrases like "I am" and "my" creates an image of independence and particularity, uniqueness. The

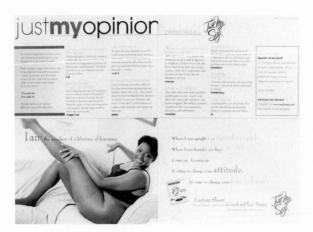

Figure 20. Just My Size (first page).

woman in the ad seems to go against the anti-age aesthetic by stressing the "lifetime of learning"; weight is somehow being associated with knowledge and experience. That experience, as suggested by the wedding ring, includes a man. Her pearls show economic stability.

The use of the words "uptight" and "bound" plays upon two contrasting ideas. The first is the idea of physical restriction. Pantyhose are normally restricting garments, but Lasting Sheer promises to be comfortable and loose. The other idea is of "looseness" as a sign of freedom from restrictions, freedom from conforming to rigid roles (like that of the slender body ideal).

It is interesting that she is clearly posed in a way that is sexual. Half-dressed, she reclines on what appears to be a couch, but there is a blanket that is half pulled off. The fact that it is clearly daytime, the couch, her state of undress, and her provocative pose suggest that she has recently had a noontime sexual rendezvous. Obviously the sight of a large-sized woman being shown in deshabille and posed sexually is new, even for the pages of *Mode*. The idea of "looseness" that the ad urges goes against most traditional ideas of advertising. As was discussed in Chapter 6, most ads urge control over "loose" bodies that threaten to go out of control. The unruly body has sex, eats, and is fat. This Just My Size ad stands in direct contrast, clearly equating a large, lived-in body with sexuality, a romantic life, and comfort.

However, it is interesting that the ad features a large-sized black woman, an image that recalls the stereotype of the mammy—a motherly, fat figure in which the supportive aspects of maternity are embraced. Similarly, the quality of the mammy is one that is wise, all-knowing. It is also perhaps more acceptable to see images of "loose" women in our culture when they are black, since racial stereotypes have it that black women's sexuality is more out of control than white women's. Yet the cultured pearls around her neck seem to explicitly work against these ideas, suggesting middle class economic stability. Similarly, the setting of the ad suggests luxurious comfort. The couch is white with an attractive cover, while the background is white and blurry but suggests the sunny openness of a house or large apartment. In this respect, her sexuality is somewhat contained, while her knowing, comforting quality is enhanced.

The power of this image, particularly for those of us who have not seen our images represented, cannot be overlooked. As seen in previous chapters, the psycho-sexual rejection of many fat women, the exclusion from "normalcy," is a powerful thing. Exclusion means that not only is one different—but in an odd way one is less than human. A fat woman loses her right to sexuality—the very thing that supposedly defines her as a woman. If she cannot appeal sexually, she loses the right not only to representation, but to things like sex, men, a home, and family. The image of a thicker woman in this ad is revolutionary in that it not only (partly) reveals a heavy body, but suggests the sexuality of a heavy body. Moreover, it associates fat bodies with not negativity or low self-esteem, but high self-esteem.

Of course, if feminists are fighting against the objectification of woman, why might it be desirable to objectify large women any more than thin women? The difference is in the right to be seen as a sexual object. Ads gain their meaning from their relationship to other ads as well as their relationship to the larger world. As Sut Jhally (1990) has observed, there is nothing inherently bad about visual objectification. It is part of human nature to objectify and to want to be objectified at times. The evaluation of that objectification as positive or negative comes from the image's relationship to other images in a system. In a sign system in which female sexuality and objectification is a sign of female success, the absence of objectified fat women as sexual means that they are symbolically annihilated from being seen as sexual beings. And, in not being shown as sexual objects, fat women lose the right to be seen as laying claim to the privileges of that objectification—love, marriage, children, and other aspects of "feminine" success. It is noteworthy that most of the ads in the campaign lack even this watered down seductive quality.

For example, in another Just My Size ad the left-hand page shows a white, young to middle-aged woman walking down a country road, smiling out at the reader. She is cropped off slightly at the head and just above the knees, giving the impression that her body is expanding off into space. Her appearance is casual. She stands with her hands in her pockets, and wears a sweatshirt over a white T-shirt and string-tied casual pants. Placed over her left breast the copy reads "I am a woman you know." The copy continues to the right-hand page, where it reads: "I am a woman you love. I am, quite possibly, you. I am unique, special, extraordinary, rare. I am truth and beauty in a perfect 14. And I am above average in every way but size. "Love," "unique," "perfect 14" and "size" are all in larger type and blue and purple print. "I am" is once again in larger type and printed in red.

Still another Just My Size ad features a coupon and a contest to win a free cruise. It features a woman on the left-hand page whose arms are raised triumphantly and open wide. She is on a beach with a cruise boat in the distance. Her smiling, open-mouthed face is also raised to the sky. Once again, she is cropped off just above the knees while one of her arms and part of her hand extend beyond the page. She wears casual clothes: jeans, with a white, button-down shirt blowing open behind her. The focal point is her bright yellow T-shirt over curvaceous breasts. Again, the copy is printed over the focal point of her breasts, it reads: "I am reserving my place in the sun." The Just My Size logo floats slightly above the copy. The type "I am" is written in large, bold-faced red type. The play of the yellow shirt with the idea of sun is clear. Once again, the idea of individuality, of proclaiming existence and subjectivity, is clear with "I am." Women's right to take up space as well as to be successful and happy is evoked with the idea of "reserving their place in the sun."

It must be noted that the presentation of women and their words in these ads seems to be formed as a reply, a response to unspoken ideas. Given our cultural context, we know what these ideas are: fat women hate themselves, are ugly, lazy, imperfect, and unlovable. The ad's copy almost hysterically refutes this notion of the fat woman as being unhappy or unbalanced. "I am the product of a lifetime of learning." Such a phrase would not be used in an ad selling a thin woman pantyhose, since her status as a learner would be irrelevant. It is as if Just My Size is desperately searching for positive things to say. Rather than concentrating on the benefits of a particular product, the ad appears to be arguing for the *right* of fat women to exist.

Is this revolutionary, or is it condescending? It is necessary to remember that media texts are always contradictory. They may be one thing at the same time they are something else entirely. There are two very different possibilities for interpreting these ads. First, the very phrase "Just *My* Size" suggests an unfortunate separation in which the *my*, the body of the fat woman, is separated from the common mass of other woman. She is thus unlike other woman, not because of the neutral qualities of being a product of a lifetime of learning (which everybody really is), but because of her needing hose in *her* size. It recalls the language of special education in which the term "special needs" children is just a way of proclaiming their difference from other children, rather than their similarities.

Again, this is a meaning formed by context. Just as the meanings of what it means to be an individual change when applied to men as opposed to women, so do they change when dealing with people outside the norm. For those in the "norm" to begin with, messages of individuality and uniqueness create a sense that the individual is moving above and beyond, For those outside the norm, the rhetoric of individuality, as seen here in Just My Size, is a rhetoric that works only to bring them up to the level of the norm. They are not above and beyond, but finally only on the same level as the "norm."

In contrast, it can equally be argued that Just My Size campaign offers its audience images of women that directly confront ideas of women as lacking subjectivity. They feature an attitude that heavily promotes ideas of individualism, physical freedom, and choice. This is not itself an unusual tactic; most ads do this. However, in contrast to many ads discussed in previous chapters, the Just My Size campaign place notions of individuality in a slightly different context, suggesting that the women are already there. These ads feature images of happy women who are happy because they already possess the right attitude. Such a woman's subjectivity will not be created by the use of a new product. Her subjectivity will occur when she recognizes she already has it. Obviously in a culture and an advertising standard that continually urge women to take up less space and control their desires, these Just My Size ads are radical in that they present an idea of the woman as being already complete.

Resistant Encoding: NARAL Ads

At least one series of ads work, not by distancing themselves from the concepts of individuality utilized by most advertisers, but, curiously, by coopting them: reframing messages of individuality, placing them in a new context in a way that does work for feminist goals. These advertising campaigns may be read as interventions in that they consciously deal with the female body as a contested terrain over which political and ideological battles are fought.

In the mainstream media, we often see the female body being depicted as a sexualized object. As an object, of course, female bodies lose subjectivity and individuality. The attitude that fosters this dehumanization of the female body is accompanied by and linked to attitudes in which the female becomes separated from her body. Depicting women as dehumanized objects removes their subjectivity, their capacity to be seen as individuals and to make individual choices. If the female body is an object to be enjoyed and controlled by others, then the female herself has no right to her body, no right to control her body against the advances of others, no right to sexual pleasure in her own body, and particularly no right to control her reproductive choices.

Obviously, there is a give-and-take relationship between cultural attitudes toward women's right to control their own bodies and their media presentations. Recent pro-choice ads have chosen a very interesting approach to transmitting their message. The NARAL (National Abortion and Reproductive Rights Action League) Choice for America campaign (1999) coopts the rhetoric and discourses of the right wing and pro-life factions. These ads frame reproductive rights as being intrinsically linked to "American" values of individuality and freedom. They also coopt the language of faith and responsibility frequently used in pro life rhetoric. By using these tactics, NARAL promotes female subjectivity at the same time the body is presented for examination, asking us to reconsider meanings of that bodily representation.

NARAL strategically uses imagery that presents America as made up of a group of individuals from all walks of life. For example, one radio ad features a "monologue" in which each line is delivered by a different voice, suggesting a range of speakers of different races and genders. It features both male and female voices.

We the people. We the people. We the people. Live in the land of the free. We live in a country founded on freedom. Freedom of speech. Freedom to vote. Freedom to choose my faith. Freedom to choose what's right for me. My family. My life. My body. We the people. Have fought for this freedom. To make sure that every pregnancy is wanted. And every woman is blessed with health and reproductive freedom. We will protect this freedom against, violence, harassment and intimidation. It's not always easy. But we live in the home of the brave. Understand and protect your right to choose. . . . The choice is yours to decide. The choice is yours to keep.

Like Nike ads, this NARAL ad plays with themes of individuality and concepts of individual freedom as essential "American" qualities. It also explicitly references the battles that Americans have fought, equating the pro-choice position with protection against the "invasion" of foreign forces. This is typical right wing rhetoric used against the perceived threat of forces that would "invade" and take over the "American" way of life—such as the Russians. The ad appeals to the history of the American military by evoking images of battle and bravery and America as a nation of fighters.

The use of the word "blessed" is telling. It presents freedom as a "natural" gift and also suggests that NARAL is articulating a religious view. In contrast to those who would argue that abortion is a godless act, the ad suggests not only that God exists, but that God sanctions abortion and NARAL is the correct interpreter of God's wishes. The appeal to the pro-life ideal of protecting life is twisted as the ad references social responsibility as including concern for the wellbeing of woman and child.

Much of the ad presents images of basic American beliefs that most people would agree with, such as free speech and religion. The use of multiple voices evokes inclusion, plurality, and the idea of the melting pot. It recalls the fact that the United States is made up of immigrants who came to America to have freedom, religious as well as economic. The inclusion of male voices changes abortion from being a "woman's" issue to one that is intrinsically connected with every American's right to individual civil liberties and our unspoken but ubiquitous notions of citizenship. It is only at the end of the ad, by now thoroughly framed within the context of this traditional rhetoric, that a pro-choice statement is revealed.

Of course radio is a medium in which sound, not sight, is the primary means of communication. The acoustic nature of radio helps divorce abstract issues like freedom and independence from the body. By removing the messy, problematic body from sight, the groundedness of the battle, the fact that it has to do with flesh and blood bodies (both of women and of the fetus) is diminished. The issue becomes abstracted. Language assumes primary importance, while the sign of women's subjugation (the messy reproductive, sexual, objectified body) becomes absent from this discourse. How, then, does NARAL deal with the medium of television, in which the hiding of the body becomes impossible?

There are several interesting ads that highlight the techniques used by NARAL to circumnavigate the traditional signification of women's bodies. For example, one 1999 NARAL ad features a montage of women of different races and ages and in different activities. Images of women in action, families, and close-ups of women's faces are juxtaposed against a sound track of the song "America" and a voiceover monologue delivered by a young to middle-aged woman. A shot by shot analysis of how this ad constructs its message is worthwhile here.

The voiceover states:

I believe there's a reason we were born with free will. And I have a strong will to decide what's best for my body. My mind. And my life. I believe in myself. In my intelligence. In my integrity, my judgment. And I accept full responsibility for the decisions I make. I believe in my right to choose. Without interrogations, without indignities, without violence. I believe that's one of the founding principles of our country. And I believe that right is being threatened. The greatest of human freedoms is choice. And I believe that no one has the right to take that freedom away. (NARAL 1999)

Visually, the ad starts with a long shot of a family, against the background of the desert. They are in the lower right hand corner of the screen framed by landscape. The landscape, gray and expansive, dominates the screen. The effect of the powerful majesty of nature is enhanced by rolling clouds, which move swiftly overhead. They are filmed with time elapse photography, a technique that emphasizes the tumultuous power of the clouds at the same time it contrasts to the stillness of the family and the landscape. The visual effect is one of timelessness, that despite the constant changes and progress of time, two constants remain: the rugged, unspoiled wilderness and the American family.

The ad crosscuts to a close up of a woman's face as she turns her head slightly to look towards the camera. She is positioned off center, on the right hand-side of the screen, with part of her face off camera. The camera angle is low so that the viewer appears to be looking slightly up at her; her image is one of power and strength. The next crosscut is a long shot of a child (whose gender is unclear), running down a desert road in slow motion. The child is in the center of the screen and moves directly towards the viewer. Once again time lapse photography is used to speed up the movement of the clouds in the background, and the child is dominated by the vast, harsh landscape.

The next crosscut reveals two young women, again in slow motion, climbing a mountain, followed by a cut to a close-up of an Asian woman. Cut to a low-angle shot of two climbers on mountain pinnacle staring triumphantly into the distance. Crosscut to a close-up of a middle-aged white woman with shadowy figures moving in the background; it appears to be an office setting. The next crosscut places the viewer in the interior of a car as it passes by an African American female construction worker. Once again, the scene is in slow motion and filmed from a low camera angle. The next cut reveals a three-quarter view close-up, from a low angle, of a young to middle-aged black woman who is looking off into the distance. In the background a flag is flying. This suggests that she is part of moving moment, reflecting upon or being part of some moment of patriotic reverence. The next shot is a slow motion view of a white woman in a business suit striding toward us in the center of the screen. Other office workers scurry by, but she continues straight on her path, her direction and pace undisturbed by their presence. She passes by an American flag on her left. The scene suggests the woman's comfort and capability in the office setting, and her presence as successful businessperson.

The next scene features a bust shot of a young white couple smiling. The crosscut is a long shot that reveals the couple standing with their children in front of their house, a "typical" middle class American family with two children. Family themes continue in the next scene, in which a middle-aged woman is pushing her daughter on her bike. The camera zooms in slightly then cuts to a shot of the woman's hands as she releases her grip on the daughter and the daughter sails away. Cut a medium shot of the woman clasping her hands and smiling joyfully and tearfully as she watches her daughter. Cut to a wide angle shot that shows the mother watching from behind as her daughter rides toward the camera.

The next shot reveals a woman, dressed in a hospital gown, sitting in a doctor's office. The setting dwarfs her and the camera dollies in toward her. Zooms create a sense of an object moving outward; dollies bring the camera and viewer closer to the object. This is the only scene in the ad in which the camera moves. Unlike other women in the ad, who do the *moving*, she is being oppressed, her space encroached upon by the invading camera. Interestingly, the second time we cut to this woman coincides with the line "being threatened."

Next there is a cut to a long shot of a woman diving from a high board into a pool. Cut to an underwater shot of a woman's body breaking surface, then cut to a medium shot as the woman swims toward the camera. The ad crosscuts to a medium shot of a woman's head above water as she turns to look toward the camera, then to a long shot that recalls the imagery of "American Gothic." An elderly couple sit in chairs in front of their house and barn, flanking an American flag blowing at full mast. A close-up of the white, older man filmed from a low angle follows as we hear the line, "I believe that's one of the founding principles of our country." This scene recalls imagery of the family farm, previous generations, and the founders of the country. It suggests that the founding "fathers," white men, who, like this old man, worked in the past to support individual freedoms, still do so today. The next shot is a medium shot of the elderly couple with the American flag waving above.

The next scenes feature a variety of close-ups of women, cutting from a white woman, again shot from a long angle, back to the woman in the hospital, to a medium shot of a black woman, to an extreme close-up of a young white woman. The next cut moves to a close-up of the elderly farmwife, then a cut to another African American woman. A crosscut follows revealing two girls, an African American and an Asian, who wear track uniforms and are standing with their arms around each other. This scene recalls not only female physicality and the rise of females in sports but suggests cross-racial friendships.

The ad concludes by returning to imagery similar to that of its beginning. The second-to-the-last shot returns us to the desert landscape. A windmill on the left-hand side stands over another family group as the clouds again race by. The crosscut is to a medium shot of a small group that consists of a bearded old man, a young man, and two young to middle-aged woman who stand with their arms around two children. One child is clearly a girl; the gender of the other child, who appears to be the one who was running in the desert earlier, is unclear. There is another cut to a close-up of an older white woman. Once again, this woman is off center, with her body extending out past the frame. The final cut is to a black screen with the words "What's freedom without choice?" printed in white.

This ad plays with several ideas that draw upon traditional right wing rhetoric and imagery. First, the ad plays with notions of individuality and American freedom. The notion of "free will" recalls typical Protestant religious sensibilities and the founding of the United States as based on religious freedom as well as the desire for self-government. In contrast to the notion that women who get abortions are "irresponsible" and uncaring about the welfare of others, the voice over states that responsibility occurs in the act of *choosing*, rather than in the final decision.

The visual imagery utilized by the ad is also interesting. Plurality is a common theme. The multiple images of the montage sequence call to mind the idea of the American "melting pot." The melting pot was formed by the immigration of people from all over the world, typically presented as coming to America to escape from oppression and persecution or in search of a better economic situation. It recalls the "American dream" that an individual from any background can, through strength of will, rise in social standing.

Visually, this ad is very interesting in the way its imagery reinforces notions of individuality and echoes themes of the American dream and social and family responsibility. In an interesting way, female bodies are fetishized. But it is done in a way that works to emphasize their unique, singular, impervious individuality—much like the figure of the cowboy hero in Zane Grey Westerns. The ad consistently juxtaposes close-ups of female and male faces with scenes of bodies in motion and bodies placed against a landscape. The entire ad is filmed in slow motion and tinted as if the film were slightly overexposed. This technique gives the images a gritty yet glowing quality.

As in the radio ad, there is a sense of plurality. The wide variety of faces creates a sense of a melting pot, as well as a shared subjectivity. While many of the faces are of women, several male faces are included. Thus, the issue of freedom is not a "woman" issue, but one that also concerns men. In addition, the close-ups of faces are always shot from a low angle. The viewer is put into a slightly inferior position to the person being viewed. The women are often slightly out of frame, caught turning toward the viewer. This breaks with the static position of woman as object. When the woman is placed slightly out of the frame, her body extends beyond the frame of the camera—she continues on, into space beyond the viewer's gaze. Thus, though we see her in close-up she resists being pinned by the gaze. Similarly, the turning body conveys a sense of moving out into space. The women in these close ups are often look-ing at the viewer, returning the gaze, a move which in music videos is said to refute the male gaze (Kaplan 1989).

Other women in the ad are shown in motion—engaged in activities, like hiking, swimming, or playing with children. Their physicality works against traditional representations of women as passive. The two hiking girls are shown on a mountain pinnacle. Again, we see them from below. Their posi-tioning recalls imagery of triumphant explorers who have conquered nature and physical hardships and climbed to the top of Everest.

The scenes featuring the mother releasing her daughter projects an all-American image of a nurturing mother. It calls upon the heavily used imagery of Americans doing battle for freedom, not only for themselves but for the protection of future generations. This again connects to military imagery in which mothers sent sons off to protect the rights of others. It calls upon not only the idea of letting one's children grow up to be responsible, productive citizens who are self-reliant and able to make their own choices, but also the imagery of "letting go," of relinquishing control over others, as a caring, nur-turing act. The sacrifices of past Americans to ensure the future is similarly referenced by the elderly couple seated in front of the flag. The presence of the flag waving at full mast in many of these scenes similarly reinforces imagery of "America" that is tied to battles.

Not least in importance is the way that the ad treats the body. For example, in many of the scenes we see individuals or groups of people being presented against the landscape. Again, this recalls several American myths, such as the American individual as an explorer in the wilderness, someone who came and conquered nature. It recalls pilgrims and pioneers and their struggle to settle the land in order to have their freedom. It also recalls ideas of the American Western cowboy hero. The hero who has a unique relationship to the natural landscape is a mythic bedrock of American culture. In Westerns, the hero is often equated to the landscape. Like the rugged terrain, the hero is rugged, wild, and untamed (Tompkins 1992).

Similarly, this NARAL ad begins and closes with shots of a group of people set against a landscape. The running figure of the child through the desert is echoed by the little girl riding her bike toward the camera. Not only are they linked to this vast, limitless landscape, but their motion, which threat-ens to crash into the viewer and move beyond the frame of the camera, hints at limitless possibilities, at a movement into the future and the progress of future generations.

There is an interesting play with images of time occurring. The ad is filmed in such a way that the sense of immanence, of being in the moment, is extended, even fetishized, thus connecting to a sense of timelessness, of infinity. For example, the movements of all the people are in slow motion. Every physical gesture is slowed down, from running to diving. Every head turn and every blink thus become emphasized and exaggerated. Simultaneously, however, time is collapsed. In every scene with a background, the clouds are moving as with time-lapse, so it seems as if the clouds are rushing overhead and time is flying by. On one hand we have the flying by of time, on the other an intense visual fascination with the small physical, momentary gesture. Individuality bleeds into a sense of infinity, fusing the momentary into the timeless. The transitory, passing nature of physicality is transcended and becomes linked to infinity, the future as well as the past. The blurring of time is further enhanced by the use of the montage, which moves back and forth from images of the young to the old to the middle aged. This recalls the narrative link from past battles, to the current situation, to the future of our coming generations.

This "timeless" quality is further enhanced by the use of color and the overexposed quality of many of the images. The ad's gritty, overexposed appearance is not realistic, but instead seems hyperrealistic at the same time it signals a break with reality. Color works to create a sense of a time outside time in which the visual world is heightened—whites become whiter, dark colors are grayed down, colors are tinged to create at times an almost water color effect. Color in these ads moves beyond a "realistic" representation and heightens the visual importance of what we're seeing.

In this ad, the visual fetishization of the moment, through camera work, slow motion and time lapse techniques, and color, does something else. It *heightens* the importance of the body at the same time it strengthens the female body. After all, it is not the use of the body as a photographic object that is harmful to women—men, after all, are regularly photographed without losing their subjectivity. The different interpretations of these images are informed not only by the differing cultural connotations in which they are perceived but by the *way* in which their bodies are filmed. Male bodies, even when filmed in a slightly fetishistic manner, as they are in action movies and Westerns (Tasker 1995; Tompkins 1992), inspire different cultural connotations about their owners, relative power and penetrability than do images of women (Bordo 1999). One reason that male subjectivity is reinforced is that they are always *more* than their bodies.

Similarly, in this NARAL ad, the body becomes linked to a sense of eternity, infinity, and always-existing values. By this means, the body becomes imbued with an overdetermination of meaning connected to individuality. In this way we have moved from the body as object to the body as a sign of individuality—of movement and identity bursting beyond restraint. This visual technique is one that has been found in other media forms which represent the female body in new and different ways, such as the female action hero (Heinecken 1999).

This imagery has been carefully crafted to appeal to people from all political positions. While most Republicans may be against a lot of Democratic reforms, many would agree that women have the right to work and be independent. The NARAL ads are quite clever, coopting the language and imagery of NARAL'S adversaries. The rhetoric of motherly love as both protective and encouraging of self-reliance is one that appeals to all sides of the political spectrum, as does the American mythology of the successful individual. The ads also work to create a sense of timelessness—that the values NARAL supports are natural, "blessed" by God, and eternal.

In recent years, advertisers seem to have recognized that women are tired of being presented with uniform, unrealistic visions of the "ideal" woman. As a result, they have created campaigns that on one hand seem to address women's concerns, while on the other hand offer only "a wink" toward women. The wink is a way of addressing the audience, suggesting that social equality for women has already been achieved. However, closer examination reveals that the wink is one way that traditionally conservative ideals are recycled into a more palatable "feminist" or progressive framework, while in fact achieving no real significant change in how women are represented.

Nonetheless, there are an increasing number of media forms that seem to be seriously trying to present more positive images of women. *New Moon* magazine is an example of a publication that works to promote positive feelings of self-esteem and a sense of community for girls. *Mode* magazine presents itself as an "anti-sizist" fashion magazine. While *Mode* often fails to present truly progressive images, it has been somewhat successful in normalizing some images, like those of large-size women, that have previously been outside the dominant frame. The success of such ads can at least partly be measured by letters to *Mode*'s editor that consistently express the joy readers feel at finally recognizing themselves in ads. However, one possible reason for the success of *Mode*'s ads is that there is really very little difference between them and mainstream ads. The different sizes and shapes of *Mode's* models, no matter how revolutionary, remain contextualized within a traditional discourse of individuality and choice.

Such rhetoric has, however, been co-opted by at least one ad campaign that is truly revolutionary and progressive, consciously dealing with the female body as a site where political and ideological battles are fought. Like *Mode* ads, NARAL's recent campaign reinforces notions of individuality. Its use of camera work, slow motion, and color fetishizes the female body, but does it in a way that emphasizes the body's unique, singular, and seemingly impervious qualities. Recalling the way that men's bodies have been glorified in western and action films, the women of the NARAL ads always seem to be more than their bodies, imbued with an overdetermination of meaning connected to individuality. In this way NARAL ads present the female body as a sign of subjectivity, tying their imagery to a truly feminist goal.

9. Final Thoughts

Feminist writers in scholarly and popular venues have argued persuasively that when viewed cumulatively media images that promote an unattainable beauty standard as an ideal for *all* women contribute to harmful effects upon gender relations and hopes for gender equality. On a societal level, the ubiquity of the "perfect" female form and, more specifically, the objectification of the female body, has been linked to social pathologies such as sexual harassment, subordination in the workplace, and rape. This body objectification of women has also been linked to such psychological pathologies as eating disorders, obsessive dieting and low self-esteem among women.

This book has explored a particular, complex relationship between the idealized images of gender we see in advertising and the everyday thoughts, feelings, and behaviors of men and women in relation to those images. The goal was to better understand different links between gender, media, and culture. It is now clear that advertising does play a significant part in the way gender roles, relationships, and identities are continuously assigned and reproduced in this culture. It is my hope that a clearer understanding of how both men and women, but women especially, live with advertising and give meanings to these messages will yield insight into how unhealthy and socially unproductive relationships with advertising images can be changed.

Gender and Decoding

In the preceding chapters we have explored how men and women experience particular images that saturate our daily media: advertising images of idealized female bodies. Granted, women are much more affected by and involved with these images than are men, and this research was not intended as a direct comparison of male and female reactions to particular ads. Instead, this book seeks to understand what part gender plays in how these *common* yet often *destructive* images of women are decoded by real people. Those participating in this study revealed not only their reactions to particular ads, but also how advertising has had an impact on the way they see themselves as gendered human beings and what effects their relationships with advertising have had on their thoughts, emotions, and behaviors across their lifetimes.

This study found that male responses to idealized female bodies in advertising are generally framed in terms of compliance to dominant prescriptions of gender in advertising content, the male gaze, and male looking in advertising, personally and in society. Men rarely "negotiated" with dominant images or prescriptions of femininity. When not in compliance with these dominant prescriptions of gender and dominant ways of seeing and looking, males in this study offered stark oppositions to these dominant messages.

When male participants gave dominant readings of the image of the new working woman, they were demonstrating that their comfort level and familiarity with ideal femininity was not confined to traditional representations, but was elastic enough to accommodate the incorporation of new, "progressive" images. However, this comfort level seemed to reach its limits with the alternative aesthetic of the female runner. Male respondents insisted on reading this image through the dominant conventions so easily applied to the image of the new working woman, conventions with which they were most familiar. Therefore, this alternative image of the female runner was generally deemed unattractive.

A definitive concept in male comfort levels with dominant images of gender is *distance*. Boys and men in this society possess a certain psychological distance from these dominant images. For the women in this study, the need to negotiate with or accommodate an image is generally indicative of a close psychological connection to it. Men rarely felt this kind of connection. For example, responses from the gay male perspective offered an interesting mix of opposition and compliance. Although extremely oppositional in his responses to dominant gender messages in advertising and larger society about heterosexual lifestyles, Camron's description of looking at potential romantic interests gave all indications of compliance with seeing through the male gaze.

The distinguishing feature of female responses to advertising with perfect female bodies depicted were ongoing negotiations with and accommodations of dominant images of ideal femininity. The women in this study were involved in ongoing struggles to achieve psychological distance from these images and the dominant messages about gender that these images help to promote throughout society. Women were extremely aware that the address of dominant images of gender was male-defined, and therefore, female spectatorship always implied a comparison between the image and themselves.

The particular moments of compliance with dominant images of femininity in female responses were very specific. For example, women in this study have internalized a hate of fat. Whether the reference to fat applies to themselves or to others, fat was seen as something to loathe and to fear. Other moments of compliance for female respondents showed up in responses to the image of motherhood in advertising. Motherhood was read as good, wholesome, a sign of positive family values. Overall, the vision of young motherhood presented in the Pier 1 ad (Figure 5), for example, was accepted by women, for the most part, as unproblematic, as "natural."

The particular moments of departure or opposition to dominant images of idealized femininity by female participants were equally specific. In the context of this analysis, perhaps the most outstanding of these moments was when several women reported that their families, and most specifically, their mothers, had served as competing influences for them against the messages in advertisements from a very early age. These women were spared much of the journey of negotiation traveled by the majority of the women in this study in relation to these images, as we saw so intimately in Elizabeth's story.

Another example of a moment of departure was when the female respondents in this study embraced the alternative aesthetic of the female runner as a positive "break" in dominant representation. The act of enjoying the ad itself was not oppositional, after all, Nike was trying to break with convention. However, the reasons these women gave for embracing this image *were* moments of opposition. Women found the image of the female runner to be a positive alternative aesthetic *because* it defies dominant, male-defined conventions of femininity in advertising. Furthermore, female respondents defined this image as alternative because it pictures a woman in the process of achieving health and fitness, not as the posed product, or result of fitness.

Moments of complete opposition by female participants to images of ideal femininity in ads were relatively rare. Instead, female negotiation with these images permeates most of the female discourse about advertising. Women do achieve a certain psychological distance when describing and identifying dominant gender images and relations, but they can rarely maintain that critical distance when they apply what they have identified or named to their personal experiences.

Female negotiations with dominant images of femininity intensify when emphasis is placed on how women see themselves as the subjects of (or the audience for) these images. Women possessed a very strong and clear sense of themselves as the objects of male looking in all aspects of their lives. Women respondents actively attributed their own internalization of this disciplining stare of the male gaze to their feelings of insecurity and self-loathing and their almost unconscious obsession with disciplining their bodies. For most women, the journeys from moments of compliance to moments of resistance with dominant images of ideal femininity are riddled with continuous struggles. These struggles usually take the form of negotiations because, when women view images of other women in this society, no matter how pleasant that viewing experience is, they are seeing the standard by which their own strengths and weaknesses will be judged.

What Can Change?

How can our relationship to the idealized image in advertising and across the media change? Sometimes the situation seems hopeless. Every time women make significant social strides, such as breaking the glass ceiling of middle management, advertising sells our achievement back to us, depoliticized and overfeminized. "You've Come a Long Way, Baby, have a cigarette and show a little more cleavage for the camera." However, there are many lessons to be gleaned from our participants in this study about how our relationship to ads might change. The women who reported that the images of women in ads had not affected them all that much growing up attributed this to the messages their families consistently gave them about being three-dimensional beings. Their families constantly gave them messages that appearance was only one small part of what they were as human beings. One question is, what if this powerful socialization process was not left solely up to the family? Could early day-care providers, church school teachers, and elementary teachers be educated in how the often subtle messages given differently to girls and boys about their bodies can serve to fuel the fire always and already lit by the media? We need to identify all the most influential social structures of a child's early life, and try to become cognizant of what messages children are receiving about their gendered bodies. If too much emphasis is being placed on appearance for the girls, the situation needs to be changed.

Media Literacy

Altering the relationship of the audience member to the message is another change that must occur. Media literacy courses are very appropriate for the elementary school level and beyond. But the reality is that most students don't experience any kind of media literacy training until college, and most college campuses do not include such courses in the general education requirements. There are competing schools of thought about what media literacy is and what a media literacy curriculum should look like. However, at the National Leadership Conference on Media Literacy held in 1992, participating scholars and policy makers agreed upon the following definitions: "Media literacy is the ability to access, analyze, evaluate and communicate messages in a variety of forms." Media literate people, therefore, "can decode, evaluate, analyze, and produce both print and electronic media" (Christ and Potter 1998, 7–8). Furthermore, most conceptualizations of media literacy include the following elements: "Media are constructed and construct reality; media have commercial implications; media have ideological and political implications; form and content are related to each medium, each of which has a unique aesthetic, codes, and conventions, and receivers negotiate meaning in media (7–8).

Sut Jhally and Justin Lewis propose a cultural studies approach when explaining that "media literacy should be about helping people to become sophisticated citizens rather than sophisticated consumers." They advocate media literacy programs that do much more than teach students to analyze media messages. "To appreciate the significance of contemporary media, we need to know why they are produced, under what constraints and conditions and by whom" (1998, 111).

A feminist media studies approach to media literacy shares the concerns of a cultural studies approach especially as explained by Robert Kubey. This approach takes audience pleasures of media seriously as well as audience sense-making of particular viewing experiences. In this approach the unifying concern would be around representations of gender and sexual stereotypes, "with the purpose of 'denaturalizing' the media" (1998, 64). One of the major goals of such a curriculum would be deconstructing how the media impart particular cultural values, such as women's subordination to men.

In this media-saturated society all citizens need to be media literate. The media should no longer be seen as outside serious scholarly pursuits or serious curricula in schools. Media are indeed one of the most influential social educators we have and they begin educating us as young as two or three years of age.

Media Watchdogs

Advertisers respond to a loss in revenue much more quickly than to accusations of sexism. Media watchdog groups such as Adbusters, based in Vancouver, and Media Action Alliance, based in Minnesota, have used different approaches to try to show up particularly sexist and misogynistic ad campaigns. In many cases they were successful in getting the campaign dropped or getting the sponsor to pull their advertising money from the magazine or television program. A major goal of *Adbusters* magazine is to link the commercial world and ecological disaster (Savan 1994). The magazine participates in "subvertising" — "an ad is not merely attacked but elements of its own campaign are twisted and used against it. This might take the form of guerrilla ads or political art—or art that looks like ads" (316). The most notable *Adbusters* anti-campaign was against Absolut vodka. "Seeing alcoholism where Absolut sees sales, the ad pictures a coffin with the headline 'Absolut Silence,' and in tiny print adds, 'The birthdays, graduation, and wedding day . . . We were there to toast them all. So from one great spirit to another, here's to the most enduring ritual of all" (Savan 1994, 317).

Media Action Alliance does not attempt to produce counter-advertising messages, but instead is committed to the media literacy of women and men and the power of boycotting ad campaigns that are sexist and demeaning to women. The group's brochure lists their goals as the following:

• Act as an educator by providing the community with a speaker's bureau and a forum for discussing how images of women in the media impact attitudes and behavior.
• Act as a watchdog group by identifying and collecting examples of negative, as well as positive media.
• Act as a research group by finding out who is responsible for reaping profits from harmful media and who allows the objectification of women to continue.
• Act as a disseminator of information by publishing our findings with action steps in our newsletter to members and other organizations.
• Act as a social change agent by providing individuals and groups with all the information and tools they need to make an impact.

In 1997 Media Action Alliance targeted the sponsors of the *Sports Illustrated* annual swimsuit edition. They encouraged citizens who were offended by the annual spectacle to target individual advertisers with a goal to boycott *SI* and the swimsuit edition in particular. Media Action Alliance (1997) provided easy-to-use postcards with the heading: "Reminder: Women Are Human Beings." As a result of the watchdog campaign, Reebok decided to pull its endorsement of the swimsuit issue in 1998 and in the future. Over thirteen other companies were contacted. Many suggested in their responses that a discontinuation of their endorsement of the swimsuit issue would be taken under serious consideration.

The Media Action Alliance also provides the following "Guidelines for Advertisers":

Negative/Destructive Elements in Advertising
1. Does my ad contain threats of violence, either subtle or blatant? Does it promote violence as glamorous, seductive and/or desirable?
2. Are individuals portrayed in my ad as sexual ornamentation or the product rather than intelligent, informed persons?
3. Is the woman in my advertisement portrayed by parts or portions of her body, or treated as an object, rather than a complete person?
4. Does my ad play on people's insecurities about their roles, such as their adequacy at parenting or on their insecurities about their bodies' size, shape or age?
5. Are women shown in positions subordinate to, or as being subservient to men, by placement or implied role?
6. Are women of color portrayed in harmful and/or limiting stereotypical roles?
7. Are the women in my ad neurotically obsessed with household cleanliness?
8. Is a single person shown as being an incomplete person?
9. Are the women in my ad incapable of, or confused about financial decisions?
10. Do the women in my ads appear threatening or predatory?
11. Are the items strictly differentiated between boys' and girls', implying that they are intended for use by one sex only?
12. Does my ad trivialize the status or efforts of professional women?
13. Are female children shown in makeup and/or attire that is more appropriate for adult females or vice versa?
14. Are elderly women portrayed in dowdy, out-of-date clothing which contributes to an image of foolish uselessness?

Positive and Constructive Elements in Advertising
1. Do my ads reflect the fact that women achieve success in careers traditionally considered to be male domain?
2. Do I include in my ads older people, people of color, people of all sizes, and are they portrayed in a constructive (non-stereotypical) manner?
3. Does my ad show women, children, and men sharing the responsibilities of maintaining a household?
4. Does my ad reflect the fact that a growing percentage of American families are headed by a single parent?
5. Are standards for physical appearance for people in my ads the same for men as for women?
6. Are women and men portrayed as people who are capable of relating to one another other than sexually (being friends, companions and/or co-workers)? (Media Action Alliance 1997).

I believe the guidelines speak to all of us—educators, students, parents, media producers, media consumers, and citizens of this culture. They could be called "questions we can ask in place of: how do we measure up?"

Changes in the Visual Landscape

Many people say the recent improvement in representation of women in advertising is the result of more women in the ad industry. While more women enter the advertising industry each year it is important to caution against the assumption of a the direct cause and effect relationship. Not all female doctors have good bedside manners and not all female ad executives are feminists. After all, we are all socialized into particular cultural ways of seeing. For most people in creative fields, these stock images of objectified female bodies continue to play themselves out consciously and subconsciously.

There are exceptions, however, that do show the power of bringing a feminist sensibility to a successful advertising campaign directed at women. Jane Champ was the writer behind the Nike campaigns for women between 1990 and 1996. The campaigns—"Did You Ever Wish You Were a Boy," "Falling in Love in Six Acts," and "If You Let Me Play Ball"—offer interventions in the traditional fabric of female representation. They do not merely "wink" toward women, they speak to women and to girls. A *Mirabella* magazine article on Champ asks the question that in many ways informs this book: Isn't this all about selling a pair of shoes? Yes, but what if the message got through to dads and boys and teachers and moms, as well as to the girls themselves? What if Champ's words really do help us reshape our self-image into one of power and self-acceptance? What if they encourage us to get and stay in shape just because we like ourselves that much? What if baby boomers hitting fifty had the esteem to celebrate their strength and smarts and not anguish over every wrinkle? What if girls didn't take an automatic drop in self-esteem when they hit puberty? What if offering up a larger spectrum of body sizes, colors, and gender roles in ads, on TV, and in film actually helped to lower the epidemic number of eating disorders among college women?

Nike's ads have been quite popular with female consumers. These ads have commonly been read as presenting a more positive view of the female body and promoting female athletics. Nike's "Just Do It" campaign features a series of ads in which women engage in a variety of sports. These ads are generally noticeable for their black and white, often grainy texture, their depiction of female athletes in motion, and their use of perhaps more "realistic" models.

The power of Nike's advertising to convey a "feminist" image of the female body to female consumers which is more appealing is evidenced in comments from women (and some men) in this study. Many of the participants selected Nike's ads as personally appealing specifically because they were seen as offering an image outside society's ideal of femininity. Many commented on the Nike ad and others featuring athletic women, acknowledging explicitly not only that these ads broke with traditional norms, but that they found this breakage both pleasurable and inspiring, reading them as offering more positive, liberating images:

I think it's a really neat ad. Once again, the "Just Do it" part, I really like that. The fitness aspect, how she's doing something for herself . . . I like it, it's real. I like that a lot . . . "Just Do It." That's what she's doing. She's not waiting for anyone else. . . . She's just doing it. And that's just a nice little motto for anybody. And you can relate that over to yourself, that doesn't have to stay on the page. (Collette, 21)

Such statements serve as a testimonial to the fact that the ads that currently fill mainstream media are so confining and restrictive that very small changes may be noticed and seen as signs of improvement by female audiences. Women are aware of the ways in which the female form is traditionally presented, and a break from that, no matter how small or slight, is instantly recognized and applauded as a movement forward. (Tellingly, some male respondents found the image less appealing.) They also serve to show that the messages of female "independence," bodily integrity, and individuality coded in the ads find an eager audience in female as well as male audiences; female audiences are as much invested in the American myth of the individual as are men.

However, these statements are as telling for what they *don't* reveal as for what they do. During the summer of 1996, Nike's business practices in developing countries made headlines when it was widely reported that the company employed Pakistani children to make soccer balls for $.06 an hour (Goldman and Papson 1998; Schanberg 1996). Nike's treatment of female workers in countries like Vietnam, China, and Indonesia has also been widely debated (Goldman and Papson 1998; Shaw 1999), as has its exploitation of the poor in the United States (Gonzalez 1997). Even though Nike claims to have made improvements in its practices, such as installing a Code of Conduct for its manufacturing facilities, critics still contend that there is plenty of room for abuse to occur (Anonymous 1997). Nike and its supporters' statements that its workers are better off earning a low wage in their factories than not earning *any* money ignores a central issue: that unequal power relations always dominate commodity chains.

There was little recognition among our participants of the chains of production and consumption outside the ad. Ironically, while Nike's ads and self-promotion in other areas stress the fact that they encourage women to break out of the confining molds of traditional, passive femininity, the actual practices of Nike and other corporations are based upon an ethos of domination that continues to oppress women and children throughout the world.

Thus, the rhetoric of individuality seen in ads for Nike and even in the Just My Size campaign are tied to neoconservative positions that are inextricably linked to a capitalist marketplace and consumer ethics. Female consumers find pleasure and a sense of self-empowerment and self-esteem in images that depict women as powerful individual subjects. As individuals, this can be read as a step forward. Nike ads give women a sense that their bodies are strong, durable, and active. Magazines like *Mode* can change women's lives, healing the scars of the psychosexual rejection caused by being "too fat," "too ethnic." *Mode* offers women a space where they can feel beautiful—worthy of love and positive attention for the first time in their lives.

As Abra Fortune Chernik writes, "Gaining weight and getting my head out of the toilet bowl was the most political act I'd ever committed" (1995, 81). Women's internalization of negative self-images is a major way in which the potentially powerful and positive social forces of women to work for change is kept under wraps (Chernik 1995; Wolf 1991). No matter how positively these ads may affect women's self-esteem and their consequent willingness to stand up and fight for themselves and others, the irony remains that at the same time women buy into the idea, they also buy into the products and ethics major corporations offer. Nevertheless, the ability of women to claim themselves as beautiful—as having a right to own their sexual and physical selves, as having the right to take up space—is one that is critically important to helping individual women free themselves from self-hatred, an act that will ultimately benefit society.

References

Abercrombie, Nicholas and Brian Longhurst (1998). *Audiences: A Sociological Theory of Performance and Imagination*. London: Sage.

Anderegg, K. (1996). "Jane Champ." *Mirabella* (March/April): 32–33.

Ang, Ien (1985). *Watching Dallas: Soap Opera and the Melodramatic Imagination*. Trans. Della Couling. London: Methuen.

——— (1989). "Wanted: Audiences. On the Politics of Empirical Audience Research." In Ellen Seiter, H. Borchers, G. Kreutzner, and E. Warth, eds., *Remote Control: Television, Audiences, and Cultural Power*. New York: Routledge. 80–95.

——— (1990). "Melodramatic Identifications: Television Fiction and Women's Fantasy." In Mary Ellen Brown, ed., *Television and Women's Culture: The Politics of the Popular*. London: Sage. 75–88.

Ang, Ien and Joke Hermes (1991). "Gender and/in Media Consumption." In James Curran and Michael Gurevitch, eds., *Mass Media and Society*. London: Arnold. 307–28.

Anonymous (1997). "Watching the Sweatshops." *New York Times*, August 20, A22.

Bacon-Smith, Camille (1992). *Enterprising Women: Television Fandom and the Creation of Popular Myth*. Philadelphia: University of Pennsylvania Press.

Ball, Colleen D. (1998). "Ally, Real Life Has No Commercial Breaks." *USA Today*, November 24, 27A.

Barrett, Michelle (1987). "The Concept of Difference." *Feminist Review* 26: 29–40.

Barthes, Roland (1974). *Mythologies*. Trans. Annette Lavers. New York: Hill and Wang.

——— (1977). *Image, Music, Text*. Trans. Stephen Heath. New York: Noonday Press.

——— (1988). *The Semiotic Challenge*. Trans. Richard Howard. New York: Hill and Wang.

Belkaoui, Ahmed and Janice Monti-Belkaoui (1976). "A Comparative Study of the Roles Portrayed by Women in Print Advertisements: 1958, 1969, 1972." *Journal of Marketing Research* 13: 168–72.

Berger, John and others (1972). *Ways of Seeing*. London: BBC.

Betterton, Rosemary (1985). "How Do Women Look? The Female Nude in the Work of Suzanne Valadon." *Feminist Review* 19: 3–24.

Bird, S. Elizabeth (1992a). *For Enquiring Minds: A Cultural Study of Supermarket Tabloids*. Knoxville: University of Tennessee Press.

——— (1992b). "Travels in Nowhere Land: Ethnography and the 'Impossible' Audience." *Critical Studies in Mass Communication* 9, 3: 250–60.

Blumer, Herbert (1969). *Symbolic Interactionism: Perspective and Method*. Englewood Cliffs, N.J.: Prentice-Hall.

Bobo, Jacqueline (1988). "The Color Purple: Black Women as Cultural Readers." In E. Deidre Pribram, ed., *Female Spectators: Looking at Film and Television*. London: Verso. 90–109.

Bordo, Susan (1993). *Unbearable Weight: Feminism, Western Culture, and the Body*. Berkeley: University of California Press.

———— (1999). *The Male Body: A New Look at Men in Public and in Private*. New York: Farrar, Straus and Giroux.

Botta, Renee A. (1999). "Television Images and Adolescent Girls' Body Image Disturbance." *Journal of Communication* 49, 2: 22–41.

Bretl, Daniel J. and Joanne Cantor (1988). "The Portrayal of Men and Women in U.S. Television Commercials: A Recent Content Analysis and Trends over 15 Years." *Sex Roles* 18, 9/10: 595–609.

Brophy, Beth (1998). "Insider: Smart Women, Foolish Choices." *TV Guide*, December 19, 6.

Busby, Linda J. (1975). "Sex-Role Research on the Mass Media." *Journal of Communication* 25, 4: 107–31.

Chernik, Abra Fortune (1995). "The Body Politic." In Barbara Findlen, ed., *Listening Up: Voices from the Next Feminist Generation*. Seattle: Seal Press. 75–84.

Christ, William G. and J. Potter (1998). "Media Literacy, Media Education, and the Academy." *Journal of Communication* 48, 1: 5–15.

Clark, Kathleen and Brenda Dervin, eds. (1999). "Exemplars of the Use of Sense-Making Methodology." *Electronic Journal of Communication / Revue électronique de communication* 9, 3.

Coleman, Robin Means (2000). *African American Viewers and Black Situation Comedy: Situating Real Humor*. New York: Garland.

Connell, R. W. (1987). *Gender and Power: Society, the Person, and Sexual Politics*. Stanford, Calif.: Stanford University Press.

Courtney, Alice E. (1983). *Sex Stereotyping in Advertising*. Lexington, Mass.: Lexington Books.

Courtney, Alice E. and Sarah Wernick Lockeretz (1971). "A Woman's Place: An Analysis of the Roles Portrayed by Women in Magazine Advertisements." *Journal of Marketing Research* 8, 1: 92–95.

Courtney, Alice E. and Thomas W. Whipple (1974). "Women in TV Commercials." *Journal of Communication* 24, 2: 110–18.

Coward, Rosalind (1982). "Sexual Violence and Sexuality." *Feminist Review* 16, 11: 9–22.

———— (1985). *Female Desires: How They Are Sought, Bought, and Packaged*. New York: Grove Press.

Craig, Steve, ed. (1992). *Men, Masculinity, and the Media*. Newbury Park, Calif.: Sage.

Day, Heather (2000). "Can't Lick It." *Mode*, February, 32.

Dervin, Brenda (1983). "An Overview of Sense-Making Research: Concepts, Methods, and Results to Date." Paper presented at the International Communication Association annual meeting, Dallas, Texas.

———— (1990). "From the Mind's Eye of the 'User': The Sense-Making Qualitative-Quantitative Methodology." In Jack D. Glazier and Ronald R. Powell, eds., *Qualitative Research in Information Management*. Englewood, Colo.: Libraries Unlimited.

———— (1991a). "Comparative Theory Reconceptualized: A Prerequisite for a More Powerful Communication Analytic." *Communication Theory* 1, 1: 59–69.

———— (1991b). "The Content Analysis of Sense-Making Responses: An Introduction to Methodology and Method." Paper, Ohio State University.

———— (1993). "Verbing Communication: Mandate for Disciplinary Invention." *Journal of Communication* 43, 3: 45–54.

Dervin, Brenda and K Clark (1993). "Communication and Democracy: A Mandate for Procedural Invention." In Slavko Splichal and Janet Wasko, eds., *Communication and Democracy*. Norwood, N.J.: Ablex.

Dominick, Joseph R. and G. E. Rauch (1972). "The Image of Women in Network TV Commercials." *Journal of Broadcasting* 16, 3: 259–65.

Dow, Bonnie J. (1996). *Prime-Time Feminism: Television, Media Culture, and the Women's Movement Since 1970*. Philadelphia: University of Pennsylvania Press.

Erni, John (1989). "Where Is the Audience? Discerning the (Impossible) Subject." *Journal of Communication Inquiry* 13, 2: 30–42.

Ewen, Stuart (1976). *Captains of Consciousness: Advertising and the Social Roots of the Consumer Culture*. New York: McGraw-Hill.

Faludi, Susan (1999). *Stiffed: The Betrayal of the American Man*. New York: William Morrow.

Fejes, Fred (1984). "Critical Mass Communications Research and Media Effects: The Problem of the Disappearing Audience." *Media, Culture and Society* 6: 219–32.

Ferguson, J. H., Peggy J. Kreshel, and S. F. Tinkham (1990). "In the Pages of *Ms.*: Sex Role Portrayals of Women in Advertising." *Journal of Advertising* 19, 1: 40–51.

Ferrante, C. L., A. M. Haynes, and S. M. Kingsley (1988). "Image of Women in Television Advertising." *Journal of Broadcasting and Electronic Media* 32, 2: 231–37.

Fisher, B. Aubrey (1978). *Perspectives on Human Communication*. New York: Macmillan.

Foucault, Michel (1977). *Discipline and Punish: The Birth of the Prison*. Trans. Alan Sheridan. London: Penguin Press.

Fredrickson, George M. (1988). *The Arrogance of Race: Historical Perspectives on Slavery, Racism, and Social Inequality*. Middleton, Conn.: Wesleyan University Press.

Freire, Paulo (1974). *Education for Critical Consciousness*. New York: Seabury Press.

Friedan, Betty (1963). *The Feminine Mystique*. New York: Dell.

Furnham, Adrian (1989). "Gender Stereotypes in Italian Television Advertisements." *Journal of Broadcasting and Electronic Media* 33, 2: 175–85.

Garfinkel, Perry (1985). *In a Man's World: Father, Son, Brother, Friend, and Other Roles Men Play*. New York: New American Library.

Geertz, Clifford (1983). *Local Knowledge: Further Essays in Interpretive Anthropology*. New York: Basic Books.

Geis, Florence L., V. Brown, J. Jennings, and N. Porter (1984). "TV Commercials as Achievement Scripts for Women." *Sex Roles* 10, 7/8: 513–25.

Gerbner, George and Larry P. Gross (1976), "Living with Television: The Violence Profile." *Journal of Communication* 26, 2: 172–99.

Gilday, Katherine (1990). *The Famine Within*. Kandor Productions. Santa Monica, Calif.: Direct Cinema.

Gilly, Mary C. (1988). "Sex Roles in Advertising: A Comparison of Television Advertisements in Australia, Mexico, and the United States." *Journal of Marketing* 52: 75–85.

Gledhill, Christine (1988). "Pleasurable Negotiations." In E. Diedre Pribram, ed., *Female Spectators: Looking at Film and Television*. London: Verso. 64–89.

Goffman, Erving (1976). *Gender Advertisements.* New York: Harper and Row.

Goldman, Robert and Stephen Papson (1996). *Sign Wars: The Cluttered Landscape of Advertising.* New York: Guilford Press.

Gonzales, D. (1997). "Youthful Foes Go Toe to Toe with Nike." *New York Times*, September 27, B-1.

Gould, Steven J. (1987). "Gender Differences in Advertising Response and Self-Consciousness Variables." *Sex Roles* 16, 5/6: 215–25.

Gray, Ann (1992). *Video Playtime: The Gendering of a Leisure Technology.* London: Routledge.

Griffin, Michael, K. Viswanath, and D. Schwartz (1992). *Gender Advertising in the U.S. and India: Exporting Cultural Stereotypes.* Minneapolis: University of Minnesota School of Journalism and Mass Communication.

Gross, Larry P. (1991). "Out of the Mainstream: Sexual Minorities and the Mass Media." In M A. Wolf and A. P. Kielwasser, eds., *Gay People, Sex, and the Media.* Binghamton, N.Y.: Harryton Park/Haworth Press. 19–46.

Hall, Stuart (1980). "Encoding/Decoding." In Hall, D. Hobson, A. Lowe, and P. Willis, eds., *Culture, Media, Language: Working Papers in Cultural Studies, 1972–79.* London: Hutchinson. 128–38.

——— (1981). "The Determinations of News Photographs." In Stanley Cohen and Jock Young, eds., *The Manufacture of News: Social Problems, Deviance, and the Mass Media.* Beverly Hills, Calif.: Sage. 226–43.

——— (1996) *Representation and the Media.* Video. Amherst, Mass.: Media Education Foundation.

Hawkes, Terence (1977). *Structuralism & Semiotics.* London: Methuen.

Hawkins, Joellen W. and Cynthia S. Aber (1993). "Women in Advertisements in Medical Journals." *Sex Roles* 28, 3/4: 233–42.

Hay, James (1989). "Advertising as a Cultural Text (Rethinking Message Analysis in a Recombinant Culture)." In Brenda Dervin, Lawrence Grossberg, B. J. O'Keefe, and Ellen Wartella, eds., *Rethinking Communication.* Newbury Park, Calif.: Sage. 129–51.

Heinecken, Dawn (1999). "The Women Warriors of Television: A Feminist Cultural Analysis of the New Female Body in Popular Media." Dissertation, Bowling Green State University.

Heywood, Leslie (1998). "Hitting a Cultural Nerve: Another season of Ally McBeal." *Chronicle of Higher Education*, September 4, B9.

hooks, bell (1992). "Representing Whiteness in Black Imagination." In Lawrence Grossberg, Cary Nelson and Paula A. Treichler, eds., *Cultural Studies.* New York: Routledge. 338–46.

Jhally, Sut (1987). *Codes of Advertising.* London: Frances Pinter.

——— (1990). *Dreamworlds.* Video. Amherst, Mass.: Media Education Foundation

Jhally, Sut and Justin Lewis (1998). "The Struggle over Media Literacy." *Journal of Communication* 48, 1: 109–20.

Johnson, Richard (1986). "The Story So Far: And Further Transformations?" In David Punter, ed., *Introduction to Contemporary Cultural Studies.* New York: Longman. 277–313.

Kaplan, E. Ann (1989). *Rocking Around the Clock: Music, TV, Postmodernism, and Consumer Culture.* New York: Routledge.

Kaufman, Michael (1998). "The Construction of Masculinity and the Triad of Men's Violence." In Michael S. Kimmel and Michael A. Messner, eds., *Men's Lives*. 4th ed. Boston: Allyn and Bacon. 4–17.

Kellner, Douglas (1990). "Advertising and Consumer Culture." In John Downing, Ali Mohammadi, and Annabelle Sreberny-Mohammadi, eds., *Questioning the Media: A Critical Introduction*. Newbury Park, Calif.: Sage. 242–54.

Kilbourne, Jean (1987). *Still Killing Us Softly: Advertising Images of Women*. Film. Cambridge.

——— (1989). *Slim Hopes*. Video. Amherst, Mass.: Media Education Foundation.

——— (1999). *Deadly Persuasion: Why Women and Girls Must Fight the Addictive Power of Advertising*. New York: Free Press.

Kimball, Meredith M. (1986). "Television and Sex-Role Attitudes." In Tannis MacBeth Williams, ed., *The Impact of Television: A Natural Experiment in Three Communities*. New York: Academic Press. 265–84.

Kimmel, Michael S. and Michael A. Messner, eds. (1998). *Men's Lives*. 4th ed. Boston: Allyn and Bacon.

Kubey, Robert (1998). "Obstacles to the Development of Media Education." *Journal of Communication* 48, 1: 58–69.

Kuhn, Annette (1985). *The Power of the Image: Essays on Representation and Sexuality*. Boston: Routledge and Kegan Paul.

Lacan, Jacques (1968). *The Language of the Self: The Function of Language in Psychoanalysis*. Trans. Anthony Wilden. New York: Dell.

——— (1977). *Ecrits: A Selection*. Trans. Alan Sheridan. New York: Norton.

Lamm, Nomy (1995). "It's a Big Fat Revolution." In Barbara Findlen, ed., *Listen Up: Voices from the Next Feminist Generation*. Seattle: Seal Press.

Lazier, Linda and Alice Gagner Kendrick (1993). "Women in Advertisements: Sizing Up the Images, Roles, and Functions." In Pamela J. Creedon, ed., *Women in Mass Communication*. 2nd ed. Newbury Park Calif.: Sage. 199–219.

Lazier-Smith, Linda (1988). "The Effect of Changes in Women's Social Status on the Images of Women in Magazine Advertising: The Pingree-Hawkins Sexism Scale Reapplied, Goffman Reconsidered, Kilbourne Revisited." Dissertation, Indiana University, Bloomington.

Leeds-Hurwitz, Wendy (1993). *Semiotics and Communication: Signs, Codes, Cultures*. Hillsdale, N.J.: Erlbaum.

Leiss, William, Stephen Kline, and Sut Jhally (1986). *Social Communication in Advertising: Persons, Products, and Images of Well Being*. London: Methuen.

Lewis, Lisa (1990). "Consumer Girl Culture: How Music Videos Appeal to Girls." In Mary Ellen Brown, ed., *Television and Women's Culture: The Politics of the Popular*. London: Sage. 89–101.

Lovdal, Lynn Terry (1989). "Sex Role Messages in Television Commercials: An Update." *Sex Roles* 21, 11/12: 715–24.

Lull, James (1995). *Media, Communication, Culture: A Global Approach*. New York: Columbia University Press.

Lundstrom, William J. and Donald M. Sciglimpaglia (1977). "Sex Role Portrayals in Advertising." *Journal of Marketing*: 72–79.

Masse, Michelle A. and K. Rosenbaum (1988). "Male and Female Created They Them:

The Depiction of Gender in the Advertising of Traditional Women's and Men's Magazines." *Women's Studies International Forum* 11, 2: 127–44.

Mazzella, Carmela, Kevin Durkin, Emma Cerini, and Paul Buralli (1992). "Sex Role Stereotyping in Australian Television Advertisements." *Sex Roles* 26, 7/8: 243–59.

McKinnon, L. M. (1995). "*Ms*.ing the Free Press: The Advertising and Editorial Content of *Ms*. Magazine, 1972–1992." In David Abrahamson, ed., *The American Magazine: Research Perspectives and Prospects*. Ames: Iowa State University Press. 98–107.

McRobbie, Angela (1984). "Dance and Social Fantasy." In McRobbie and Mica Nava, eds., *Gender and Generation*. London: Macmillan. 130–61.

Means Coleman, Robin R. (2000). *African American Viewers and Black Situation Comedy: Situating Racial Humor*. New York: Garland.

Media Action Alliance (1997). Promotional materials. Minneapolis, Minnesota.

Mellencamp, Patricia (1995). *A Fine Romance: Five Ages of Film Feminism*. Philadelphia: Temple University Press.

Miles, Rovert (1989). *Racism*. London: Routledge

Millium, Terry (1975). *Images of Women: Advertising in Women's Magazines*. London: Chatto and Windus.

Modleski, Tania (1982). *Loving with a Vengeance: Mass-Produced Fantasies for Women*. London: Routledge.

Moores, Shaun (1993). *Interpreting Audiences: The Ethnography of Media Consumption*. London: Sage.

Morley, David (1980). *The "Nationwide" Audience: Structure and Decoding*. London: British Film Institute.

——— (1986). *Family Television: Cultural Power and Domestic Leisure*. London: Comedia.

——— (1989). "Changing Paradigms in Audience Studies." In Ellen Seiter, H. Borchers, G. Kreutzner, and E. Warth, eds., *Remote Control: Television, Audiences, and Cultural Power*. London: Routledge. 16–43.

Morrison, B. J. and Sherman (1972). "Who Responds to Sex in Advertising?" *Journal of Advertising Research* 12, 2: 15–19.

Morse, Margaret (1987–88). "Artemis Aging: Exercise and the Female Body on Video." *Discourse* 10, 1: 20–53.

Mulvey, Laura (1975). "Visual Pleasure and Narrative Cinema." *Screen* 16, 3: 6–18.

Myers, Kathy (1982). "Fashion 'n' passion." *Screen* 23, 2–3: 89–97.

——— (1986). *Understains: The Sense and Seduction of Advertising*. London: Comedia.

NARAL (1999). *Choice for American Initiative: TV Ads*. Washington, D.C.: NARAL.

Nichols, Bill (1981). *Ideology and the Image*. Bloomington: Indiana University Press.

Nicholson, Daniel R. (1997). "The Diesel Jeans and Workwear Advertising Campaign and the Commodification of Resistance." In Katherine Toland Frith, ed., *Undressing the Ad: Reading Culture in Advertising*. New York: Peter Lang. 175–96.

Omi, Michael and Howard Winant (1986). *Racial Formation in the United States from the 1960s to the 1980s*. London: Routledge.

O'Sullivan, Tim, J. Hartley, D. Saunders, M. Montgomery, and J. Fiske, eds. (1994). *Key Concepts in Communication and Cultural Studies*. 2nd ed. London: Routledge.

Orbach, Susie (1976). *Fat Is a Feminist issue: The Anti-Diet Guide to Permanent Weight Loss*. London: Hamlyn.

Parker, S., Mimi Nichter, N. Vuckovic, C. Sims, and Cheryl Ritenbaugh (1995). "Body Image and Weight Concerns Among African American and White Adolescent Females: Differences That Make a Difference." *Human Organization* 54, 2: 103–14.

Peirce, Kate (1989). "Sex-Role Stereotyping of Children on Television: A Content Analysis of the Roles and Attributes of Child Characters." *Sociological Spectrum* 9: 321–28.

Pharr, Suzanne (1995). "Homophobia: A Weapon of Sexism." In Sheila Ruth, ed., *Issues in Feminism: An Introduction to Women's Studies*. 4th ed. London: Mayfield. 276–86.

Pingree, Suzanne, Robert P. Hawkins, and William Paisley (1976). "Equality in Advertising: A Scale for Sexism. *Journal of Communication* 26, 2: 193–200.

Pipher, Mary (1994). *Reviving Ophelia: Saving the Selves of Adolescent Girls*. New York: Ballantine.

Press, Andrea (1991). *Women Watching Television: Gender, Class, and Generation in the American Television Experience*. Philadelphia: University of Pennsylvania Press.

———— (1996). "Toward a Qualitative Methodology of Audience Study: Using Ethnography to Study." In James Hay, Lawrence Grossberg and Ellen Wartella, eds. *The audience and Its Landscape*. Boulder, Colo.: Westview Press. 113–30.

Radway, Janice (1984). *Reading the Romance: Women, Patriarchy, and Popular Literature*. Chapel Hill: University of North Carolina Press.

———— (1986). "Identifying Ideological Seams: Mass Culture, Analytical Method, and Political Practice." *Communication* 9: 93–123.

———— (1988). "Reception Study: Ethnography and the Problems of Dispersed Audiences and Nomadic Subjects." *Cultural Studies* 2, 3: 359–76.

Rakow, Lana F. (1986). "Rethinking Gender in Communication." *Journal of Communication* 36, 4: 11–26.

Roach, Jacques and Peter Felix (1989). "Black Looks." In Lorraine Gamman and Margaret Marshment, eds., *The Female Gaze: Women as Viewers of Popular Culture*. Seattle: Real Comet Press. 130–42.

Root, Jane (1984). *Pictures of Women: Sexuality*. Boston: Pandora Press.

Rossi, Susan R. and Joseph S. Rossi (1985). "Gender Differences in the Perception of Women in Magazine Advertising." *Sex Roles* 12 9/10: 1033–39.

Rowe, Kathleen (1995). *The Unruly Woman: Gender and the Genres of Laughter*. Austin: University of Texas Press.

Sabo, Donald F. (1998). "Pigskin, Patriarchy, and Pain." In Paula S. Rothenberg, ed., *Race, Class and Gender in the United States: An Integrated Study*, 4th ed. New York: St. Martin's Press. 325–27.

Sabo, Donald F. and Ross Runfola (1980). *Jock: Sports and Male Identity*. Englewood Cliffs, N.J.: Prentice-Hall.

Sadker, Myra and David Sadker (1994). *Failing at Fairness: How America's Schools Cheat Girls*. New York: Scribner's.

Saunders, Carol S. and Bette A. Stearn (1986). "Women's Adoption of a Business Uniform: A Content Analysis of Magazine Advertisements." *Sex Roles* 15, 3/4: 197–205.

Saussure, Ferdinand de (1956). *Course in General Linguistics*. Trans. Wade Baskin. London: Peter Owen.

Savan, Leslie (1994). *Sponsored Life: Ads, TV, and American Culture*. Philadelphia: Temple University Press.

Schanberg, S. (1996). "Six Cents an Hour." *Life*, June, 38–42, 45–48.

Seiter, Ellen (1998). *Television and New Media Audiences*. New York: Oxford University Press.

"The Sexism Watch" (1989). *U.S. News and World Report*, March 27, 12.

Shaw, Randy (1999). *Reclaiming America: Nike, Clean Air, and the New National Activism*. Berkeley: University of California Press.

Shields, Vickie R. (1990). "Advertising Visual Images: Gendered Ways of Seeing and Looking." *Journal of Communication Inquiry* 14, 2: 25–39.

——— (1994). "The Constructing, Maintaining and Negotiating of Gender Identities in the Process of Decoding Gender Advertisements." Dissertation, Ohio State University.

——— (1996). "Selling the Sex That Sells: Mapping the Evolution of Gender Advertising Research Across Three Decades." In Brant B. Burleson ed., *Communication Yearbook* 20. Thousand Oaks, Calif.: Sage.

Shields, Vickie R. and Brenda Dervin (1993). "Sense-Making in Feminist Social Science Research: A Call to Enlarge the Methodological Options of Feminist Studies." *Women's Studies International Forum* 16, 1: 65–81.

Shimanoff, Susan B. (1980). *Communication Rules: Theory and Research*. Beverly Hills, Calif.: Sage.

Skelly, Gerald U. and William J. Lundstrom (1981). "Male Sex Roles in Magazine Advertising, 1959–1979." *Journal of Communication*: 52–57.

Spitzack, Carole (1990). *Confessing Excess: Women and the Politics of Body Reduction*. Albany: State University of New York Press.

Spradley, James P. (1979). *The Ethnographic Interview*. New York: Holt, Rinehart and Winston.

Stacey, Jackie (1994). *Star Gazing: Hollywood Cinema and Female Spectatorship*. London: Routledge.

Strate, Lance (1992). "Beer Commercials: A Manual on Masculinity." In Steve Craig, ed., *Men, Masculinity, and the Media*. Newbury Park, Calif.: Sage. 78–92.

Tasker, Yvonne (1995). *Spectacular Bodies: Gender, Genre, and the Action Cinema*. New York: Routledge.

Tompkins, Jane P. (1992). *West of Everything: The Inner Life of Westerns*. New York: Oxford University Press.

Tuchman, Gaye, Arlene Kaplan Daniels, and James Benét, eds. (1978). *Hearth and Home: Images of Women in the Mass Media*. New York: Oxford University Press.

Valdivia, Angharad N. (1997). "The Secret of My Desire: Gender, Class, and Sexuality in Lingerie Catalogues." In Katherine Toland Frith, ed., *Undressing the Ad: Reading Culture in Advertising*. New York: Peter Lang. 225–50.

Wagnor, L. C. and J. B. Banos (1973). "A Woman's Place: A Follow-Up Analysis of the Roles Portrayed by Women in Magazine Advertisements." *Journal of Marketing Research* 10: 213–14.

Waldman, Diane (1989). "Film Theory and the Gendered Spectator: The Female or the Feminist Reader?" *Camera Obscura* 18: 80–94.

Whipple, Thomas W. and Alice E. Courtney (1985). "Female Role Portrayals in Advertising and Communication Effectiveness: A Review." *Journal of Advertising* 14, 3: 4–8.

Williamson, Judith (1978). *Decoding Advertisements: Ideology and Meaning in Advertising*. London: Methuen.

——— (1986). "Woman Is an Island: Femininity and Colonization. In Tania Modleski, ed., *Studies in Entertainment: Critical Approaches to Mass Culture*. Bloomington: Indiana University Press.

Winship, Janice (1981). "Handling Sex." *Media, Culture and Society* 3: 25–41.

——— (1985). " 'A Girl Needs to Get Street-Wise': Magazines of the 1980s." *Feminist Review* 21: 25–46.

Wise, G. L., A. L. King, and J. Paul Merenski (1974). "Reactions to Sexy Ads Vary with Age." *Journal of Advertising Research* 14, 4: 11–16.

Wohleter, M. and B. H. Lammers (1980). "An Analysis of Male Roles in Print Advertisements over a 20-Year Span: 1958–1978." In Jerry C. Olson, ed., *Advances in Consumer Research*, vol. 7. Ann Arbor, Mich.: Association for Consumer Research.

Wolf, Naomi (1991). *The Beauty Myth: How Images of Beauty Are Used Against Women*. New York: Anchor Books.

Women's Action Coalition (1993). *The Facts About Women*. New York: New Press.

Wortzel, Lawrence H. and J. M. Frisbie (1974). "Women's Role Portrayal Preferences in Advertisements." *Journal of Marketing*: 41–46.

Index

Acknowledgments

This book has been a long time coming, with many stops and starts. As with any project of this scope there were many people who played pivotal roles in bringing these ideas to fruition. I want to especially thank Dawn Heinecken who lent her insight and skills of keen cultural analysis to Chapters 7 and 8 of this book. Our collaboration on many projects has been good for my mind and my soul. I am forever indebted to Dawn for breathing fresh life into sections of the book that needed it most.

I am indebted to a number of individuals at the Ohio State University, where the initial research took form. My advisor and mentor, Brenda Dervin, inspired the method and design and continues to play an integral part in my intellectual growth. Her methodology not only provided the tools for this project, it helped provide me with alternative ways of seeing human communication. Because of her commitment and intellectual spirit I continue on my quest to bring Sense-Making into cultural studies, often in the face of resistance. At Ohio State I worked through many of the theoretical ideas in this book with a group of peers who will always be my intellectual inspirations and my good friends: Rob Huesca, John Higgins, Kate Clark, Jamie Newmeyer Litty, Rich DiCenzo, Lynn O'Brien Hallstein, Helga Shugart, and Cathy Wagonner. I give a heartfelt thank you to my team of interviewers at Ohio State who made the initial data collection possible and who did such a fine and dedicated job: Marc Conte, Rich DiCenzo, Lynn O'Brien Hallstein, Michael Scarce, Pete Strimer, and Therese Wood. The richness and complexity of the data are a positive reflection of their efforts.

At Bowling Green State University there are many people to thank for their help. This project was supported by a Summer Research Alumni Fellowship Grant. This grant allowed me the time and financial support to complete four chapters of the book. I am especially grateful for that support.

My colleagues in the Department of Telecommunications and the Women's Studies Program at BGSU have provided encouragement, space, and financial support to complete this project. In particular I thank Ellen Berry, the diva of cool, for her unwavering faith in me and this project and her equally unwavering friendship, and Arlene Spoores for being the Women's Studies Program's "rock." Knowing Arlene was running the place so well allowed me the space I needed to complete this project. Also in the Telecommunications Department, warm and special thanks goes to Ewart Skinner and Peter

Shields. I continue to be inspired by my graduate students at Bowling Green State University, whose own scholarly observations and interest in this project have helped propel it forward, even when I didn't feel like going on. Special thanks go to Ann Savage, Petr Pavlik, Rodney Heiligmann, Patrick Stearns, Robin Means Coleman, Lydia Brauer, Brenda Fite, Laurie Wurth, and Nicole Monteiro. Special thanks go also to my many classes of students in Women, Mass Media, and Culture since 1994.

Kelly S. Mayhew provided me with top-notch research assistance the year I proposed this book to the University of Pennsylvania Press, and Jennifer Waldron was my research assistant extraordinaire in the heart of the writing period. You two women are awesome. Other valuable assistance was provided by Kavitha Shetty, Tom Ruggiero, and Tim Gleason.

I thank a collection of people who have made major differences in this project. First, I want to thank Patricia Smith at the University of Pennsylvania Press for believing in the worthiness of this project in its infancy and for never seeming upset when we missed deadlines. Three anonymous reviewers pushed me to mold the book into the product it is today. Thank you for taking the time to help me make this so much better than it was before. I thank Sue Curry Jansen and Anghharad Valdivia for their ongoing interest in this project and the inspiration their own work has given me over the years. I thank the Feminist Division of the International Communication Association for allowing me to work out many of these ideas through conference presentations. I also want to thank the Departments of Communication at St. Cloud State University and Butler University for inviting me to give keynote addresses on these ideas. The audience feedback has made its way into the book.

Most important, I thank my family, who mean everything in the world to me. My life partner, soul mate, and colleague, Peter Shields, has endured this writing process and all the other life challenges with me. Your love, support, and advice are invaluable. I want to thank my loving parents, Jeannette and Norm Rutledge. And finally I thank my little feminists-in-progress, Claire and Ava Shields, for bringing sunshine into my life every day and for always reminding me why research for women is so important.